"My Will Is Absolute Law"

"My Will Is Absolute Law"

A Biography of Union General Robert H. Milroy

Jonathan A. Noyalas

McFarland & Company, Inc., Publishers
Jefferson, North Carolina, and London

LIBRARY OF CONGRESS CATALOGUING-IN-PUBLICATION DATA

Noyalas, Jonathan A.
"My will is absolute law" : a biography of Union general Robert H. Milroy / Jonathan A. Noyalas.
        p.   cm.
Includes bibliographical references and index.

ISBN 0-7864-2508-3 (softcover : 50# alkaline paper)

1. Milroy, Robert Huston, 1816–1890. 2. Generals—
United States—Biography. 3. United States. Army—
Biography. 4. United States—History—Civil War, 1861–1865—
Campaigns. I. Title.
E467.1.M54N69   2006
973.7'3092—dc22   2006009911

British Library cataloguing data are available

©2006 Jonathan A. Noyalas. All rights reserved

No part of this book may be reproduced or transmitted in any form or by any means, electronic or mechanical, including photocopying or recording, or by any information storage and retrieval system, without permission in writing from the publisher.

Cover image: Portrait of Brig. Gen. Robert H. Milroy, USA (Library of Congress)

Manufactured in the United States of America

McFarland & Company, Inc., Publishers
  Box 611, Jefferson, North Carolina 28640
  www.mcfarlandpub.com

Table of Contents

Preface   1
Introduction   5

1: "Desirous of fame and renown"   7
2: "The Swamp Devils"   18
3: "I fear I shall not like Fremont"   32
4: "West Point Science"   55
5: "To play the tyrant among these traitors"   79
6: "Halleck hates me without cause"   116
7: "Spreading death and fire"   142
8: "The army of eternal peace"   165

Appendix A: "Sketch of the Military Career of R.H. Milroy"   177
Appendix B: Troops Commanded by Milroy in Combat   184
Notes   186
Bibliography   201
Index   209

Preface

In recent years Civil War historians have been publishing biographies of the war's lesser figures—division, brigade, and sometimes regimental commanders. While each story is important the value of some of these biographies to a larger understanding of Civil War history is limited. Biography can be a way not only of understanding facts about people, but understanding the times in which they lived and how they influenced that period. Too often biographers fail to explain the broader context of the history that their personalities influenced. This work attempts to go beyond the traditional biography and illustrate how Gen. Robert H. Milroy influenced the time in which he lived and how he was impacted by those times.

As a graduate student at Virginia Tech under the guidance of two of the world's premier Civil War historians, Dr. James I. Robertson Jr. and William C. "Jack" Davis, I began research on Gen. Robert H. Milroy's Civil War career, particularly the time he spent in Winchester, Virginia, during the first half of 1863. Since graduating from Virginia Tech's MA program in history I became interested even more in the man known as the "Gray Eagle" and began contemplating the value, to the wider literature of the Civil War, of a biography of this lesser-known general. I asked myself—why should anyone read a biography of Robert Milroy? There are several reasons.

First, a study of Milroy's early life reveals what motivated individuals who grew up in the antebellum United States to seek a military career. Second, a biography of Milroy reveals a large amount of information about the lesser-known operations in western Virginia during 1861 and 1862. Third, Milroy's story sheds a tremendous amount of light on the bond between commander and men as well as the seemingly sharp divide between West Point–trained officers and volunteer generals. Fourth, and most importantly, a book of this nature provides a case study of how an abolitionist general enforced his will as an occupation commander in various regions throughout the Confederacy and how President Abraham Lincoln's Emancipation Proclamation was enforced from the moment it was formally issued on January 1, 1863.

In reconstructing Milroy's life I have relied heavily upon his personal letters, the lion's share of which are housed in the Robert H. Milroy Collection at the Jasper County Public Library in Rensselaer, Indiana. Other primary documents from various archives are used to not only let Milroy's voice sound from the past, but so, too, are letters from both his soldiers and his enemies used to illustrate how people reacted to him and his policies.

Maj. Gen. Robert H. Milroy (Jasper County Public Library, Rensselaer, Indiana).

Writing this book has been a tremendous undertaking and would not have been possible without the help of countless individuals. The people I recognize have in some way aided in the maturation of this manuscript, but in no way are at fault for any of its errors. Dr. Brandon H. Beck, the Hugh D. and Virginia McCormick Chair in Civil War History at Shenandoah University who supported me in this project and who continues to provide professional guidance; Glenda Brown and the staff of the Jasper County Public Library in Rensselaer, Indiana, who worked so diligently to provide me with copies of Milroy's letters and without whose support this book would never have been a reality; the library staff at Lord Fairfax Community College, especially Linda Harper and Viv Dewitt, who aided me in acquiring countless volumes through interlibrary loan; the staff at Duke University, who graciously aided me in locating pertinent materials; the staff at the Kreitzberg Library at Norwich University, who shed a tremendous amount of light on Milroy's days as a student at Captain Partridge's Military Academy; the staff at the Library of Virginia Archives who aided me in searching Gov. John Letcher's Papers; the staff at the Pennsylvania

State University Archives; the staff at the Stewart Bell Jr. Archives at the Handley Regional Library in Winchester, Virginia, who always seem tireless in helping me; the staff at the University of Miami, Ohio, who pulled pertinent materials from Gen. Robert C. Schenck's letters; the staff at the Virginia Historical Society for providing me with the petition from the Jonah H. Lupton papers; and my thesis committee at Virginia Tech — Dr. James I. Robertson Jr., Dr. Richard Hirsh, and William C. "Jack" Davis — who for nearly two years guided me in my research on Milroy which provided the foundation for this biography. Last but certainly not least I would like to thank the love of my life, my wife, Brandy, a fine historian, whose research assistance and advice has been invaluable.

Jonathan A. Noyalas
Martinsburg, West Virginia
April 2006

Introduction

Ten years after Gen. Robert H. Milroy's death in 1890, Joseph Warren Keifer, who served under Milroy in western Virginia and the Shenandoah Valley in 1862 and 1863, published his wartime experiences. In the two volumes Keifer shared many Milroy stories and defined his former superior's Civil War legacy: "The colored people of America, should erect a monument to his memory. He was their friend when to be so drew upon him much adverse criticism."[1]

While Milroy does not rank among the pantheon of the Civil War's legendary battlefield commanders, and for that reason has largely been forgotten, Milroy played a significant role in the war — occupation commander and active enforcer of President Abraham Lincoln's immortal Emancipation Proclamation, arguably the Civil War's greatest legacy.

When Lincoln issued the preliminary proclamation in September 1862 the Union army was sharply divided on whether to support the measure, and many Union officers despised the document's intention. Milroy, among the minority in admiration of Lincoln's proclamation, was ecstatic and believed that the only way the war could be won was if slavery was abolished.

Milroy's sometimes irrational behavior on the battlefield made many of his contemporaries skeptical of his abilities and have caused some historians to glance over his involvement in the war altogether or treat him as some sort of misfit. True, Milroy had a penchant for fighting and loved combat, but those were not the only reasons he exhibited a sometimes excited behavior on the battlefield. Ultimately he wanted to preserve the United States and end the South's "peculiar institution." "He was a man of intense patriotism," recalled Col. E.P. Hammond after the Civil War. "The cause which he was fighting, his country, the integrity of the Republic, the freedom of the slaves, was constantly present in his mind."[2]

This study traces Milroy's development as a child interested in being a soldier to his military education at Captain Partridge's Military Academy in Vermont, through the Mexican War, the Civil War, and the Gray Eagle's postwar life.

This book presents Milroy for what he was—an ardent abolitionist and patriot—qualities which at times blocked his vision for the creation of his legacy as one of the best leaders of men in combat. It does not attempt to cover up his shortcomings or enhance his faults; it merely presents Milroy the person in the hope that readers will come to better understand this dynamic individual and the role that he played in America's epic conflict, the Civil War.

1

"Desirous of fame and renown"

From a tender age Robert Huston Milroy dreamed about battlefield fame and glory. He confessed in his adult years, "I have from the very earliest boyhood been ambitious and intensely desirous of military fame and renown as a general."[1] The Civil War provided Milroy with the opportunity to obtain distinction and greatness as a battlefield commander. His ambitions and sometimes zealous behavior plagued his bid for elevation to the pantheon of legendary commanders, but those same characteristics won the admiration of many of his men and the mere mention of his name struck fear and anger into many Confederates. Not considered unique among commanders of men in combat, Milroy nonetheless left his mark on the Civil War as he was one of the first to actively enforce President Abraham Lincoln's Emancipation Proclamation — perhaps the conflict's greatest legacy.

Robert Milroy's path to the battlefield began on June 11, 1816, when he was born in Washington County, Indiana.[2] That same year, Indiana entered the Union, and Milroy frequently boasted in later years he was "as old as the State of Indiana."[3] Milroy grew up listening to the heroic exploits of his father, Maj. Gen. Samuel Milroy, during the War of 1812 as well as his father's involvement in other conflicts between the Indians and white settlers in Kentucky and Indiana.[4] Military service aside, Samuel served on the first constitutional convention of Indiana and also was a member of the state's legislature.[5]

Milroy's familial connections to power and combat, however, do not begin with his father's exploits as an officer against the British or Indians. Milroy's great-grandfather, John McElroy was the earl of Annandale in Scotland. Connected to England's King George II, McElroy fled Scotland after Scottish clans rose up in support of the Second Jacobite Rebellion in 1745 led by Charles Edward Stuart (better known as Bonnie Prince Charlie). Although the rebellion failed to restore the Stuart kings to the English throne, McElroy, fearing for his family's safety, fled to Ireland.[6]

McElroy spent several years in Ireland and changed his name to "Milroy," wanting to eliminate all connections to King George II. After a stint in Ireland the Milroys came to Pennsylvania and settled near Carlisle, where they took up farming. In Carlisle his wife bore him two sons and three daughters. One of his sons, Henry, was Robert Milroy's grandfather and settled in Mifflin County, Pennsylvania, where Robert Milroy's father, Samuel, was born. Samuel grew up in Pennsylvania, but in 1809 moved to Kentucky where he married Martha Huston. The couple then moved to Indiana.[7]

When Robert was 10 years old Samuel and Martha Huston Milroy moved to Delphi, Indiana, where Samuel pursued farming and young Robert would have the opportunity to learn. The school he attended in Delphi consisted of nothing more than a log schoolhouse, but as primitive as it might have been Milroy began to hone his skills in the hopes that one day he might attend West Point.[8]

As a teenager Milroy undoubtedly carried on many conversations with his father about attending West Point. At every turn Milroy received constant resistance from his father — Samuel Milroy did not believe in a standing national army, nor did he believe in the professional training of military officers. One can only speculate as to the origin of Samuel Milroy's animosity toward West Point, but the fact that he was a Democrat in the purest sense of the ideology could not have helped Robert's bid for a military education. "The old gentleman," remembered Milroy, "was so much of a Democrat in theory and practice that he had unconquerable prejudices."[9]

By the age of 24 Milroy became disgusted with his situation in Indiana. Robert knew that all hopes of an appointment to West Point disappeared as he got older, but he still desired a higher education. His father refused to pay because he also did not favor higher education. Samuel was a "self made and self educated man" who believed that a "collegiate education was more injurious than beneficial."[10] His father told him that if he wanted to learn he should teach himself by using the family library. As extensive as the Milroy family library might have been, it did not satisfy Robert's thirst for a military education. So adamant was Robert about going to college, particularly a military school, that he pleaded with his father to give up all rights to his estate in exchange for tuition, but to no avail.[11] Samuel Milroy would not budge.

Samuel tried to appease his son's desire for a formal education in the winter of 1840–41 when he sent him to visit an uncle in Mifflin County, Pennsylvania. Aside from seeing some of his relatives, the visit had another purpose — to collect $200 from his grandfather's estate. When Robert collected the money his father told him to use it to "see the world."[12] Samuel wanted Robert to visit Washington, D.C., and other cities in the East. With money in hand Robert thought it could be put to better use, college tuition. He heard favorable remarks about many schools, but one in particular caught his attention — Norwich University. The institution possessed all of the trappings of a fine mid-nineteenth century college education with a twist; it was also a military academy.[13] Without notifying his parents Milroy packed up his meager belongings and made his way to Vermont where he enrolled in Captain Partridge's Military Academy at Norwich University.[14] Upon hearing the news, Samuel must have been disgusted, but instead of lashing out at his son he offered to help pay the tuition.[15]

Incorporated by the Vermont legislature in 1834, Norwich University stood as one of the most successful private military academies during the antebellum years.[16] It ranked second only to West Point in the number of officers it supplied to the Union army during the Civil War.[17]

Regarded as "one of the most powerful men ever at the University," Milroy undoubtedly enjoyed every moment and excelled at every endeavor.[18] Daily life at Norwich for the cadets echoed that of a typical day at West Point. Every morning at sunrise reveille sounded, marking the start of a hectic day. Cadets had to dress hastily and prepare for morning roll call. Afterward the cadets had no more than 15 minutes to tidy up their quarters for inspection by the officer of the day. Following these daily inspections students ate breakfast promptly at 6:00 A.M. in spring and summer and 7:00 A.M. in fall and winter. Days were filled with morning prayer in the chapel, intense classroom instruction not only in military science, but math, physics, philosophy, and history. Practical military applications such as drill also consumed time each week.[19] Sunday for the cadets was a day of rest and worship. University faculty strongly urged cadets to attend Sunday worship services, and those who did not attend had to spend much of the day reading scriptures.[20] Sundays aside the faculty encouraged students to read the "Holy Scriptures ... during their leisure hours."[21] A Presbyterian, Milroy probably had no problem with attending worship and contemplating Holy Scripture.[22]

Milroy listened intently as his professors lectured on topics ranging from to literature to artillery.[23] Studiousness aside Milroy excelled at nonacademic activities as well. He received the admiration of his classmates for athletic prowess and undoubtedly was regarded as a talented musician for his flute-playing skills.[24]

While students had little time to leave the university — only twice a year, once after commencement and once after the conclusion of the winter quarter — they did have exposure to the world beyond the walls of academe. Cadets frequently took part in parades and other commemorative activities throughout New England. For example, on Independence Day

1843, the corps of cadets, under the command of Gen. Truman B. Ransom, gave several exhibition drills and the cadets, Robert Milroy among them, delivered speeches in commemoration of the Declaration of Independence.[25]

By 1843, Milroy had succeeded at every task and in a class of 10 students Milroy graduated first.[26] At the commencement exercises on Thursday, August 17, 1843, he received three degrees — master of arts, master of military science, and master of civil engineering.[27] As he delivered the valedictory address that Thursday, Milroy must have been dreaming about the opportunities this education might create; would this win him the fame and glory he dreamed about as a child and make him one of the most revered names in American military history?

Almost immediately after graduation he tried every avenue to secure a commission as a lieutenant in the Army, but he failed. As his options for serving in the military, aside from enlisting as a private, deteriorated with each passing day Milroy began to recognize the favoritism to "the royal priesthood of West Point."[28]

Dejected, Milroy spent several months after graduation touring New England as a fencing and drill instructor for local militia companies. Milroy's passion for fencing materialized in his days as a student at Norwich and like everything he excelled at that. Throughout his life, not just during the months in New England, Milroy was known to have given private lessons. Among his students was Lew Wallace, later a Union general and famed author of *Ben-Hur*. Wallace wrote of Milroy's fencing prowess: "In fence with sabers his wrist was like flexible steel; besides which he had a reach to make another swordsman, though ever so skillful, choosy of engaging him. This I know, having been one of a class under his instruction."[29] While initially this may have been enough to quench Milroy's thirst for something military he soon realized that it did not and so he returned home in the spring of 1844.[30]

Not knowing what path to take Milroy enrolled in law school at the Indiana State University. While he may have excelled academically, Milroy's heart was not in the study of law — he wanted adventure. In 1845 Milroy's "restless disposition" directed him to Texas where he took the oath to the "Lone Star" Republic.[31] Even though Milroy never explained his reason for going to Texas, he may have done so to seek some sort of military post with his mother's second cousin, Sam Houston, who was then serving his second term as the republic's president.[32]

Milroy's time in Texas was short-lived. In the fall of 1845 Milroy received a disturbing letter from his mother — his father and oldest brother had died. Putting his family's needs above personal ambitions Milroy returned home to Indiana to assist in caring for the family farm.[33] In Indiana Milroy divided his time between the study of law and the farm, yet the whole time his thoughts were of grandeur on some glorious battlefield. Unfortunately for Milroy there was no war and he began to resign himself to the fact that he would lead a dull, ordinary life. Unhappy with his lot, the moment that Milroy waited for had arrived in 1846 — war.

When the United States went to war with Mexico in the spring of 1846 Milroy saw an opportunity to test his military education and begin steps toward military glory. Men from all corners of the country rushed to the Federal government's call for troops. Robert and his younger brother Samuel offered their services. While Samuel (who came into service as a lieutenant and was promoted to captain) undoubtedly enlisted because of pressure from peers, Robert unquestionably mustered into service as he saw this as the perfect stepping stone for life in the professional army. Eager to fight and have rank, Milroy expelled every bit of energy in the organization of a company. In June 1846 Captain Milroy's company mustered in for a period of one year as Company C, 1st Indiana Volunteers, which bore the sobriquet of Wabash Invincibles.[34]

When the 1st Indiana reached Mexico many of the men were fearful, yet Milroy dreaded nothing. Dr. E.H.M. Beck, serving in the same regiment, noted that "Rob is very anxious for a fight."[35] Other members of the regiment witnessed Milroy's eagerness for combat. Lew Wallace, who served in the 1st Indiana with Milroy, recorded that Milroy "was one of the very few whom I have met actually lovers of combat. Eager, impetuous, fierce in anger."[36]

With 61 men under his command, Milroy longed for action, but the long-awaited moment for combat never materialized. Throughout the Wabash Invincibles' service the company guarded posts at Matamoras and Monterey. Milroy grumbled that Mexico was a "miserable cheerless place."[37] He and his command soon learned what all veteran soldiers knew — military life, except on the battlefield, was very mundane. The Indiana captain bemoaned that "we have the same daily routine of military duty to perform each day."[38] Some of Milroy's time in Mexico was spent combating illness brought on by an improper diet.[39]

The mundane existence in Mexico made Milroy and his troops eager for a fight. While they waited for a major battle, that for the Wabash Invincibles would never come, Milroy directed his anger at his family. As he would during the Civil War Milroy grew furious when people would not answer his letters in a timely fashion. In the spring of 1847 he lambasted his sister for not writing him quickly enough. "I felt so vexed," Milroy explained, "that I swore not to write home again." Even though he was aggravated Milroy informed his sister that he would write her to set a

"Christian example by returning good for evil."⁴⁰ Although irritated because his sister did not write him as much as he would have liked Milroy's impatience with his family was undoubtedly magnified by the fact that as the months grew on the likelihood of him leading his company in a grand and glorious battle diminished.

The only action that the Wabash Invincibles witnessed in Mexico was on a foraging expedition from Monterey to Matamoras. In the latter part of 1846 Gen. Zachary Taylor ordered four companies of the 1st Indiana under Milroy's command to move by land and then via the Rio Grande from Monterey to Matamoras. Milroy's superiors speculated that the movement would not take any more than four days, yet they were gravely mistaken. The expedition would take almost twice as long. As a result Milroy's men were forced to forage. After the four-day period Lew Wallace simply wrote, "a famine struck us, and it became necessary to forage."⁴¹ A detachment of five Hoosiers set out to secure cattle for Milroy's command, but guerilla forces under Gen. Jesus Maria Carvajal ambushed the unsuspecting Indiana soldiers. With three of the soldiers dead, the other two took to their heels and headed for the main body of Milroy's force. When the soldiers returned they found their comrades on the Rio Grande aboard the *Enterprise* headed for Matamoras.⁴²

Frightened, the soldiers recounted their horrific experience to Milroy. Incensed over the act of Carvajal's men, Milroy, according to one witness, "buckled on his sword, jumped ashore, and called for volunteers."⁴³ Every man in the detachment answered Milroy's energetic plea for volunteers to reclaim the slain bodies and to seek retribution against Carvajal's guerillas.

The enraged soldiers set out into the countryside. They soon discovered the bodies—men who had once been their brothers in arms were now "horribly mutilated" corpses. The sights of the butchered men energized Milroy's command to find Carvajal. In a small, nameless village atop a bluff, the Indiana troops located Carvajal. With an opportunity for revenge and finally to get into some real combat, Milroy ordered his men to form in battle lines, proceed through the fields, and move up the slopes to the Mexican position. When the order came for the men to advance the Hoosiers rushed headlong for the high ground. Lew Wallace who experienced the attack wrote of the charge: "Heavens! What furnace heat there was in that go!" The steepness of the hill slowed Milroy's advance and soon Carvajal and his guerilla band escaped with little loss—one man killed and four wounded.⁴⁴

After the quick fight Milroy's command awaited further orders. Prior to setting off in search of Carvajal, Milroy vowed to burn the town where

Carvajal was found. His men prepared to perform the act, but Milroy, using his better judgment, opted to rescind the order and take care of the wounded troops.[45] The small affair with Carvajal — hardly anything to brag about — marked the highest point of Milroy's military career in Mexico. Following the incident his men resumed guard duty of various posts until their enlistments expired in June 1847.

As the Hoosiers' enlistments neared an end, Milroy made preparations to organize a company of mounted infantry. Many of his own men agreed to join the mounted infantry company. With a full company Milroy made preparations prior to June 1847 to have the men mustered in and attached to Gen. Zachary Taylor's force. When Milroy approached Taylor to have the mounted infantry mustered into service Taylor refused. Taylor stated he could accept them only as regular infantry. The general's response did not please Milroy and his men, as they "refused to be mustered in for a second term except as a cavalry or mounted infantry."[46] Taylor probably did not accept Milroy's offer of mounted infantry as he feared the extra supply problems horse soldiers might create.

Not wanting to totally demoralize Milroy, Taylor recommended that the Indiana captain offer his services to the Texas government, which had recently been authorized to raise an additional regiment of rangers. Milroy met with Texas officials, however, they too declined the offer as the quota for rangers had been filled. Dejected, Milroy made a final plea to the War Department, but for a third time was turned down. With the term of enlistment expired in June 1847 the 1st Indiana went to New Orleans where it mustered out of service.

After the Indiana troops disbanded Milroy returned to Mexico for several weeks. His reason for returning is unclear, but more than likely he was searching for a way to get back into the field. If in fact that is what he was attempting to do, those efforts also failed. By the end of July 1847 Milroy returned home to Delphi.

The Mexican War presented Milroy with an opportunity that he thought could be used to launch an epic military career, but in the end it did not. Disgusted, Milroy lamented: "I unfortunately got into [a] Regiment ... that was cursed by an incompetent Colonel ... the shortness of [the] war prevented me from acquiring any reputation."[47]

With his hopes for military success dashed, Milroy returned to the study of law at Indiana State University. Between 1847 and 1850 Milroy began to hone the skills that would launch his legal career. Also during this time Milroy found love. He courted Mary Jane Armitage and on May 17, 1859, the two wed in Delphi.

Ten months after they were married the couple had their first child, a son, Edwin Bruce. Unfortunately for the Milroy family Edwin's health deteriorated and the following year, at the age of one, he died. The Milroys' second child, Ella Gertrude, was born on Christmas Day 1851 and less than two years later, on November 21, 1853, the couple had another son, Edgar. Unfortunately Edgar too succumbed to illness and at the age of two he died in 1856. Despite the heartache of having suffered the deaths of two sons, something that was commonplace in mid-nineteenth century America, Robert and Mary Milroy were determined to build a family. In August 1855 another son, Valerius, was born and two years later in August 1857 another son, Walter. The family continued to grow with the birth of another son, Robert, in September 1859.[48]

Throughout the joy and heartache of marriage and birth, Milroy continued to pursue a career that would allow him to provide for his family. He successfully completed his legal studies at Indiana University at Bloomington. After being admitted to the Indiana bar, Milroy launched a somewhat successful legal career. In 1851 Milroy served as a member of the Indiana State Constitutional Convention. The same year Milroy was appointed circuit judge for the 8th district. He moved from Delphi to Rensselaer in 1854 and continued his legal pursuits.

During the 1850s, as Milroy established a legal career and dealt with the severe blows of the deaths of two his sons, he also became increasingly interested in the debate over the expansion of slavery. Undoubtedly he read of the horrific events that drove a wedge between North and South — bloody events in Kansas, the caning of Massachusetts senator Charles Sumner and John Brown's raid to name a few. As the events transpired Milroy became increasingly concerned that the United States was on a path to civil war and that it was the institution of slavery that would lead to armed conflict.

His suspicions of a divided union began to materialize on December 20, 1860, with the secession of South Carolina, followed by six other Deep South states. Milroy intently read the newspapers and he must have been awestruck when he received word that on February 4, 1861, the seceded states met in Montgomery, Alabama, to form a provisional Confederate government. He viewed this as treason and as an act of war.

Anguish ran rampant among many United States citizens, but they did not necessarily equate the meeting in Montgomery with an armed rebellion — Robert Milroy did. Two days after the initial meeting in Montgomery, Milroy drafted a patriotically charged message, to be published in the local newspaper, to his friends and neighbors in Rensselaer to "Prepare for War." He started the ad by writing: "Fellow citizens, the glorious Flag of our country has been fired upon — torn down by traitor hands and trampled upon.... The sovereignty of our government has been insulted — defied and set aside within its own rightful limits by traitors led by a disappointed demagoguery whose motto is rule or ruin." Some northerners saw these actions as treason and Milroy explained: "Treason and rebellion have raised their ... head under a strange banner within six of the southern states of our Union ... the time has come to test the strength of our government to determine whether it ... will tremble into discordant fragments before the first breath of treason."[49]

Milroy also used the ad to condemn President James Buchanan's handling of the situation — doing nothing to prevent secession and not responding to the failed attempt of the *Star of the West,* in January 1861, to resupply Fort Sumter in Charleston Harbor. He firmly believed, and rightly so, that the situation was spiraling out of control because of the lack of leadership from the Buchanan administration. Buchanan of course cared not at all because by the time secession occurred he had become a lame-duck president with Abraham Lincoln's election. Milroy labeled Buchanan's presidency as an "imbecile administration whose pusillanimous conduct has given strength and confidence to this impious treason." Although disgusted with Buchanan's lack of action he reminded his fellow friends and neighbors that within one month Abraham Lincoln would be inaugurated and would do whatever was necessary to make certain that "the union must and shall be preserved."[50]

Although the Civil War had not begun in February 1861 Milroy, as well as many others in the nation, could see that armed conflict would be the ultimate consequence of secession. Perhaps viewing the impending conflict as another opportunity to gain renown as a battlefield officer, Milroy requested that the people of Rensselaer prepare for war and enlist in a company he was organizing to put down the rebellion. He pleaded with the people: "The new administration will doubtless require thousands of volunteers to assist in crushing out this rebellion.... Volunteers in the Union states should therefore be everywhere organized and ready at a moments warning. It is desired to organize a company of such volunteers in Rensselaer." Milroy requested that anyone interested should send their names directly to him and when he had sufficient numbers a meeting would be held to elect officers.[51]

At the end of his appeal Milroy called to mind the memory of the nation's ancestors who fought to create an independent nation. "Shall the flag of our country whose glory and honor have been sealed by the blood of a thousand battles be thus disgraced," wrote Milroy. He continued: "Shall the ... sovereignty of our government whose foundations were laid and established by the wisdom of our forefathers to secure the blessings of liberty to ourselves and our posterity and before which tyrants have trembled and that has never yet been defied or questioned with impunity."⁵² The heartfelt appeal yielded little result. Only two men answered Milroy's initial plea for volunteers. Although many throughout the country believed conflict was imminent few wanted to take immediate military action and hoped that perhaps another compromise — as they had since the beginning of the republic—could alleviate the problem. Nonetheless, Milroy firmly held that civil war could not be avoided and he continued to make preparations to raise a company.

On April 12, 1861, the opening guns of war resounded in Charleston Harbor, marking the beginning of four years of bloody conflict. When news of the attack reached Jasper County, Indiana, Milroy hastened to the county courthouse to recruit men to put down the rebellion. This time he would have no difficulty in recruiting men. The citizens of Rensselaer were energized to preserve the Union after the attack on Fort Sumter. The *Rensselaer Weekly Gazette* reported on April 17: "The proud flag of the brave and the free no longer waves over Sumter. It is trampled in a dismantled fortress by rebel feet, while above them defiantly floats the rattlesnake banner. The thought sends the blood quick and hot through every patriots' vein, burning with unquenchable fire until the shame shall be wiped out with a terrible blow."⁵³

Quickly Milroy filled the ranks of an infantry company and when Indiana's governor Oliver P. Morton was required to raise six regiments from Indiana Milroy offered his unit. Eventually the company became Company G, 9th Indiana Infantry with Milroy as its captain. Following the mustering in of the company Milroy addressed the recruits of the Iroquois Guards and warned them about the hardships of military life. Milroy informed them that their lives would be difficult as soldiers and that if any man wanted out of the company he should step forward now. Ten men stepped out of the ranks and their places were almost immediately filled by eager volunteers. Milroy intended to clear out the weak with this speech as people who knew him felt that he wanted to "have a company of fighting devils." Everyone who knew Milroy predicted that if the Iroquois Guards ever witnessed action "every man will die on the battlefield or return home a hero, with a halo of glory encircling his brow."⁵⁴

Milroy's tenure as captain of the company, however, would be short lived. On April 25, 1861, Milroy received a commission as colonel of the 9th Indiana and would be charged with leading the regiment in its first campaign. When Milroy became the 9th's colonel the citizens of Rensselaer were elated and wanted to commemorate the occasion and present Milroy with a token of their appreciation for fighting to defend the Union. The item they chose to commemorate his commission was a horse. The horse, named

Jasper, was presented to Milroy in an elaborate ceremony. After he received the four-year-old "dapple gray horse" Milroy delivered remarks of gratitude. "I have not the vanity to suppose for a moment that this fine horse comes to any private worth or merit that I may possess, but he comes to me and I receive him as Colonel of the 9th Ind. Vols. as a gift of the military head of this splendid Regiment of patriotic soldiers who I have the proud honor to command," Milroy told the crowd. He then proclaimed to the crowd that he would cherish his new steed and use it to crush the rebellion. "I feel assured that this war horse is presented to me ... as a small token of the deep interest in the glorious cause in which we are all engaged & to be used in the promotion of that cause and let me assure my generous friends ... that this horse shall be rode by me during the present campaign whenever duty calls." Sternly he told the onlookers: "It shall be my endeavor to find that the path of duty leads to where traitors are found most plenty, and the battle of defense of the Star Spangled Banner falls thickest."[55]

After he received his commission and the pageantry of various presentations to the regiment and to Colonel Milroy concluded, he tried to prepare his men for war. He drilled his soldiers vigorously, employing what he learned as a student at Norwich in the hopes that they would become the finest combat unit in service and aid in creating his military legacy as one of the finest officers to ever command troops in combat.[56] Unfortunately for the 9th Indiana and every other Union regiment, time was of the essence and the public demanded action. Soon Colonel Milroy would be on his way to the front lines in western Virginia, embarking on his second opportunity to gain renown as a battlefield commander.[57]

2

"The Swamp Devils"

From his headquarters in Cincinnati, Ohio, on May 26, 1861, Gen. George B. McClellan penned a message to his men moving into western Virginia. The general, who would become likened to Napoleon by many for his bombast and braggadocio, proclaimed: "Soldiers— You are ordered to cross the frontier and enter upon the soil of Virginia. Your mission is to restore peace and confidence, to protect the majesty of the law, and to rescue our brethren from the grasp of armed traitors."[1]

Five days after McClellan wrote his inspirational words Colonel Milroy's 9th Indiana entered western Virginia ready to preserve the Union or at least for the moment help Unionists in the region create their own state government. The following day, June 1, Milroy's regiment along with other Indiana soldiers entered Grafton with Brig. Gen. Thomas A. Morris at their head.[2]

Milroy thirsted for action. He would not have to wait long. Two days prior to Milroy's arrival Col. Benjamin F. Kelley's 1st Virginia (U.S.) Infantry drove a small Confederate force under Col. George Porterfield out of Grafton. Porterfield's troops sought refuge about 15 miles south of Grafton in Philippi — a notoriously Confederate town.[3] As long as Confederates operated in the region, Union military planners on the front lines and in Washington, D.C., feared the failure of Unionist efforts to create a new Virginia government.

When the Indiana troops arrived the officers immediately went into a council of war to discuss plans for attacking Porterfield's Confederates. Colonel Kelley had been planning an attack against Phillipi since earlier that day but Morris, being the ranking officer in the field, tweaked the plan slightly — instead of moving Federal soldiers south in one column it would be a two-pronged offensive. One column under Col. Ebenezer Dumont moved south on the Beverly-Fairmont Road. The other wing commanded by Colonel Kelley, of which Milroy's regiment was part, proceeded east on the Baltimore & Ohio Railroad. Morris intended Kelley's force to create the illusion that they were moving to Harpers Ferry, but in fact they rode the rails for only six miles to Thornton where they got off and marched to Philippi.[4] Dumont's and Kelley's columns, according to the plans, were supposed to converge on Philippi at 4:00 A.M.; however, circumstances hampered the effort.

Dumont's column arrived on time, but Kelley's did not. Determined to succeed despite Kelley's absence, Dumont ordered the attack. Terrible weather, rugged terrain, and the misdirection of Jacob Baker, a civilian guide, caused Kelley's column to arrive too late to cut off a Confederate retreat. Porterfield's men, outnumbered by Federal forces, took to their heels and retreated southward. Had everything worked out as planned Milroy's 9th Indiana should have been positioned at a well-known landmark on the Beverly-Fairmont Pike known as the "Big Rock" to block Porterfield's withdrawal, but again a local guide took the Hoosiers off track, more than a mile from where they were supposed to position themselves.[5] Disgusted at being able to say only that he "participated in the affair" at Philippi, Milroy questioned the loyalties of the guides who misdirected Kelley's column.

While Milroy undoubtedly lamented over not being involved in the fight at Philippi, Confederate military planners in Richmond gasped as they saw western Virginia slipping from their grip. Gen. Robert E. Lee, serving as an advisor to Confederate president Jefferson Davis sent a trusted subordinate, Gen. Robert S. Garnett, to command the troops in western Virginia and salvage the region for the Confederacy.[6] Milroy would soon get another opportunity for combat.

As Garnett strengthened his two key defensive positions at Rich Mountain and Laurel Hill, McClellan began receiving exaggerated reports of Confederate troop strength. Fearing for the safety of western Virginia and his soldiers, McClellan felt it best to leave his headquarters in Cincinnati and go to western Virginia. When he arrived in Grafton on June 20, McClellan immediately took steps to strengthen his force and draft plans to drive out the Confederates.

McClellan decided to take three brigades and attack the Confederate position at Rich Mountain, while one brigade, including Milroy's 9th Indiana, under General Morris struck 16 miles north at Laurel Hill. Morris' brigade was supposed to amuse the Confederates at Laurel Hill and prepare to cut off a Confederate retreat from Laurel Hill.

On July 7, with Milroy's regiment in the van, Morris' brigade arrived at the small village of Belington, two miles west of Laurel Hill.[7] Sensing the opportunity to command his regiment in a battle Milroy ordered his men to attack the Confederate pickets. The Hoosiers easily drove in the pickets and wanted to pursue, but Milroy had to order them to halt. Milroy saw this as a serious error in judgment on the part of his superior, General Morris. He later lamented that his regiment would "have driven them into their fortifications had I not been restrained."[8] Despite Milroy's disgust at not being able to pursue, Morris was only following McClellan's directive to "amuse" the Confederates at Laurel Hill until the three Federal brigades were in position at Rich Mountain. Even though Milroy might have exhibited his displeasure with Morris the 9th Indiana was in no condition to pursue the enemy even if the order came. "Notwithstanding the strain of the day and the terrible march through which we had passed," recorded an officer of the regiment, "General Milroy was anxious to pursue the rebels and only desisted when it became apparent that his worn out command could not endure further marching."[9]

Throughout the next four days Morris' Federals skirmished with Confederates atop Laurel Hill. Impatience brewed among many officers and men. On one occasion several dozen men from Milroy's regiment, after exchanging shots with the enemy became so infuriated that "by a common impulse ... [they] ran forward into the woods and attacked the Confederate works."[10] The soldiers soon recognized the folly of their advance and as

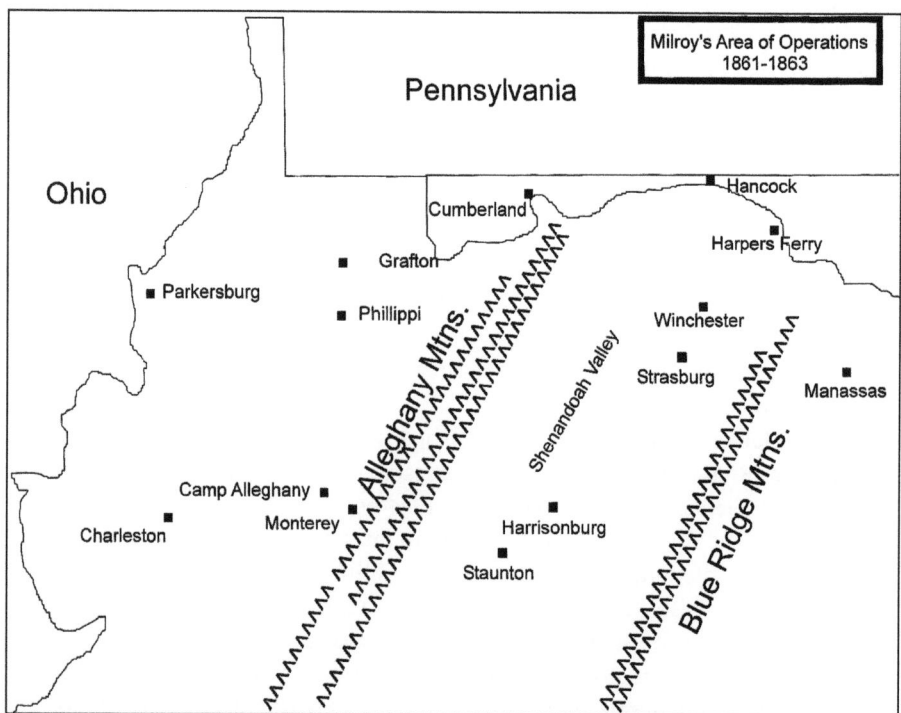

Ambrose Bierce, a soldier in the 9th, recorded, "we came out of the woods faster than we went in."[11]

While Milroy's men grew impatient at Laurel Hill, the bulk of McClellan's force bore down on Lt. Col. John Pegram's Confederates at Rich Mountain. In the early afternoon of July 11, the Federal attack column commanded by Brig. Gen. William S. Rosecrans climbed up the slopes and struck the Confederate position. By day's end the force defending Rich Mountain had been defeated and Garnett at Laurel Hill had to examine his options.

Garnett decided that since the Federals held Rich Mountain and with Morris' Federals in his front he had to withdraw. As news of the Confederate withdrawal reached the regimental commanders on the morning of July 12, Milroy according to some accounts did not wait for permission to pursue the enemy and cut them off as was one of General Morris' original orders; he simply ordered his regiment to pursue. Soon other regiments followed. The pursuit was rapid, Milroy recalled, but impeded by Morris' orders to halt and rest on the night of July 12. Initially Garnett retreated south toward Beverly, however, when he received erroneous information from his scouts that Federal soldiers occupied Beverly, Garnett changed direction and headed northeast. On July 13, Morris' men caught up to Garnett's rear guard at Carrick's Ford and obliterated them. Among the casualties was Garnett. By evening the fighting was over at Carrick's Ford and Milroy's regiment, along with the brigade returned to Laurel Hill.

Throughout June and July Milroy tasted action, but the grand battle that he hoped for never materialized. Shortly after Milroy's "Swamp Devils," as the 9th came to be called, returned to Laurel Hill, they went via train to Indianapolis. There the regiment mustered out of service on July 30.[12]

Milroy earned no military distinction during his first campaign. In fact the only thing he did earn was his nickname — "The Gray Eagle." Many of the soldiers who served with Milroy recorded why they felt he was given this sobriquet. One soldier suggested that Milroy's long sharp nose, watchful gaze, and overbearing demeanor made him appear as an eagle. Col. Joseph Warren Keifer believed that it was Milroy's "head of white, shocky, stiff hair that led his soldiers to dub him the Gray Eagle."[13]

As the regiment prepared to muster out of service Milroy communicated with Congressman Schuyler Colfax — a member of the U.S. House of Representatives from Indiana — to try to secure a command for Milroy in the regular army. Milroy believed that a post in the "old Army" would give him the best chance for earning a heroic reputation. On July 13, Colfax wrote Milroy: "I have not yet given up all hope of securing an app[ointment]t for you and shall keep on trying.... I shall try to get you in the old

Army if it is at all possible. I have been discouraged by my present failures; but shall keep on trying." Not encouraged by the letter Milroy was uncertain about his prospects of getting into the regular army, but felt somewhat confident at least that he would be able to recruit another regiment, command it, and earn the military glory he desired.[14]

While Milroy schemed with Colfax he made plans for his 9th Indiana to reenlist. Before his men mustered out of service Milroy told them that if they wished to reenlist they should rendezvous at La Porte, Indiana. Excited about future prospects of combat Milroy returned home, but only remained for four days. Milroy made preparations during the first week of August and the early part of the second week for the recruits who would flock to the defense of the nation's flag.

The first recruits streamed into La Porte on August 12. By August 27, Milroy had nearly 700 men ready for service. Even though it was not at full regimental strength the 9th Indiana mustered into service. Milroy, however, did not rest on his laurels and continued to recruit throughout the next several weeks to get the regiment to full strength—1,000 men. By September 12, the ranks swelled to about 960 troops. Milroy filled up the remainder of his ranks with recruits from the 28th Indiana.[15] As Milroy prepared to bring the 9th to full regimental strength he received some welcome news—he had been promoted to brigadier general to rank from September 3, 1861.[16] Although a brigadier's star graced the shoulder of his frock coat, he had not yet been assigned a brigade and for the time being remained in command of the 9th Indiana.

Although obviously disgusted at not being assigned a

Schuyler Colfax, a congressman from Indiana during the Civil War, became one of Milroy's supporters during the early months of the conflict. Colfax tried desperately at that time to secure Milroy a more active field command, but he did not succeed. After the Civil War Colfax served as vice president of the United States in Ulysses S. Grant's administration.

brigade Milroy's time in Indiana did afford him one opportunity to strike a blow against treason. In early September Milroy ordered the arrest of John C. Brain. Brain, a Confederate spy and member of the Knights of the Golden Circle — an organization aimed at disunion and aiding the Confederate war effort — was arrested in Michigan City, Indiana. Milroy and other members of the 9th Indiana suspected Brain of espionage and after they arrested him their suspicions proved true. Testimony from Mary Fraley stated that Brain had established a network to smuggle contraband goods — guns, food, medicine, etc. — into the Confederacy. Milroy turned Brain over to government officials who made a strong case against him and detained him.[17]

After the excitement of Brain's arrest passed, Brigadier General Milroy continued the efforts to fill the ranks of the 9th. By September 14, Milroy's regiment reached capacity and he was ordered with all possible haste to proceed to western Virginia to assist Gen. Joseph Reynolds, commanding Federal forces in the Cheat Mountain District, who was being "hard-pressed by the Reb Gen. [Robert E.] Lee."[18]

A West Pointer and native Kentuckian, Reynolds was supposed to harass the Confederates in his front. As September neared an end Reynolds' soldiers dreamed of leaving Cheat Mountain. Seen as a "veritable realm of enchantment" by some, Cheat Mountain was anything but to the soldiers from Indiana and Ohio in the early fall of 1861.[19] Torrential rains, gusty winds, and frigid temperatures made Cheat Mountain one of the least enchanting places on earth for Reynolds' men.[20] While the men in the ranks wanted to leave Cheat Mountain for a better place, such as the Shenandoah Valley to the southeast, Reynolds and his subordinates planned a movement against the Confederates at Camp Bartow — a fortified Confederate position in the hills that overlooked Traveller's Repose.[21]

The plans for attack were finalized on September 27 and 28 — Reynolds' force would conglomerate on Cheat Mountain Summit, about 10 miles from Camp Bartow and then launch the attack. Milroy's 9th Indiana was at Camp Elk Water when word came. The Hoosiers eagerly prepared for battle. Milroy's men moved out in a "terrible rain storm" on the 27th that continued for two straight days.[22] The men spent two miserable nights shivering in the cold, wet weather. Milroy sympathetically recalled that his men were "without tents or shelters of any kind" and they "suffered terribly."[23]

By October 2, Reynolds' force amassed on the summit and final preparations were made for the assault. At the stroke of midnight Reynolds gave the order to advance and the Federal column of nearly 5,000 troops began its march down Cheat Mountain. Leading the column was the 32nd Ohio. Milroy's 9th Indiana followed.

The march to Camp Bartow was cumbersome. Milroy remembered

that "the night was intensely dark" and the column moved at a snail's pace as the 32nd Ohio stopped on occasion to clear a fallen tree.[24] Although clearing fallen trees slowed the column it was essential to allow the artillery and ambulances to pass freely on the road. As the sluggish column marched, the 32nd Ohio became disgusted with being in the front and allowed the 9th Indiana to take the lead. Eager for a fight Milroy quickly ordered his men to advance to the front after the 32nd "went to hell."[25] The Hoosiers picked up the pace and encountered Confederate pickets around dawn at the bridge on the Parkersburg-Staunton Turnpike that spanned the Greenbrier River.[26] The Confederates opened fire first and struck two members of Milroy's regiment, but the 9th promptly answered with a volley that made the Rebels take to their heels. Three more of Milroy's men became casualties when men of the 9th mistakenly fired on their own comrades— one man was killed and two others wounded.[27]

The Confederate pickets fell back to a picket post about one mile from Camp Bartow and sent word of the coming attack. As the Federals advanced Col. Edward Johnson of the 12th Georgia Infantry was roused from his peaceful sleep at his headquarters in Traveller's Repose with a message from Col. James Ramsey, officer of the day, that the Federals were attacking.[28]

This would be the first of three times that Johnson and Milroy would clash during the war. Johnson decided to form his Georgians about one mile from the main Confederate position at Camp Bartow and slow the Union advance. Reynolds deployed his line of battle and Milroy's men formed up on the left bank of the Greenbrier.[29] As the advance commenced, Confederate Brig. Gen. Henry Jackson scurried to form a defensive position. With approximately 1,800 troops, Jackson's strength paled in comparison to Reynolds.' Jackson hoped his three artillery batteries could halt the Union attack.[30]

Reynolds' men rushed Johnson's position around 7:00 A.M. and after a fight of about 45 minutes broke that part of the Confederate line. Milroy's men and Col. Nathan Kimball's 14th Indiana moved forward at the double-quick and fired as they went. After Johnson's men gave way after a spirited fight in the face of overwhelming odds—Johnson having only about 100 men—Milroy pressed his men forward to within one-half mile of Camp Bartow. Federal progress halted as Reynolds ordered the advance to stop to allow enough time for the Union guns to get into position to support the assault.[31]

Around 8:00 A.M., with 13 Federal guns in place, iron shot and shell filled the air. Confederate artillery from atop Camp Bartow replied, belching forth the same. For nearly three hours an intense artillery duel commenced. The barrage achieved little and as Milroy noted caused "much more noise than harm to either side."[32]

As the bombardment continued fear turned into boredom and some soldiers even reportedly fell asleep during the whole affair.[33] Milroy, however, feared for his men's safety as they were pinned down in the middle of the artillery duel. Without orders he began to move his men several hundred yards to the Union left out of harm's way. As he commenced this maneuver a courier called him to a council of war with General Reynolds.

All officers gathered around Reynolds and Milroy "strenuously urged an immediate attack upon the Reb works."[34] Other regimental officers, incensed over the stalemate, concurred with Milroy. Reynolds, at least for the moment, agreed. He ordered all troops to form opposite the Confederate trenches and wait for the order to advance, but the command never came.

After the council of war Reynolds changed his mind and ordered four of his regiments to move against the Confederate right — the 7th, 14th, and 15th Indiana and the 24th Ohio. These four regiments met disaster as they neared the Confederate right flank. Captain Shumaker's guns poured canister into them and sent them reeling for the rear.[35] As the Indiana and Ohio regiments retreated, General Reynolds mistook portions of the 52nd Virginia Infantry as a major reinforcement that would give the numerical advantage to the Confederates, bolstering his reason for ordering the withdrawal.[36] Somehow in the confusion of battle Milroy never received the order to retire and his Hoosiers remained in position until all regiments left the field.[37] Casualties on both sides were limited — the Federals reported 43, while Brig. Gen. Henry Jackson reported 52.[38] The Union withdrawal meant more time on wretched Cheat Mountain.

Milroy's Hoosiers suffered only eight casualties in the melee. Following their withdrawal the Indiana men marched in the direction of Cheat River and spent the night of October 3 in camp near it. The following day the men returned to Camp Elk Water. For the next week Milroy's men remained at Camp Elk Water performing the mundane tasks of soldiers and Milroy contemplated when he would finally receive command of a brigade. That welcome news reached Milroy on October 10.[39]

That day Milroy and the 9th Indiana headed back to Cheat Mountain Summit where Milroy took command of a brigade consisting of the 9th Indiana and the 24th, 25th, and 32nd Ohio Infantry regiments.[40] When Milroy arrived at Cheat Mountain Summit later that day he began to prepare for what he thought would be an imminent movement against Camp Bartow. He enacted a regular system of scouting in all directions around his post, but paid special attention to scouting in the direction of Camp Bartow.[41]

Milroy firmly believed that General Reynolds would make another attack against Camp Bartow very soon. As the remaining weeks of October passed it became clear that Reynolds had no intention of attacking Camp Bartow. Incensed over this West Pointer's reluctance to attack, Milroy pleaded with Reynolds to strike at "the inferior enemy," but to no avail.

Disgusted, Milroy's scouts continued to gather information and his brigade went about its daily camp and guard routine. Near the end of October a surprise visitor interrupted the monotony of camp life. The visitor was a mulatto simply named Ben. Part Cherokee and part African American, Ben lived and worked in Arkansas prior to the Civil War, but when conflict broke out his master, an unidentified Confederate officer, took him along as a servant. Seeking his freedom, Ben fled his master and entered Milroy's camp carrying a white flag. When he came before General Milroy, Ben promised to provide the Federals with intelligence about the Confederates. The only thing Ben wanted in return was the guarantee of freedom.

Ben could not have come into a better camp. General Milroy, an abolitionist and as the war progressed an active enforcer of emancipation, eagerly took in the runaway. Milroy told Ben that he would have to earn his freedom. Milroy named the former slave Benjamin Summit and initially employed him at his headquarters and used him as a guide. After a stint with Milroy's brigade in the fall of 1861 Milroy sent Ben to the Milroy home in Indiana in December 1861. There Milroy's wife schooled the former slave and paid him for doing odd jobs around the Milroy residence. Ben also performed similar tasks for Milroy's neighbors. He remained with Mrs. Milroy throughout much of 1862, but by August Ben wanted to do more to serve the Union and he became a servant for the staff of the 73rd Indiana Infantry. His stint with the Indiana regiment lasted several weeks, ending when Union Gen. Stephen Burbridge, a native Kentuckian and antiabolitionist, demanded Ben prove his freedom. Ben could not and fearful of what Burbridge might do he returned to Rensselaer and continued to work for various people in the town. In December 1863 Ben left Rensselaer and enlisted in the 23rd U.S. Colored Troops. He finished the war a sergeant and was among the first soldiers to enter Richmond in 1865 after the Confederacy surrendered.[42]

The care Milroy gave Ben was not customary for most Union officers in the conflict's early days. In fact Milroy was in a small minority in the war's infancy as he favored immediate emancipation. Only a handful of Union commanders—most notably Gens. Benjamin Butler, John C. Frémont, and David Hunter—openly exhibited abolitionist tendencies in the war's early stages.[43]

The distraction of Benjamin Summit did not occupy Milroy for long, however, as he fumed over not being able to attack the Confederates at

Camp Bartow. Incensed over his superior's lack of aggressiveness, Milroy frequently wrote to Schuyler Colfax to secure a more active command for his old regiment and himself. On December 12, Colfax gave Milroy assurance that he was doing everything in his power to secure a better, more active command for the Gray Eagle. Colfax informed Milroy that he had President Lincoln write a letter to General McClellan specifically asking to move the 9th Indiana and Milroy to a "place where they would have an opportunity of seeing the enemy and fighting him."[44] Colfax tried to strengthen Milroy's spirits further by writing: "I wrote a strong letter to General [McClellan] also for the 3rd time, asking it as a personal favor to myself."[45]

As Colfax bargained with Lincoln and McClellan, Milroy's hunger for battle was about to be sated. Throughout the first half of December Milroy probed Col. Ed Johnson's outposts south of Cheat Mountain Summit. Federal troops made daily patrols south along the Staunton-Parkersburg Pike toward Camp Alleghany but failed to gain enough intelligence about Johnson's strength and intentions. Some suspected that Confederates were withdrawing from the region but suspicion did nothing to bolster confidence. Indeed Federal suspicion was correct. Confederate forces under Gen. William Loring began withdrawing from the region to Staunton and then proceeded to the Shenandoah Valley to join forces with "Stonewall" Jackson in Winchester. Jackson wanted all available troops in the area to converge on Winchester and then make a move against Romney — a strategic town located less than 40 miles northwest of Winchester. Jackson believed the occupation of Romney would yield control of the South Branch Valley and from this location, he could ensure the safety of Winchester. That move would put his command between Federal forces west of Staunton and Union regiments along the Potomac River line to protect the lower Shenandoah Valley. The movement was heavily debated in the Confederate command and among those who spoke out was Col. Ed Johnson. He felt that a withdrawal of all forces from the area would leave Staunton — a vital rail center — vulnerable to capture. His pleas fell on deaf ears and the movement began.[46]

As the Confederate high command in western Virginia moved Loring's approximately 6,000 troops to Winchester, the Gray Eagle, from atop his perch on Cheat Summit, searched for a way to confirm the troop withdrawal and enemy weaknesses near Camp Alleghany. Near the end of the first week of December the confirmation of Confederate strength Milroy waited for had arrived. Five Confederate deserters entered Milroy's camp. These deserters from Lt. Col. George W. Hansbrough's 9th Battalion Virginia Infantry informed Milroy that Johnson's men were weak and demoralized.

The Confederates told Milroy that if he attacked they would guide the Union forces in the assault.[47] Even though these deserters gave what appeared to be vital information to Milroy it was a ruse. Johnson's men were neither demoralized nor weak and were ready for anything the Gray Eagle threw their way.[48]

Despite the apparent good news from these Confederate deserters Milroy needed to be cautious in assaulting Camp Alleghany. Union forces in the region throughout early December departed for service in Kentucky and western Maryland, drastically depleting Federal troops strength.[49] General Reynolds also left in December for family reasons. His brother died, and he returned home to Indiana to help run the family grocery business. By December 10, the only available Union forces around Cheat Mountain were the 9th Indiana, 25th and 32nd Ohio and 2nd Virginia (U.S.).[50]

When Reynolds departed Milroy assumed command of the remaining forces in the Cheat Mountain District. With his regiments spread out at Beverly, Huttonsville, Elk Water, and Cheat Mountain and armed with the information from the five deserters, Milroy prepared plans for an attack against Camp Alleghany.[51] With forces leaving and many soldiers either sick or on furlough Milroy's task at assembling a sizable force to attack Johnson would not be easy. He issued a plea for volunteers—in all about 2,000 men answered the call.[52]

On the morning of December 12, two companies from the 9th Indiana moved out from Cheat Mountain Summit with orders to capture Camp Bartow—abandoned by the Confederates on November 22—and hold it until the main body arrived.[53] As Milroy's van neared Camp Bartow 106 men of the 52nd Virginia under command of Maj. John Ross ambushed the Hoosiers.[54] While two men of the 9th Indiana were killed the Confederates fled for Camp Alleghany.[55]

As the men of Milroy's old regiment secured Camp Bartow the main body of Milroy's force marched off Cheat Mountain Summit around noon. Milroy and his men had confidence that soon they would be cooking coffee at Camp Alleghany. The volunteers from Rigby's artillery exuded such confidence that "they went along without arms, expecting to take possession of the enemy's guns when captured."[56]

By nightfall Milroy's command arrived at Camp Bartow. While his men rested, the Gray Eagle made the final preparations for battle. Milroy proposed dividing his force into two columns. One column, under the command of Col. Gideon Moody, would move against the Confederate left via the Greenbank Road and the other column, commanded by Milroy, would aim at the Confederate right via the Staunton-Parkersburg Turnpike.[57] If coordinated properly both columns would strike the Confederate position simultaneously.

With the attack plan prepared Milroy needed to make sure that these two columns, approaching from different directions, converged on Camp Alleghany at precisely the right time. In order to achieve a precision march over rugged terrain Milroy would need help. He employed two local Unionists as guides. Moody's column was guided by a local Unionist who lived only several miles from Camp Alleghany, a man identified only as Slater. Milroy's column proceeded to Camp Alleghany with the aid of another Unionist from northwestern Virginia named Shipman.[58] Moody's force departed Camp Bartow around 11:00 P.M. and Milroy's column deployed one hour later. The two columns marched toward the prize of Camp Alleghany. Victory meant not only control of Alleghany, but possibly the vital rail center of Staunton, western Virginia's link with Richmond.

Around 4:00 A.M. on December 13, Confederate pickets fled for the main line at Camp Alleghany, alerting Johnson that an attack was underway. As the Confederate pickets fled for the rear, Milroy's column aimed at the Confederate right, marched on a narrow trail leading to the Confederate flank. By 7:15 A.M. Milroy's attack force was in place and launched its offensive against Johnson's right flank.[59]

The 13th Indiana struck first and broke the Confederate line. Milroy described the scene: "The enemy's line broke in confusion and retreated back among their houses and tents and over their trenches, leaving the ground covered with their dead and wounded."[60] After the initial attack Milroy's men held the advantage as they took cover behind trees and shot at their foe, but Johnson's men advanced and drove the Federals from their position. Some of Milroy's men immediately "broke to the rear in confusion" at the first intimation of a Confederate counterattack, while other stalwart troops remained in position and engaged in hand-to-hand fighting.[61] The Union troops of the 25th and 32nd Ohio and 13th Indiana who remained tested their foe admirably. From a Confederate perspective Lieutenant Colonel Hansbrough penned: "The fight here was almost hand to hand, the roar of musketry was incessant and deafening, but above the roar rang the shouts of officers and men. It must be admitted that not much order was observed."[62]

For the next three hours Federal assaults against the Confederate right continued, but to no avail. As the battle raged many of Milroy's men became discouraged as they heard no fighting on the Confederate left. Where was Moody's column? Milroy wondered. As the hours passed and Moody's column was nowhere in sight and the ammunition ran low in Milroy's ranks the Federals had no choice but to withdraw. About three hours after the attack commenced Milroy decided to pull out but not before he launched one more attack to gain ground momentarily so that the wounded could be taken from the field. "By great and active exertions" wrote Milroy, "was this attack successful and the Federals carried many of their dead and wounded brethren down the mountain."63

As Milroy's column retreated down the mountain and gathered near the Staunton-Parkersburg Turnpike, Moody's attack against the Confederate left commenced and with the same result as the attack against Johnson's right flank. By 2:00 P.M. the battle ended and Milroy's men marched back to Cheat Mountain, 20 miles to the northwest.64

Confederate Maj. Gen. Edward "Old Alleghany" Johnson, a graduate of West Point and veteran of the Seminole and Mexican wars, was perhaps Milroy's biggest nemesis during the first half of the Civil War. The two fought against each other in western Virginia in 1861 and 1862. In 1863, at the Second Battle of Winchester, Johnson's division put the finishing touches on Milroy's battered command, helping clear the way for a Confederate invasion of Pennsylvania (*Battles and Leaders*).

Defeated, the Union troops headed back to their camps. Many soldiers in the ranks blamed Milroy's overconfidence in the report of the Confederate deserters for the defeat. Milroy blamed a myriad of reasons for the loss. First, he pointed out the obvious—had Moody's attack commenced simultaneously the result would have been different. He lamented after the war: "There is little doubt but had Col. Moody attacked simultaneously as ordered it would have been a complete success and the Reb. Genl. Johnson with all his forces captured."65 Second, Milroy blamed the men in the ranks for deserting under fire. Scores of men fled to the rear, a phenomenon not uncommon in the war's early stage, weakening Milroy's attack force. Milroy lambasted these "cowards" in his report of the engagement: "too much execration cannot be poured upon the many base cowards who deserted the battlefield and left their brave companions, in violation of orders. They should be remembered in eternal infamy." Finally Milroy blamed an unnamed Union deserter who apprised the Confederates of Milroy's plan prior to the battle. The Gray Eagle bemoaned: "The enemy was fully apprised and prepared to meet us at all points, and we have since learned from prisoners that they were fully apprised not only of our coming, but of the plan of attack, two days before, by a deserter from our camp."[66]

Regardless of who should shoulder the blame, Milroy's first major test in battle as a brigadier was a dismal failure. In the immediate wake of the battle Milroy portrayed the action as a victory. He stated that his forces defeated Johnson. In a message to his superiors immediately following the action Milroy stated: "General Milroy ... met General Johnson, of Georgia ... at Alleghany Camp ... and after 3 hours' hard fighting defeated Johnson.... Johnson burned his camp and retreated to Staunton."[67] Johnson had not retreated and his men hunkered down for the winter at Camp Alleghany just as Milroy's men did the same at Cheat Summit.[68] In fact Johnson's victory earned him a promotion to brigadier general to date from the battle and the eternal sobriquet of "Alleghany Johnson."[69]

Even though, in the immediate wake of the fighting atop Camp Alleghany, Milroy and the northern press depicted the affair as another great victory in western Virginia, Milroy knew that the fight delivered anything but victory. In his formal report Milroy did not use victorious rhetoric, but rather lambasted some of his command for fleeing and admitted that that was the ultimate reason for the Union loss.[70]

A week after the battle at Camp Alleghany Milroy was officially assigned to command of the Cheat Mountain District by Brigadier General Rosecrans commanding the Department of Western Virginia.[71] Official assignment to command must have pleased Milroy, but no assignment could remove the bitter taste of defeat. Confined to a miserable, frigid, and bleak winter atop Cheat Mountain, Milroy longed for another battle and a chance to avenge his defeat at the hands of Old Alleghany.

3

"I fear I shall not like Fremont"

Throughout the early months of 1862, as snow blanketed the ground atop Cheat Mountain, a depressed Milroy turned his thoughts to home. Among his chief concerns in the early months of 1862 was the future of Ben Summit. Summit, the runaway slave Milroy sent home to Indiana, had been the cause of some debate in Rensselaer as some of the area's citizens questioned whether or not Ben had the legal right to be in Indiana. Article XIII of the 1851 Indiana Constitution placed severe restrictions on free blacks coming into their state; however, as was the case with similar laws in other states, it was difficult to enforce. The law did stipulate that anyone who employed a free black would be subject to a fine. When a fellow named Ballard questioned Ben's right to remain in Rensselaer the citizens held an "indignation Meeting" and decided that the state's laws forbidding free blacks to be brought into the Hoosier state were "not effective." Ben would be allowed to remain.[1]

Although Ben's troubles worried Milroy his preeminent concern was his children's health. They were sick with measles. Seeing many of his own men suffering and dying from them on a daily basis could not have bolstered his confidence that his children would survive. "My poor boys of the 9th are suffering from them — about 300 of them are down with them last week — 13 had died and some 4 or 5 more are expected to die."[2] Finally in early February Milroy received good news from Mary that the children were recovering. Knowing that his precious loved ones were safe and on a path to recovery he focused wholly on military matters.

One of his concerns in the early part of 1862 was trying to find a more suitable command — one that would allow him to see action and earn distinction. Much of Milroy's free time during January and February 1862 was spent writing letters to Congressman Schuyler Colfax trying to convince him to speak with General McClellan to see if "Little Mac" might be able to find Milroy a better command, one in which he could see more action.

By early February Milroy received a message from Colfax with McClellan's endorsement stating that by the end of February Milroy would be given a command in Kentucky that would be part of a Union invasion of Tennessee.[3] Confidently Milroy wrote his wife: "I will be ordered to K[entuck]y between this time and the 20th and if they will then let me have a Hoosier brigade and let me pitch into Tennesse and on the South that will be glorious."[4] Excited at the prospect of being assigned to a command in Kentucky, Milroy was somewhat disappointed in his inability to create more havoc in western Virginia and capture Alleghany Summit. "But I will regret to have to leave this country as much as I detest it, without taking them devils on Allegany Summit," Milroy explained to his wife.[5] He blamed his shortcomings on his superiors and argued that with two or three more regiments he could have captured the Confederate stronghold. "I have been prevented from [taking Alleghany Summit] for the want of two or three more Regts. This is horribly annoying when I see hundreds of Regts. laying idle elsewhere," Milroy lamented, "practicing the new system invented by our commander in chief called the setting hen tactics."[6]

Bitterness over the restrictions placed on his movements in western Virginia could have only increased his excitement as February neared an end and he awaited his new orders with anticipation. Joy at the prospect of being reassigned soon turned into disappointment as February came to a close and he received no word of a new command. "I am still here," Milroy cried on March 6, "and have nearly lost all hopes of orders for leaving this state as was promised me."[7]

As spring approached and Milroy's hopes for a new command were dashed he focused his attention on Confederate activity in western Virginia and became keenly aware of the crimes against Unionist families in the region. He aimed to do something about it. Milroy's first attempt at dealing with bushwhackers came near the end of February when he sent about 200 troops from the 2nd Virginia (U.S.) Infantry into Pendleton County, Virginia, "to clear out a nest of traitors and horse thieves who made that place their headquarters." The Virginia Unionists attacked the bushwhackers and captured 28 of them.[8]

During the first two weeks of March, Milroy ordered similar expeditions, but had limited control over the operations when General Rosecrans sent Milroy to Beverly, Virginia, to assume a temporary position on the Board of Examiners—an arm of the army to determine the ability of officers. The purely administrative duty was monotonous for Milroy as he questioned junior officers and determined their capability to command and their knowledge of military duties. For the next week while Milroy performed his role in Beverly he could not conceive how West Pointers like

Rosecrans saw more importance in quizzing junior officers while Unionists in western Virginia were being "murdered at their own doors and the people ... begging and praying for us to come over and relieve them from the horrible oppression."[9] Milroy understood the importance of aiding the Unionists who constantly sought refuge with Milroy's command and told many "tales of wrong, oppression and outrage" at the hands of Confederates. He recognized their importance to curbing the activities of partisan forces in western Virginia as well as serving as scouts for Union forces in the region. Milroy feared that not doing everything in his power to protect Unionists would slowly chip away at the Unionist support that existed in the area and only make it more difficult for Federal forces to conduct military operations.[10]

Although Milroy's expeditions failed to permanently halt irregular partisan operations in western Virginia they hampered their efforts. Scores of these partisans had been captured and among them was a noted bushwhacker, Frederick W. Chewning.[11] Chewning initially stood at the mercy of General Milroy, who wanted to execute the bushwhacker by hanging. Milroy did not get his wish and Chewning instead served time in prison.[12]

Throughout March Union forces in western Virginia began mobilizing for the spring campaign and the Lincoln administration restructured the high command. On March 11, 1862, Lincoln created the Mountain Department. It encompassed western Virginia, parts of Kentucky, and Tennessee. Lincoln gave command of the newly minted department to Maj. Gen. John C. Frémont. Nicknamed the "Pathfinder" for his expeditions across the Rocky Mountains in the 1840s, Frémont replaced General Rosecrans, a Democrat who oftentimes did not see eye to eye with the Republicans in Washington.[13] Frémont officially took command on March 29.

News of Frémont's promotion to command of the Mountain Department pleased Milroy and he saw an opportunity. Once again enlisting the aid of Representative Colfax, Milroy penned him a note asking him to speak to Frémont on his behalf. On the evening of March 17, Colfax visited Frémont and his wife, Jessie, and told him about Milroy's situation. Colfax painted a very positive image of Milroy and as Colfax informed Milroy: "I went up to Fremont's ... and told him and Jessie all about you. He says you are the very man he wants with him — took your name in his note book — and told me to tell you that he would in a few days put himself in communication with you.... He will ... give you every opportunity for fighting and distinction, and will counsel with you about the campaign." The message seemed encouraging and also highlighted the prospect of Milroy's promotion to major general. "I told him," Colfax wrote of his conversation with Frémont, "I should ask no appointments of him, only that he should let you loose and let you earn a Major Generalship by fighting." Milroy undoubtedly viewed this as good news, but as happy at the prospect of getting into some real combat and earning a second star as Milroy might have been, he was melancholy over the departure of his beloved 9th Indiana to Kentucky. "Much as your heart's with the 9th," Colfax wrote to Milroy, "I think ... your best fighting sphere will be with Fremont. In K[entuck]y and T[ennessee] there are so many Generals you might be overstaffed again."[14] Weighing his options Milroy decided that remaining in western Virginia would afford the best chance for personal advancement. After reading Colfax's dispatch the Gray Eagle firmly believed that Frémont would cut him loose and "help the Devil to a large supply of traitors."[15] Surely, Milroy believed, because of Colfax's communiqué, Frémont would not be as idle and complacent as Rosecrans. By the first week of June Milroy would realize the error in his judgment.

While the command structure in western Virginia changed, the spring campaign season opened in the nearby Shenandoah Valley. On March 12, 1862, Maj. Gen. Nathaniel P. Banks seized Winchester, Virginia — the first of many times the town would be occupied by Federal troops.[16] Eleven days after he seized Winchester, Federal forces under Gen. James Shields defeated Jackson at the First Battle of Kernstown. After Jackson's defeat at Kernstown on March 23, Stonewall marched south, up the Shenandoah Valley and reorganized his command.

As part of the reorganization Jackson ordered Brigadier General Johnson's troops from Camp Alleghany to the Shenandoah Valley. Johnson's Army of the Northwest filed down the mountain to the Valley beginning on April 2.[17] The day following Johnson's withdrawal, Frémont cut Milroy loose with strict orders to advance no farther east than Monterey. En route to Monterey Milroy saw an opportunity to seize the site of his first major loss — Camp Alleghany. On April 6, Milroy's flags fluttered in the breeze atop Camp Alleghany — finally the prize had been gained, but not in a glorious battle as Milroy had hoped.[18]

After Milroy and his troops settled in at Camp Alleghany the Gray Eagle strolled through the camps and fortifications of his old nemesis — Old Alleghany Johnson. "I was greatly surprised at the great extent and immense strength of the rebel fortifications and winter quarters here," wrote Milroy to his wife, Mary.[19] Milroy knew that during the fight for Camp Alleghany on December 13, Johnson's men were not this well protected. He somehow felt slightly vindicated by the extra work done on the earthworks after the battle. On April 7, he wrote to his wife: "We must have given them a tremendous scare at that time for their whole force seems to [have] worked on the fortifications incessantly since then and it is wonderful to see the amount of labour they have performed."[20] Milroy took great pride in knowing that the fighting of December 13, 1861, prompted the Confederates to strengthen their fortifications. Assessing those fortifications Milroy noted: "The place is now almost a Gibraltar for strength both by nature and with a brave garrison, a good cause, and sufficient supplies it would be almost impregnable to any force that could be brought to bear against it."[21]

Exciting though it may have been for Milroy and his troops to walk the ground at Camp Alleghany, they were soon reminded of the horror of the battle fought in December. As they traipsed through the earthworks and log winter huts they discovered the unburied bodies of two of their comrades—one from the 2nd Virginia and another from Milroy's old 9th Indiana. Although "much decayed," Milroy remembered, the bodies were identified by the "spots where they were known to have fallen."[22]

During the short time at Camp Alleghany Milroy's command received kind treatment from civilians in the area. They helped them any way they could and Milroy informed Mary that "we acknowledge that our neighbors have been somewhat neighborly and will remember them."[23] Milroy's stay at Camp Alleghany was short lived. On April 8, only two days after marching into Johnson's old camps, Milroy pressed on with the bulk of his troops to Monterey, about 10 miles east of Camp Alleghany. After Milroy's Federals reached Monterey he sent out scouting parties on a regular basis and they frequently skirmished with the enemy.[24]

On April 12, a small band of Confederates from Johnson's command tested Milroy at Monterey, but the heavily outnumbered Confederates withdrew east to Johnson's main line on Shenandoah Mountain. Milroy praised his men for their splendid performance and knew now that a battle was near. Eagerly awaiting battle, the sound of cannon and muskets energized Milroy. Like music to his ears, Milroy exclaimed to his wife that on the fight of April 12, "the firearms sounded splendidly through the mountains."[25]

The Gray Eagle's forces at Monterey not only had to deal with repeated Confederate incursions during the second week of April they also had to contend with a constant flow of contrabands coming into their camps. On April 13, for example three contrabands arrived in Milroy's camp. He described the band as "black as coffee." The contrabands informed Milroy that their master was sending them south, and they fled. They were hungry, frightened, and weak, and Milroy's heart undoubtedly ached for these troubled runaways. One of the female contrabands who entered Milroy's camp that night was so exhausted with "hunger and fatigue" that she "fell off her seat when she sat down," recalled Milroy.[26]

As contrabands poured into Milroy's camps in Monterey before and after the small clash of arms on April 12, Milroy decided to disobey Frémont's order to not go beyond Monterey and he pursued his foe. The day following the small engagement, April 13, Milroy sent some of his force 10 miles east of Monterey to the small Virginia hamlet of McDowell. When Federal soldiers arrived in McDowell the civilians of the town informed them that Confederate forces under General Johnson — nearly 3,500 soldiers and 2,000 African Americans— were in the process of fortifying Shenandoah Mountain several miles to the east.[27] When he received the news Milroy peered to the east and speculated in a letter to his wife that "our next fight will be on the Shenandoah if they do not leave there soon."[28]

Circumstances in the Shenandoah Valley, however, would not allow a battle with Johnson atop Shenandoah Mountain. Six days after contact with Milroy's force near Monterey, Old Alleghany Johnson received a message from Gen. Robert E. Lee, advisor to Confederate president Jefferson Davis, which informed Johnson that forces under Stonewall Jackson were withdrawing up the Shenandoah Valley toward Staunton — Banks was in pursuit. The terse message read in part: "I have received information that Genl Jackson has fallen back to Big Spring, some 9 miles from New Market, and that the enemy is still pressing him in the direction of Staunton."[29]

Several hours after receiving the message from Lee, a courier delivered another note to Johnson — this time it was from Jackson. Stonewall wanted Johnson to come to his headquarters. When Johnson arrived at Capt. Asher Argenbright's home near Conrad's Store, Jackson ordered Old Alleghany to move his men off of Shenandoah Mountain. Obedient to orders, Johnson sent a dispatch to Col. John B. Baldwin of the 52nd Virginia Infantry in command of forces on Shenandoah Mountain to be prepared for a move.[30] While en route to his Army of the Northwest on April 20, Johnson learned that his men had pulled back from Shenandoah Mountain to a small village known as West View, a mere six miles west of the vital rail center at Staunton.[31]

After the withdrawal of Johnson's Army of the Northwest from Shenandoah Mountain, Milroy deployed a small force of infantry and cavalry to North Mountain — 10 miles east of Shenandoah Mountain. Milroy accompanied the small scouting party. Federal infantry and horsemen easily brushed aside some of Johnson's pickets and came within site of the tracks of the Virginia Central Railroad. The Virginia Central was Stonewall Jackson's lifeline. It ran north from Richmond to Hanover Junction, then Northwest to Gordonsville. From Gordonsville the rails went southwest to Charlottesville. From Charlottesville the tracks moved west, traversing the ridges of the Blue Ridge Mountains into Staunton.[32] If Milroy seized Staunton, Jackson's lines of communication and supply would be cut off with the Confederate capital.

Since the late fall of 1861 Milroy had wanted to capture Staunton, but circumstances prevented him from doing so. Now he saw another opportunity. In late April part of Milroy's force was within sight of Staunton, but Frémont ordered Milroy to keep calm and return to McDowell. He withdrew his force to the western slope of Shenandoah Mountain. Again on May 4, Milroy with a force of three infantry regiments, an artillery battery, and one company of cavalry crossed to the east side of Shenandoah Mountain. While he wanted to provoke a battle his judgment got the best of him and he decided to obey Frémont's order to not engage the enemy. Milroy ordered his command back to McDowell but he did leave one of his regiments, the 32nd Ohio, east of Shenandoah Mountain as an advance picket — to sound the alarm should Johnson attempt to strike Milroy.[33] While Milroy returned to McDowell with the remainder of his command Stonewall Jackson implemented plans to lash out at the Federal forces.

Near the end of April, General Banks' force of 19,000 stood near Harrisonburg, while Frémont's army of nearly 20,000 was to the west of the Shenandoah Valley in the Alleghany Mountains. While Jackson's ultimate objective was to prevent Banks from moving east of the Blue Ridge to assist in the Union movement against Richmond via the Virginia Peninsula he first had to deal with the threat that Frémont's vanguard, under Milroy, posed to Staunton. Furthermore Jackson needed to silence Frémont's force west of the Shenandoah Valley and prevent a link-up between Frémont and Banks which could easily have been achieved in the spring of 1862 by a march on the Warm Springs Turnpike. Before Jackson could go after Banks he needed to first deal with the threat to the west.[34]

Jackson's plan to strike west of the Valley was brilliant. Reinforcements under Gen. Richard S. Ewell would occupy Conrad's Store, the site of Jackson's old camp. From this location Ewell could hamper any movement against Staunton made by Banks. While Ewell blocked Banks, Jackson would take his force of 6,000, combine it with General Johnson's 2,800 troops and strike at Milroy, deterring Frémont from linking with Banks. Following this Jackson and Johnson would move into back into the Shenandoah Valley, combine with Ewell and with a force of nearly 17,000 annihilate Banks.

Jackson's plan unfolded on April 30, when he began a circuitous march to the east, making it appear as if he was leaving the Shenandoah Valley. Once Jackson reached Mechum's River Station his men boarded the trains of the Virginia Central Railroad and steamed toward Staunton.[35] Jackson's men arrived in Staunton on May 4. Three days later the combined force of Jackson and Johnson, nearly 9,000 strong, marched west toward McDowell.

That day, May 7, the lead elements of the Confederate force encountered the 32nd Ohio— Milroy's advance picket — and drove the Federals off with ease.³⁶ The Confederate attackers allowed no time for the Ohioans to gather any of their gear and as Milroy explained to his wife the Confederates attacked "my 32nd Ohio so suddenly that thay had to fall back leaving their tents and most of their baggage."³⁷ When Milroy received word of the skirmish he rode to the hot spot. Undoubtedly Milroy wanted to attack his enemy, however, General Frémont explicitly prohibited Milroy from bringing on a general engagement. As impetuous for a fight as Milroy might have been, his eagerness for combat waned when he noticed a Confederate force much larger than his own marching over Shenandoah Mountain. "Observing them coming down in force," Milroy penned to his wife, "I thought it prudent to fall back to McDowell."³⁸

Milroy sent a message to the Federal force at Franklin, 30 miles distant, under command of Gen. Robert C. Schenck. Milroy needed reinforcements. At approximately 11:00 A.M. on May 7, Schenck prepared his men to march from Franklin to McDowell. Over the next 23 hours Schenck pressed his 1,500-man brigade to McDowell. While Schenck's men marched speedily to Milroy's aid the Gray Eagle concentrated his forces in McDowell.³⁹

By the afternoon Milroy's regiments were in McDowell and he could see the Confederates marching down the west side of Shenandoah Mountain via the Staunton Parkersburg Turnpike. Witnessing the gray column descend the mountain Milroy ordered two guns from the 9th Ohio Battery on Shaw's Ridge to open fire and halt the Confederate advance. "This they did with such effect," recalled Milroy, "as to cause the enemy to retire beyond Shenandoah Mountain." Milroy's joy at driving off the Confederates soon turned to sorrow as he noticed another Confederate force crossing the mountain two miles in the distance. Milroy decided to retire.⁴⁰

The remainder of the day was quiet as Milroy waited for Schenck's arrival. With sunrise on May 8, Milroy decided to test the Confederate position. The Federals awoke that morning to the sight of Confederates atop Bull Pasture Mountain. Fearing an attack Milroy needed to do something to spoil whatever plans the Confederates had in mind. Milroy ordered his guns to begin shelling the enemy as he deployed skirmishers to ascertain the amount of Confederates in his front.⁴¹

Around 10:00 A.M. on May 8, Schenck joined Milroy in McDowell giving Federal forces there an aggregate strength of about 3,500.⁴² When Schenck arrived in McDowell he noticed that this small hamlet surrounded by mountains afforded no opportunity for a good defense. Schenck recorded of the scene: "A little observation served to show at once that McDowell, as a defensive position, was entirely untenable, and especially against the largely outnumbering force that was ascertained to be advancing."⁴³ Furthermore Schenck observed that the combined force could not remain there because supplies were low and there was nothing left to forage in the area.[44] Unable to remain and defend the position Schenck, senior to Milroy, conferred with the Gray Eagle and both determined it best to withdraw.

Even though both commanders decided that a withdrawal in the direction of Franklin was necessary both understood that leaving McDowell had its problems. If the Federals retreated from McDowell during the day their movements would be observed by the Confederates on the heights. Schenck and Milroy knew that Stonewall Jackson's men would not allow them to fall back without a fight. Schenck especially was concerned. "Such a movement, however, could not with any safety or propriety be commenced before night," Schenck wrote in his report of the battle of McDowell, "nor did it seem advisable to undertake it without first ascertaining or feeling the actual strength of the rebel force before us." Furthermore even though Schenck had been directed by Frémont to make certain that the two brigades retreated safely to Franklin and should not bring on a general engagement Schenck, and especially Milroy, felt obligated to at least test the Confederates and disrupt their operations as much as possible. If nothing else, Schenck and Milroy hoped to paralyze the Confederates' ability to pursue the retreating Union brigades. Schenck believed that the Union forces in McDowell had to take "some step that would serve to check or disable" the enemy "from his full power or disposition to pursue."[45]

Throughout the day on May 8, as Milroy's forces skirmished with the Confederates and Milroy and Schenck made preparations to evacuate McDowell, General Johnson's troops began fortifying positions on Bull Pasture Mountain atop an eminence known as Sitlington's Hill. One mile to the west was McDowell and the Federal forces. As Johnson's men reinforced the high ground Milroy received a disturbing communiqué from Capt. George R. Latham of the 2nd Virginia (U.S.) Infantry — "the rebels were endeavoring to plant a battery upon the mountain."[46] Milroy knew if the Confederates placed artillery on that high ground his men would become easy targets for Rebel artillerymen. Milroy immediately sought permission from General Schenck to make "a reconnaissance for the purpose of obtaining accurate information of their strength and position." Schenck approved and Milroy readied five regiments to make a reconnaissance in force — the 25th, 32nd, 75th, and 82nd Ohio, and 3rd Virginia (U.S.) More than 1,700 strong these Federals were supposed to reconnoiter the enemy position and do whatever they could to prevent artillery from being placed atop the heights.[47] In reality Milroy was not launching a reconnaissance in force, he was launching an assault.

In actuality the Confederates were not planting guns atop Sitlington's Hill and in fact were having difficulties getting infantry to the top. The

3. "I FEAR I SHALL NOT LIKE FREMONT"   41

slope up to Sitlington's Hill was steep and the trails narrow, making it difficult for soldiers to get into position, let alone cannon. Nonetheless Latham's report convinced Milroy that his situation was hazardous. The only option he had was to launch an attack up Sitlington's Hill and capture the Confederate position.

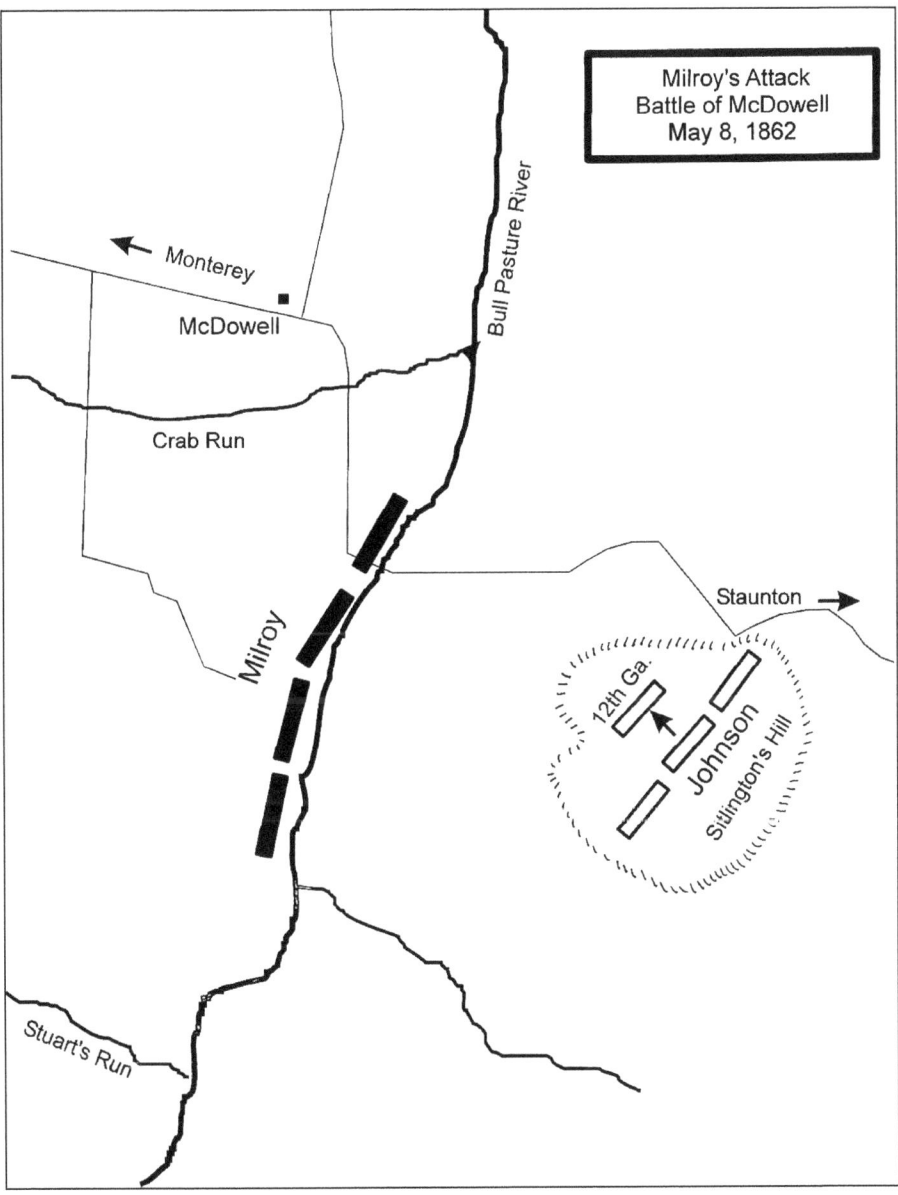

Around 4:30 P.M. Milroy took his five regiments, crossed a bridge over the rain-swollen Bull Pasture River and launched an assault against the seemingly impregnable Confederate position atop Sitlington's Hill.[48] With his sights set on the enemy position and a chance to avenge his first defeat at the hands of Ed Johnson, Milroy sent the 25th and 75th Ohio and struck near the left end of the Confederate line. These two Ohio regiments "advanced in the most gallant manner up the face of the hill" and struck the Confederates.[49] Milroy boasted that the Ohioans attacked the Confederates "most splendidly — received and returned the enemy's fire with such spirit that they fell back when my boys charged and drove over them over the top of the first ridge behind which there is a high ridge covered with woods."[50]

When the attack commenced it would have appeared that the Confederates held an impenetrable position. Terrain coupled with the advantage of numbers would make anyone believe that the place was untenable, but Johnson believed the contrary. While the flanks of the Confederate line were strong, bolstered by Virginia regiments, the center was weak. Johnson's old 12th Georgia held the center of the line. The center jutted out toward the Federal advance like a nose and was vulnerable to fire not only from the front, but from the flanks as well.[51] Complicating Johnson's position was that Milroy ordered two cannon to be placed atop a hill adjoining Sitlington's Hill — Hull's Hill.[52]

While the two Ohio regiments battled against the Confederate left the other three regiments struck at the Confederate right. Milroy ordered the 82nd and 32nd Ohio, along with the 3rd Virginia (U.S.) to "turn the right flank of the enemy, and, if possible, attack them in the rear."[53] One of the Confederate regiments defending the position, the 31st Virginia, had been raised in the area around Clarksburg, Virginia, the same hometown of many of the men from Milroy's 3rd Virginia. At times during the battle some of the western Virginia men shouted at each other amid the sounds of the whizzing shells and bullets.[54]

As the Federal line made repeated attacks against a seemingly impenetrable Confederate defense, Johnson feared for the safety of his position — particularly the center. Fearing the same, Jackson ordered reinforcements to the Confederate center. At the precise moment that Milroy's men began to crack the Confederate center, defended initially by the 12th Georgia, reinforcements from Brig. Gen. William B. Taliaferro's brigade arrived on the scene and stemmed the tide.[55]

The arrival of reinforcements did not deter Milroy's assaults. As the sun set the fighting continued. Milroy's men had a slight advantage as darkness fell over the field at McDowell. Due to the steep slopes of Sitlington's

Hill the Confederate defenders had to stand and fire. When a Confederate soldier stood he was silhouetted against the sky, making an easier target for Federal infantry as opposed to the Union soldiers who were masked in an ethereal atmosphere of darkness, smoke, and trees. Nonetheless the Federals had a difficult time choosing their targets. The 75th Ohio's Col. Nathaniel McLean wrote that as darkness descended over the field, "our men could only see the enemy by the flashes of their guns. The moon was shining, but did not give us sufficient light to enable the men to shoot with accuracy."[56] Around 8:30 P.M. after repeated attempts to shatter the Confederate position and with ammunition running low Milroy ordered his men to withdraw.[57]

Once again Old Alleghany defeated Milroy. "I found after repeated charges," explained Milroy to his wife, "that it was impossible to dislodge them with my force."[58] As the order to withdraw came many of Milroy's command pleaded to hold their position until morning, but using his better judgment Milroy decided to withdraw his men and wait to fight for another day. "I deemed it prudent," recalled Milroy, "in their exhausted condition to withdraw them."[59] Although Milroy knew that it was prudent to fall back it was a bitter pill for him to swallow knowing that he would "have to fall back before traitors and relinquish to them any portion of the country I had struggled so hard to recover from Va."[60] Around 2:00 A.M. on May 9, bruised and battered, but not demoralized, Milroy and Schenck returned their men to Franklin — the location where Frémont's main column was converging.[61]

Despite being driven from the field Milroy felt that his men had fought ably. He had nothing but praise for them. Union soldiers received Milroy's commendation in his report of the fight: "Our force engaged with undaunted bravery a force of the enemy ... displaying courage and zeal which has merited the thanks of the country and proven them true representatives of the American citizen soldier."[62] While he reveled in the fighting prowess of his command he also would have taken comfort, had he known at the time, that he had inflicted more casualties on the Confederates than they on his troops. The Federals lost 259 men as compared to 416 Confederate casualties.[63]

General Schenck as well was quite impressed with the fighting ability of the troops from Ohio and western Virginia as well as Milroy's ability to conduct the troop movements. "Too much praise cannot be awarded to General Milroy," Schenck penned in his after-action report. Of the men in the ranks who made the attacks and held their ground, Schenck praised them, writing: "No veteran troops, I am sure, ever acquitted themselves with more ardor, and yet with such order and coolness, as they displayed in marching and fighting up that steep mountain side in the face of a hot and incessant fire."[64]

The morning following the battle, at approximately 5:00 A.M., Stonewall Jackson pursued the fleeing Federals—fearful that once the retreating column joined with Frémont's main army at Franklin that the "Pathfinder" would attempt to link with Banks in the Shenandoah Valley. To prevent the two Federal armies from joining forces Jackson ordered his cartographer, Jedediah Hotchkiss, to gather cavalry and block the mountain passes into the Shenandoah Valley. These Confederate horsemen did everything in their power to block those routes—felling trees, burning bridges, and blocking the roads with boulders.[65]

While Hotchkiss prevented any possibility of the two Union armies combining forces Jackson followed the fleeing Federals. For two days after the battle Jackson's men pursued but never fully engaged their foe. On the afternoon of May 10 Confederates struck at Milroy's advance pickets.[66] To hamper Jackson's pursuit Federal soldiers set fire to the woods along the road, cloaking it in an eerie atmosphere of smoke and haze out of which Union troops ambushed their pursuers.[67]

By May 12, Milroy's and Schenck's brigade completed their withdrawal to Franklin and established strong defensive positions on a hill that dominated the surrounding area. At the first intimation of a Confederate attack against the position Milroy's artillery from the high ground fired on Jackson's advance. Jackson realized that he could not make an attack and so he withdrew—he felt he had neutralized Frémont and now set his sights on Banks. News of Jackson's withdrawal pleased the Federal soldiers, but Milroy wanted more. He asked Frémont for permission to follow the Confederates, but Frémont told Milroy to stay put and rest his men. Milroy boasted that even though his men enjoyed the respite they would "much prefer being after the rebels."[68]

For nearly the next two weeks Frémont's army remained idle around Franklin. The Pathfinder's lack of willingness to pursue Jackson into the Shenandoah Valley aggravated Milroy. "I fear I shall not like Fremont," complained Milroy to his wife, "he is not sufficiently free, sociable, and approachable for me, and he don't dash on after the rebels in a style to suit me."[69] Milroy, however, may have been slightly unfair in judging his superior so harshly. Frémont did not necessarily remain idle at Franklin because he did not want to fight—he could not fight. Franklin lay nearly 60 miles from his supply base at New Creek. With no rail line between New Creek and Franklin, Frémont's supply line depended upon one wagon road which had become nearly impassable due to heavy rains.[70]

While Milroy complained to his wife about Frémont's inactivity and the Pathfinder's army remained plagued by supply problems Jackson battled General Banks' force in the lower Shenandoah Valley. On May 23, Confederates overwhelmed a small garrison at Front Royal and two days later drove Banks from Winchester.[71]

The day prior to Banks' defeat at Winchester, May 24, President Lincoln ordered Frémont to march his army from Franklin to Harrisonburg and cut off Jackson from his supply base at Staunton. Lincoln informed Frémont that "this movement must be made immediately."[72] Despite Frémont's reluctance to abandon western Virginia and leave Gen. Jacob Cox's forces isolated in southwestern Virginia, he obliged Lincoln and went to Banks' aid.[73]

The route from Franklin to Harrisonburg spanned 40 miles over rugged, mountainous terrain. With the advice of his staff Frémont opted not to obey Lincoln's plan. Instead he decided to march his army north, closer to his supply base at New Creek, feed his army and then move against Jackson.[74]

Frémont's army departed Franklin on May 25, and marched north to the vicinity of Petersburg the following day. At Petersburg, Frémont knew that a rapid march was essential if he was going to aid Banks at all. When the army reached Petersburg he issued an order to all of his commanders that they leave all unnecessary baggage behind — tents, extra cooking utensils, etc.— for the march to the Shenandoah Valley. Although a necessary move to produce greater rapidity on the march, many soldiers suffered because of it. Especially difficult for the soldiers to handle was the lack of sufficient shelter. The deficiency of tents "has proven a great hardship to both officers and men who have been compelled to lay out exposed to all kinds of weather day and night," grumbled Milroy.[75]

On the morning of May 27, Frémont's army marched about a dozen miles and reached Moorefield. When he reported his position to Lincoln, the chief executive was enraged. He sent a terse message to the commander of the Mountain Department: "I see that you are at Moorefield. You were expressly ordered to march to Harrisonburg. What does this mean!"[76] Frémont explained to the chief executive why he could not march to Harrisonburg. Lincoln in turn told Frémont to hold his column and wait for further orders from the War Department. Frémont's directive from Washington, D.C., came on May 29 — "Please have your force at Strasburg, or, if the route you are moving on does not lead to that point, as near Strasburg as the enemy may be at the same time."[77] Ideally, Lincoln now hoped Frémont's force and a division under Brig. Gen. James Shields which had left Maj. Gen. Irvin McDowell's army at Fredericksburg on May 24, would converge on Strasburg and trap Jackson in the lower Shenandoah Valley.

As Frémont proceeded to Strasburg and Shields proceeded west on the Manassas Gap Railroad toward Front Royal, Jackson received word of the Union maneuver. On May 28, Jackson carried out orders to move against Harpers Ferry to give the general impression that his army might march into Maryland or strike Washington, D.C., but his march was only hours old when he learned of Frémont's and Shields' plans. Fearful of being contained in the lower Valley, Jackson withdrew his men from the vicinity of Winchester on May 31.[78]

Jackson's speed and delays in both Frémont's and Shields' commands allowed Stonewall to escape. With the linkup between them a complete failure the two Federal commanders had a new task—to pursue and destroy Jackson. Frémont would march south, up the Shenandoah Valley, and Shields would parallel him in the Luray Valley.

By June 3, Jackson's Valley army had crossed the Shenandoah River's north fork at Meem's Bottom and rested comfortably south of New Market. After the army crossed the North Fork, Brig. Gen. Turner Ashby's cavalry set fire to the bridge, for the moment cutting off Frémont's pursuit.[79] Heavy rains swelled the river so that no point was fordable—Frémont's only option was to build a pontoon bridge. As the sun began to set on June 3, his engineers went to work constructing the pontoon bridges, but to no avail. Fierce rainstorms "raised the river so high that we did not get our pontoon bridge across the river for two days," recalled Milroy. By the afternoon of June 5, the waters receded, the pontoons bridges were laid, and Frémont's army marched across; but Jackson was gone.

While Jackson easily observed Frémont's movement he had scant idea what Shields intended to do. Knowing that all bridges over the Shenandoah River's south fork had been destroyed, Jackson surmised that Shields could enter the Valley at only one point—where a bridge crossed the North River at Port Republic. Jackson feared a pincer movement—Frémont from the north and Shields from the south. Jackson decided to redeploy his Valley army to Port Republic, a point from which he could strike at either Federal army.[80]

In the early morning hours of June 5, Jackson marched his men to Harrisonburg. The following day Federal troops entered Harrisonburg and attacked the Confederate rear guard.[81] The day after the fight Frémont ordered Milroy's brigade to "collect the dead and wounded and proceed a few miles beyond to see where the enemy was."[82]

That same day Jackson sent troops under Maj. Gen. Richard S. Ewell to the vicinity of Cross Keys, about halfway between Harrisonburg and Port Republic. Jackson hoped to entice Frémont to attack and with Milroy reconnoitering that was a distinct possibility, but Milroy restrained himself. Aside from his advance guard skirmishing with the Confederates Milroy obeyed Frémont's directive. Undoubtedly Milroy thirsted for action that day. He explained to his wife the events of the day: "I found that they were encamped a short distance ... but being positively prohibited by Fremont from bringing on a battle and ordered by him to return I did so reluctantly."[83] When Milroy returned from his mission he informed Frémont of the Confederate position at Cross Keys and that he suspected Jackson was no longer in retreat; rather, aimed to fight. Frémont would oblige Stonewall.

On Sunday, June 8, in the early hours of the morning, Frémont formed his troops and marched them to Cross Keys. The once-peaceful village that had received its name for two crossed keys on the sign of local tavern was about to become the site of a clash of arms between Frémont and Jackson. Frémont's brigades moved southeast from Harrisonburg beginning at 5:15 A.M. Milroy's brigade of 2,500 troops got underway around 6:00 A.M.[84] Around 8:30 A.M. Frémont's van under Col. Gustave Paul Cluseret marched on the Keezletown Road and engaged the 15th Alabama near Union Church. Cluseret's brigade punched through the Confederate defenders and sent them reeling for the main Confederate line to their southeast.[85]

Cluseret's brigade pursued and Frémont's other brigades filed off the Keezletown Road and formed a battle line to its south. As the brigades formed the sound of small-arms fire and the thunderous roar of Confederate cannon from atop Mill Creek Ridge must have sounded like music to Milroy. At the first sound of battle Milroy dashed ahead of his brigade and hurried his artillery into position.[86] Milroy placed his three batteries, but they were more than a mile from the Confederate line and able to do little damage. Seeing that his guns had little impact on the Confederate batteries atop Mill Creek Ridge he deployed them to near the Armentrout House, about one-half mile southeast of Union Church and much closer to the Confederate line.[87]

While Milroy watched his batteries hurl shot and shell at Mill Creek Ridge he noticed that there was no enemy presence in his front. Milroy thought if he could get his infantry and artillery closer he might be able to break the Confederate line. He sent one of his staff officers to ask Frémont for permission to advance. Consumed with a failing attack against the Confederate right, Frémont granted Milroy's request.[88] The Gray Eagle advanced his men about a half mile beyond the Armentrout House to the cover of a ravine. When his infantry advanced Milroy noticed a better position from which his artillery could wreak further havoc on the Confederate guns. Milroy's battery commanders brought their cannon forward, set them up and as Milroy told his wife, "commenced preaching to the rebels in a most eloquent and striking manner."[89]

48   *"My Will Is Absolute Law"*

With Milroy's guns checking the Confederate cannon, he rode forward to see how his infantry could get closer to the Rebel line where, as Milroy wrote to his wife, "they could use their Minnie [*sic*] and Enfield rifles."[90] About several hundred yards to his front he noticed another ravine, which connected with yet another ravine. These could be reached, Milroy believed, "without exposure."[91] The first ravine that caught Milroy's attention was

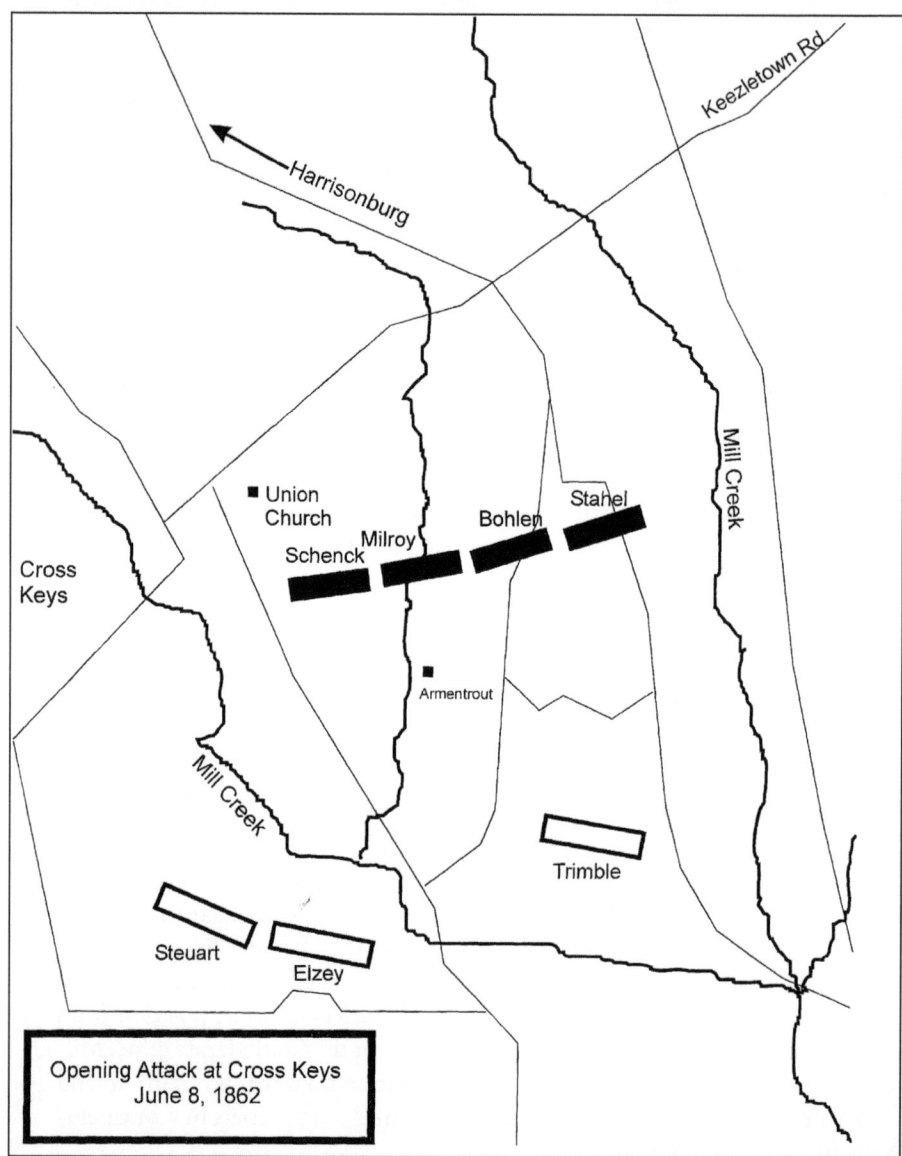

Opening Attack at Cross Keys
June 8, 1862

actually a small drainage bed that ran south into Mill Creek. The bottom of Mill Creek marked Milroy's second position.[92] From the Mill Creek bottom which "ran along the foot of the hill on which the rebel batteries were situated," Milroy believed he could "silence the batteries ... and take them at the point of the bayonet."[93]

Eager to turn the tide, Milroy deployed his brigade forward. They passed into the first ravine with ease, but as they approached to within 60 or 70 yards of the second ravine Confederate infantry, concealed in tall grass, "mowed down" the head of Milroy's column "by a deadly fire."[94] Unable to dislodge the Confederates Milroy came under heavy fire and looked to a body of woods to his right. The thick foliage seemed to be a natural safe haven to Milroy. He sent skirmishers forward — something he failed to do as he advanced to the second ravine — but they too were greeted with a "perfect storm of bullets," as they approached the woods.[95] Milroy's men fired into the woods, but the Confederate fire was destructive. The Federals, recalled Milroy, "were dropped by it rapidly." In the course of the fight Milroy's trusted horse, Jasper, received two bullet wounds. The first bullet that struck Jasper hit his hind leg and the second entered the left breast and lodged in the animal's right shoulder. The animal nearly crushed Milroy as it plunged to the ground with "blood spurting out of his breast." Milroy left the horse for dead.[96]

Now on foot Milroy attempted to rally his troops and keep up an intense fire against the Confederates. Still sensing that the Confederate left was near crumbling Milroy ordered the 25th Ohio to lead the brigade in an attack to turn the Confederate left flank. As the 25th Ohio marched off to the right to carry out Milroy's plan, one of General Frémont's aids hastily rode to Milroy and ordered him to withdraw from the field. Milroy could not fathom such an order as he felt his brigade was near success against the Confederate left. Astonished at the order, Milroy asked the courier to repeat it three times. The frightened "Dutchman" repeated the order while all around the courier "balls were whizzing around him like bees and he was dodging his head down behind his horse like a duck dodging thunder," remembered Milroy.[97] When the courier informed Milroy that he had to pull his brigade approximately one mile to the rear Milroy was standing behind the center of his brigade. "I ... felt ashamed," Milroy confessed to his wife "to order them to cease firing and file to the rear."[98]

Although ashamed, Milroy obediently commanded his brigade to pull back. He gathered the regimental commanders, explained Frémont's order, and told them to make certain that the withdrawal was orderly and that all the dead and wounded were collected. As the disheartened men of Milroy's brigade prepared to head for the rear, Milroy sought out his horse. As he approached the animal Milroy noticed Jasper was still alive and he slowly walked the animal to the rear as it hobbled on three legs.[99] The men in Milroy's brigade cursed Frémont's order to withdraw. Still believing that this had to be a mistake, Milroy halted his men about half a mile from the position in the ravine and ordered his batteries to commence firing on the Confederates. As Milroy's artillery fired, one of the Gray Eagle's staff members rode back to Frémont to seek confirmation that Milroy should withdraw. He had not changed his mind. Slowly and reluctantly Milroy obeyed the order.[100]

With the guns and infantry withdrawn from the field Milroy sought Frémont to find out the reason for the order to fall back. Milroy explained to him that his brigade, along with that of Gen. Robert Schenck's, could have possibly turned the Confederate left. Frémont pleaded ignorance. Milroy lamented to Mary: "He [Frémont] expressed surprise and said he was sorry he did not know it. He has a whole cloud of aids and it was his duty to know everything that was going on in his army when in battle."[101] While Milroy conferred and pleaded with Frémont to resume the fight he was amused to see the general and his staff scurrying around trying to dodge bullets and exploding artillery shells.[102]

After Cross Keys Milroy lost any last ounce of confidence he had in Frémont: "as a General he was a perfect failure."[103]

Following Cross Keys, Jackson capped off his splendid Shenandoah Valley Campaign with a victory over Shields at Port Republic on June 9. Frémont's army was of no great assistance in the fight at Port Republic because Jackson's men fired the bridge over the North River—the only direct route to reinforce Shields.

After Shields' defeat both Frémont and Shields worked independently to save their commands and had to assume a defensive posture. As Shields withdrew from Port Republic, President Lincoln ordered Frémont to move and remain in Harrisonburg. Lincoln wanted him to stay in Harrisonburg to block a Confederate advance against Strasburg to the north or Franklin to the west.[104] En route to Harrisonburg, Milroy became appalled at the behavior of some of the Federal soldiers in Brig. Gen. Louis Blenker's division.

Many of Blenker's men, primarily German immigrants, plundered and robbed as Frémont's army withdrew. The conduct of these men enraged Milroy; ironically, Milroy would later gain notoriety among the Confederate civilian population for doing much worse. Taken aback by their behavior Milroy penned: "The dutch brigades are composed of the most infernal robbers, plunderers, and thieves I have ever seen [and] our army is disgraced by them…. Such conduct has injured our cause very much and the name of

Blenkers dutch will be as celebrated in history as the vandals."[105] Even though Milroy despised the behavior of Blenker's men he blamed a lack of provisions as being the root of the plundering, although he believed the foraging of Blenker's men to be excessive. "The plundering," Milroy explained to his wife, "has been induced to some extent by the great scarcity of provisions, our men being most of the time on very short allowance since before we left Franklin till after we got to Harrisonburg, sometimes being a day or two without anything."[106]

While Milroy lambasted the "Dutchmen" in Frémont's army, the latter considered his position in Harrisonburg untenable. To a large army Harrisonburg had many advantages, but to a small command in the hands of an inept leader Harrisonburg could become a death trap. Frémont realized that the proximity of Harrisonburg to Staunton and the fact that Harrisonburg could be approached on any of nine roads left his lines of supply and communication vulnerable to attack. On June 11 and 12, Frémont's army, with Lincoln's permission, withdrew to Mount Jackson — a much more defensible position for the small band of wearied troops.[107]

Once at Mount Jackson Frémont's command halted and rested. Soldiers used the time to write letters home and Milroy was no different. He used the opportunity to write his wife, care for Jasper, and make preparations to send the animal home to Indiana to convalesce. On June 17, Milroy wrote a short letter to his wife explaining that one his clerks, F.W. Welton (nicknamed "Alf"), was sickly and would be making his way home to Indiana. Welton, Milroy informed his wife, would bring Jasper to her.[108] Clearly Milroy had a special affinity for this horse. After all, this horse had been with him since the beginning of the conflict and bore Milroy throughout all of his campaigns up to this point.[109] Jasper's condition improved on a daily basis and many of Milroy's soldiers visited the sick animal. Milroy wrote to his wife that "every day soldiers and officers in my brigade knows him and are attached to him and are sorry for his wound and inquire after his health with as much interest as if a brother soldier and all declare that he knows as much as a common soldier."[110]

While Milroy's thoughts turned to home and Jasper, General Frémont's turned to a Confederate attack. After about one week at Mount Jackson, he felt vulnerable in his position. He ordered his men to move farther north and by June 24 his command reached the vicinity of Middletown and joined forces with Gen. Nathaniel P. Banks and Gen. Franz Sigel.[111] Three days after Frémont reached the northern Shenandoah Valley he resigned his commission.

The resignation came as a result of a command change that occurred on June 26. Maj. Gen. John Pope had been placed in command of the armies in the Shenandoah Valley and Gen. Irvin McDowell's corps. The suggestion came from President Lincoln's secretary of the treasury, Salmon P. Chase, who suggested that a combined army of Banks, Frémont, and McDowell would be more productive. This newly minted Army of Virginia would be able to better protect the capital, guard the Shenandoah Valley, and hamper the Virginia Central Railroad — the Confederacy's lifeline in and out of the Shenandoah Valley.[112] The command change enraged the Union high command in the Valley. Banks and Frémont were senior to Pope. Banks could live with the command change, but Frémont could not. He was relieved of command on June 27, and replaced by Sigel.[113]

Frémont's departure from command pleased many, including Milroy. "Our whole [army] is rejoiced in the change that has been made," wrote Milroy. Milroy held no affections for Frémont; after all, he stood in the way of the one thing that Milroy wanted — military fame and glory. From the moment Frémont took command he constantly informed Milroy to not do anything to bring on a premature engagement with the enemy and when the opportunity presented itself to fight as it had at Cross Keys, Milroy believed Frémont's order to withdraw was premature. From Winchester, Virginia, on Independence Day Milroy wrote

German-born Maj. Gen. Franz Sigel was Milroy's corps commander during Gen. John Pope's stint as commander of the Army of Virginia in 1862. Milroy liked Sigel very much until 1864 when Sigel was given command of Union forces in western Virginia — a post for which Milroy believed he was better suited. Milroy believed that Lincoln made the appointment only because Sigel was a leader of the German American community and that by giving Sigel the command Lincoln increased his chances of receiving the German vote in the 1864 presidential election.

of his former superior: "Poor Fremont is played out and down forever. The world has been greatly deceived in that man. He is intellectually a poor thing and if it had not been for his wife Jessie and his father in law, old Tom Benton, he never would have been heard of." Milroy had no respect for Frémont and saw him as a failure.[114]

As disgusted as he was with Frémont's behavior as his superior he was optimistic about his new corps commander, General Sigel. He wrote to his wife of Sigel: "We feel now that we have a General that has been tried and one that we can rely on and will not run from rumors and imaginary dangers." Sigel had in fact performed admirably up to this point, in particular at the Battle of Pea Ridge, Arkansas, in March 1862, but undoubtedly it was not only his military record that made Milroy have such a high opinion of the native-born German. Sigel was very kind to Milroy and assigned Milroy's brigade as the advance brigade in the I Corps, Army of Virginia, a post that Milroy regarded as the post of honor.[115] "Sigel appears very favorable and friendly towards me. He has done me an honor of making my B[rigade] his advanced B[rigade] ... I feel certain that I shall get along much better with Sigel than I did with Fremont."[116]

Independence Day was spent not only complaining about Frémont, but also honoring the birthday of the United States. Milroy organized his brigade, had his artillery fire salutes, a chaplain deliver a prayer, musicians play patriotic tunes, and had a reading of the Declaration of Independence by an officer from the 25th Ohio. The ceremony was impromptu as Milroy and his men expected marching orders at any moment. After the Declaration of Independence was read Milroy prepared to dismiss the brigade. As he gave the order to dismiss the men refused to go and from the ranks a "thundering shot and call" arose from the entire brigade calling upon Milroy to make a speech. Unprepared to make any remarks Milroy at first tried to get out of it, but his men continued to chant "A speech from Gen. Milroy." "There was no getting off," Milroy told his wife, so he used a wagon as an impromptu stage and spoke to his men about the meaning of the Declaration of Independence and the importance of union. His remarks were well received by the brigade. "I wish you could have heard the thundering heart felt cheers that went up from my boys when I got up in the wagon," Milroy proudly boasted to his wife. Milroy spoke for nearly an hour and although he believed he rambled he received many flattering remarks from his men.[117]

Undoubtedly energized by his brigade's Independence Day celebration, he was further invigorated that July 4, by Frémont's resignation and the prospect of battle under Pope. With Frémont's removal Milroy's hope for battlefield glory boomed, not only because Sigel liked him, but because he knew that General Pope had a reputation as a fighter. Military victory for the Union and the creation of a heroic image for himself, Milroy surmised, was within reach now that Pope was in command. Soon, however, Milroy would come to realize the folly of his judgment and understand that Pope in many ways was like his predecessors.

4

"West Point Science"

Following Pope's appointment Federal troops awaited orders to go on the offensive. Initially Pope's army was supposed to strike Charlottesville and Gordonsville in an effort to disrupt the Virginia Central Railroad, but the situation in Virginia had rapidly deteriorated for the Union army under McClellan operating in eastern Virginia and altered the larger strategic situation. General Lee had driven McClellan from Richmond by July 1, to Harrison's Landing on the James River. Any hopes of disrupting the Virginia Central had to be abandoned by Pope and instead he had to prepare a defensive plan.

While Pope figured out what to do, Federal soldiers in the Valley used the time to relax. Milroy's brigade, encamped near Strasburg, held an impromptu Fourth of July celebration. The brigade band struck up patriotic airs, one of the regimental chaplains offered a prayer for the nation, and an Ohio soldier read the Declaration of Independence. The Independence Day celebration concluded with a rousing one-hour speech from Milroy. At first Milroy did not want to say anything but the cheers of his men pressured him to stand on a wagon and make a speech. Milroy explained the electrifying moment to his wife: "I wish you could have heard the thundering heart felt cheers that went up from my boys when I got up in the wagon. Spoke near an hour and thought I made a rambling scattering speech ... but the boys cheered me very often and were greatly pleased with it."[1]

After the celebrations concluded Milroy received orders that the army would be moving out the following morning at 6:00 A.M. The movement came as a result of the defensive scheme Pope had created. Pope ordered his army to move east of the Blue Ridge and establish a defensive line that ran from Fredericksburg to Sperryville. Pope believed that putting his troops on this line would allow his army to counter any move from the enemy, either against the capital, or northern or western Virginia.[2]

Milroy's brigade led Sigel's corps on July 5, from the vicinity of Strasburg north to Middletown. From there Milroy's brigade marched to Front

Royal where it crossed the Shenandoah River. After brushing aside a small contingent of Confederate cavalry near Front Royal, Milroy headed to Luray and on the morning of July 9, his brigade crossed the "celebrated Blue Ridge."[3] After moving through Sperryville Milroy's brigade set up camp near Woodville, in the rolling hills of Rappahannock County.

Following the march across the Blue Ridge, Milroy's brigade as well as all troops in Pope's command sat idly and awaited further orders from Pope, who directed all of his army's movements from Washington, D.C. Soldiers used the time to rest from the marches and Milroy used the opportunity to implore his wife to write more frequently. He wrote her on July 14. It had been several weeks since he received a note from his wife. Milroy feared the worst. Had someone died or gotten terribly ill? He felt his wife was keeping something from him and begged her: "If anything distressing has happened let me know the worst don't keep me in this painful suspense."[4] In reality nothing terrible had happened — the mails simply were slow and by the end of the month Milroy received a slew of letters from his beloved Mary dated July 6, 16, and 23.[5]

While he fretted over the worst possible scenario at home in Rensselaer he became enraged with the inactivity of the Union generals. His men had crossed the Blue Ridge on July 9, and after three weeks an irascible Milroy complained to his wife: "It has now been over 20 days since we crossed the Blue Ridge and have been lying idle in Camp. Oh! How horrible it is, that our Generals will thus recklessly waste the resources and energies of our country by these miserable delays."[6] Undoubtedly Milroy believed that had the army been wholly under control of volunteer officers, such as himself, the war would have been over. "Scientific West Point Generals," claimed Milroy, "and their Science is proving as detrimental to the Nation as Treason."[7]

Despite his anger with Pope and other West Pointers he could do nothing but sit and wait. Milroy occupied himself throughout July with dealing with the mass influxes of runaway slaves coming into his camps near Woodville. Almost on a daily basis slaves — men, women, and children — entered Milroy's camps seeking refuge from the horrors of the South's peculiar institution. Milroy ordered his men to construct special quarters to house the runaways until Milroy determined where they would be sent or how they would be employed. Although sympathetic to the plight of slaves Milroy would not allow them to become idle — as previously exhibited by his treatment of Ben Summit. Some of the male runaways were utilized by Milroy as wagon drivers, while others were hired by officers as personal servants. Those who could not secure employment as a driver or servant comprised a pioneer company that Milroy established. The Gray Eagle believed that these former slaves could repair roads, bridges, chop wood, dig latrines, build breastworks, etc. and free his soldiers from that sort of manual labor. Former slave women found work washing clothes and cooking.[8]

Milroy's impromptu works program improved the quality of life for many soldiers, but some initially despised the thought of sharing space with runaways. Chief among the discontented were troops in Milroy's Virginia regiments. Despite the fact they were fighting for the Union many of these soldiers were still proslavery and according to Milroy many of them initially held "prejudices against fugitive slaves and a strong disposition to abuse and drive them away from camp."[9] An abolitionist, Milroy could not watch these soldiers from western Virginia bully the former slaves. He gave the officers and men stern lectures or punished them in some fashion. Quickly Milroy regained control of these regiments and perhaps the rapidity in which he achieved control testifies to the strong rapport he had with the rank and file. Particularly throughout the first half of the Civil War Union officers sometimes had difficulty in diffusing soldiers' negative attitudes toward fugitive slaves, yet Milroy did it with relative ease.[10] "The fact is I can do with them what no other General could," boasted Milroy, "for the officers and men all have such a high regard for me that they fear to offend me and there is not one among them that would not shed the last drop of his blood for me."[11]

Helping fugitive slaves aside, Milroy's cavalry went throughout Rappahannock County and rounded up people to take the oath of allegiance to the United States. Bringing people into Union lines to take the oath was not exclusively being practiced by Milroy. Pope issued orders to all of his commanders that they force civilians to take the oath.[12] Many of the civilians brought before Milroy during July accepted the oath; only 11 refused. Those who swore their allegiance to the United States did so reluctantly. Milroy believed that many who raised their right hand and swore allegiance to the Federal government did so only to "avoid being sent off and to save their property."[13] Suspect of their loyalty Milroy warned those who took the oath that should they ever violate the oath they "would be hung or shot."[14]

While Milroy suspected that many of the civilians who took the oath did so reluctantly he knew that some accepted with sincerity. For their loyalty Milroy believed they deserved the gratitude of the army. To show his appreciation Milroy did whatever possible to protect the lives and property of civilians from rowdy Union soldiers—most notably the German immigrants. General Blenker's men frequently plundered civilian property east of the Blue Ridge throughout July and civilians frequently came to Milroy for protection from the "robbing and thieving characters of the Blenker Dutch."[15] As much as Milroy might have despised Blenker's men he hated the Confederates even more and would only post guards at the homes of those he found "to be friendly, peacable, and inoffensive, or widows, etc." Grateful for the assistance Milroy provided in protecting civilians' properties, many of the residents of Rappahannock County treated Milroy's men kindly and men vied for the duty. "The boys are fond of it," Milroy wrote to his wife, "as they are treated like princes while staying at a house as guards."[16]

Constantly throughout July Milroy and his troops dealt with many mundane tasks—helping fugitive slaves, protecting civilians, and administering the oath, but occasionally this monotonous lifestyle was broken. For example, during the last week of July, General Sigel held a great drill and "sham battle." Sigel deployed 8,000 men of his corps against Milroy's brigade. Undoubtedly both sides would have boasted to have won a "sham victory" but Milroy believed he had the upper hand in the fight. "Our long lines of infantry, artillery, and cavalry, maneuvered splendidly and everything went off splendidly," Milroy wrote his wife.[17]

Mock battles aside Milroy and his men also found considerable fun in reading captured Confederate mail. Love letters from Confederate soldiers brought some of the greatest amusement to the Federal soldiers and especially to Milroy. He was so moved by one of the Confederate love letters he sent it home so that his daughter Ella, 10 years old at the time, would have a "moddle [sic] love letter that she may learn how to write it to her beau when she gets old enough to get one."[18]

As July turned to August the monotony and sometimes lighthearted routine of camp life in Rappahannock County neared an end. On August 4, General Halleck ordered Gen. McClellan to move his army from the Virginia Peninsula to join Pope's army along the Rappahannock. Less than a week prior to Halleck's order to McClellan, Pope left the security of the capital for his army in the field. When Pope reached his army along the Rappahannock line he had specific orders from Halleck to block any Confederate advance against the capital and keep the way clear for the withdrawal of the Army of the Potomac from the Virginia Peninsula.[19]

On August 7, while inspecting General Sigel's force around Sperryville, Pope received some startling news—about 20,000 troops under Stonewall Jackson were headed toward the Rapidan River.[20] Jackson watched Pope's moves constantly during the first week of August. Jackson knew that Pope's command stretched for more than 50 miles from Sperryville to Fredericksburg. On August 7, Jackson decided to move against Culpeper. With only elements of General Banks corps at Culpeper, Jackson believed that if he moved rapidly and defeated Banks, Pope's command would be divided and rendered impotent to aid McClellan's movement from the Virginia Peninsula.[21] With Jackson's approach to the Rapidan and Culpeper, Pope decided to concentrate his entire Army of Virginia near Culpeper — to halt Jackson's advance and prevent him from crossing the Rappahannock.[22]

As Pope's lackadaisical army moved out for Culpeper, Jackson's command moved sluggishly. Nearly unbearable heat, miscommunication, and slow-moving soldiers made August 8 one of the worst marching days for Jackson's men, but it would not matter.[23] Pope's commanders showed no sense of urgency and by the morning of August 9, Banks still remained the only substantial force near Culpeper. That morning Pope ordered Banks to take position south of Culpeper and block Jackson's advance. Approximately 8,000 of Banks' troops formed near Cedar Mountain, about eight miles south of Culpeper.[24] Later during the day on August 9, approximately at 1:00 P.M., the battle of Cedar Mountain began when Banks, unconscious of Pope's wishes to avoid a general engagement while the Army of Virginia was en route to Culpeper, struck Jackson.[25]

Banks' men were no match for Jackson's command, although for the first several hours of the fight Banks' troops delivered devastating blows against their Confederate foe. While the battle raged at Cedar Mountain General Sigel's corps advanced to the hot spot. The lead elements of Sigel's corps under General Milroy arrived in the vicinity of Culpeper early on the morning of August 9, but were not immediately sent to Banks' aid at Cedar Mountain because Banks presented Pope with a false sense of security.[26] As late as 5:00 P.M. Banks sent messages to Pope that everything was under control and that Banks expressed no "apprehensions of attack in force by the enemy, nor did he ask nor intimate that he needed reinforcements."[27]

Despite Banks' assessment of the situation Pope ordered Sigel's troops to Cedar Mountain. Milroy's men, who were "impatient from the time of hearing the first shot," received the "order to march with a shout and moved off with Alacrity."[28] The lead elements of Milroy's brigade reached the battlefield around 8:00 P.M. and found everything in confusion. As Milroy's men neared the field they had difficulty moving on the road, which was clogged with wounded and frantic retreating soldiers. Disgusted at the chaotic scene and not wanting to waste any time in getting at the Confederates, Milroy left his infantry and artillery on the road "to make the best of their way toward the front," and took his cavalry detachment forward — three companies of the 1st Virginia (U.S.) Cavalry. The attempt at bypassing the retreating Federals proved futile. The cavalry tried to move forward, but they were swept up in the tide of retreating soldiers. Confederate artillery shells exploding among the fleeing Union soldiers only added to the chaos. Milroy attempted to gather the frightened troops. He had little success. Two artillery batteries and a small contingent of cavalry rallied around Milroy, but the small force was no match for Jackson. As the night wore on Milroy's brigade was fully concentrated on the field and went into camp around 2:00 A.M. on August 10.[29]

In the hours before sunrise on August 10, Milroy and his men felt confident that they would be attacked. In the early morning dawn, while Milroy's men slept, the Gray Eagle mounted his horse and surveyed the field. As he rode over the field Milroy heard the neighing of horses and voices. A thick morning haze obscured the figures and Milroy, determined to discover if they were friend or foe, approached them. Closer to the horsemen Milroy could make out the butternut color of their jackets. Initially Milroy suspected that they were local civilians trying to flee the battle, but fearful they might be spies or Confederate cavalry Milroy ordered them to stop. Milroy shouted out to the horsemen, "Who are you sir!" The men paused for a moment, sized up Milroy, and dug their spurs into their horses. When the horsemen bolted for the Confederate lines Milroy put his spurs into his horse and took out his revolver, determined to stop these men. Accidentally, when Milroy removed the revolver from his holster the muzzle got caught in the bridle rein and the pistol went off, grazing his horse in the neck. Milroy pursued the horsemen for several hundred yards all the while shooting at them, but when the aggressive Milroy sighted Confederate infantry to his front he turned his horse around and summoned his artillery into position. Quickly the gunners manned their posts and "opened on them with shell most beautifully and some made them git."[30]

Following the incident with the Confederate horsemen, Confederate skirmishers pestered Milroy's brigade with small-arms fire throughout the morning. After several hours of exchanging shots Milroy deployed his company of sharpshooters and four companies of infantry to drive the Confederates from the field, which they did with relative ease. Milroy's losses on August 10, were light — two killed and three wounded.[31]

Even though no large-scale battle had been fought that day, many wounded Union and Confederate troops were locked in a desperate struggle for survival. As the sun rose on Monday, August 11, Milroy and Brig. Gen. George Bayard, a cavalry commander in McDowell's corps, took it upon themselves to send out details to recover the wounded and bury the dead. The scene on the battlefield was hellish. Many of the dead Union soldiers had been stripped naked by Confederate soldiers and the ghastly sight of swollen corpses repulsed many veteran soldiers, including Milroy. "The battlefield was the most terrible spectacle that I have ever seen since the war commenced. Our poor wounded boys had been laying the third day where they had fallen — their wounds undressed and exposed to the hot sun by day and cold by night. The dead were scattered over a mile and a half one way and a mile and half a mile the other way," explained Milroy to his wife.[32]

Milroy sent out nearly 400 men with picks and shovels to perform the unpleasant task of burying fellow comrades and countless wagons to remove the wounded. As the Union burial details took to the field, Confederates under a flag of truce approached Milroy's men and asked if a temporary cease-fire could be granted to allow the Confederates to bury their dead and help their wounded. Milroy, with Pope's approval, negotiated a suspension of hostilities until 2:00 P.M. The day wore on, however, and with the field still littered with corpses and wounded, both sides agreed to suspend hostilities until the field was clear.[33]

Throughout that Monday thousands of soldiers, from both sides, performed the unpleasant task of burying the dead, but amid the carnage and tragic scene some soldiers used the opportunity to swap stories with their foe. They "joked and talked about their battles as free as old friends," Milroy wrote his wife.[34] Milroy too talked with some of the Confederate officers and enlisted men. Undoubtedly boasting, Milroy gloated to his wife: "I was introduced to a number of reble generals and officers. They had all heard of me and were anxious to see me.... The rebles paid me the highest complement of saying that they regarded me as one of the Most dangerous Genls. they had to contend against."[35] Although these Confederate officers may have stroked Milroy's ego, he could not help but become enraged in their presence. He did everything he could to keep himself contained as he had "so much contempt and detestation for the intelligent traitor officers" that he "could hardly treat them with civility."[36]

By the end of the day Milroy's men buried close to 500 men and many from the burial party collapsed from utter exhaustion. The following day, August 11, Milroy was ordered forward to reconnoiter the Confederate camp. When he came into view of Jackson's camp he found that the Confederates had left. Jackson began his withdrawal during the night of August 10, as burial details gathered the dead. By the following morning his command crossed the Rapidan River and headed for Gordonsville.[37] Jackson did not want to press Pope any more, at least not without the remainder of the Army of Northern Virginia.

With ambiguous orders from Pope to reconnoiter the enemy position, Milroy pushed his men closer to the Rapidan on August 12. Milroy felt that there was an opportunity at this point to pursue Jackson and eliminate his wing of the Army of Northern Virginia. He had hoped that Pope would order the entire Army of Virginia to follow Jackson aggressively but Pope, shaken by Cedar Mountain, wanted to reassess the situation.[38] Later, on August 12, Pope ordered Milroy to return to the main body of the army. Enraged at the apparent stupidity of the order Milroy complained to his wife: "*According to West Point Science*. I was getting along too fast. The rebles must be given time to fortify and prepare to receive us.... If our Govt. fails to put down this rebellion, so called West Point Science will be the cause of it."[39] At this point Milroy's hatred for the apparent lack of common sense among West Pointers grew and continued to do so for the remainder of his Civil War career. He grumbled after Pope issued the order that "if the Devil had swallowed that institution 40 years ago, this rebellion would have been crushed Months ago—Our Genls. would now have been governed by common sense instead of West Point Slavery."[40]

While Milroy grumbled about Pope's stupidity, General Lee gained a clearer understanding of the Union's strategic plan. Following Jackson's victory at Cedar Mountain persistent rumors circulated in the Confederate capital that McClellan was removing his command from the Virginia Peninsula to Washington, D.C., and would reinforce Pope. Once tales of McClellan's withdrawal turned into confirmed reports, Lee promptly responded. Lee decided to consolidate and destroy Pope before McClellan's forces could join with the Army of Virginia. On August 13, Lee ordered Gen. James Longstreet to send 10 brigades to Jackson at Gordonsville.[41] The following day Longsteet's lead elements arrived in Gordonsville—a day Jackson set aside for thanksgiving for the recent success at Cedar Mountain.[42]

Pope received news of Lee's plan on August 17, after Federal cavalry captured one of Confederate cavalry commander Gen. J.E.B. Stuart's aides, who surrendered official correspondence. Among the dispatches was a letter dated August 16, from Lee to Stuart. The communiqué alerted Pope to Lee's intentions to crush the Army of Virginia before reinforcements from the Army of the Potomac would arrive.[43] With the Rapidan to his front and the Rappahannock to his back Pope felt trapped and ordered his men on the 18th to move north across the Rappahannock and block a Confederate advance north. By moving here Pope would be able to protect both his supply base at Manassas Junction and Fredericksburg, the gateway for many reinforcements from the Army of the Potomac.[44]

With Pope's army in position by August 20, Lee needed to find a way to strike Pope before McClellan's troops arrived. Lee not only needed to strike quickly, but he also needed to attack as far away from Fredericksburg as he could—distancing his army as greatly as possible from Federal reinforcements. With Pope's left flank not an option Lee decided to move against Pope's right.

Lee's men attempted to cross the Rappahannock on August 21 and succeeded momentarily at Beverly's Ford, but Federals quickly hurled the attackers back. The following day Lee's subordinates engineered more attempts to cross the Rappahannock. Early on the morning of August 22, J.E.B. Stuart's horsemen reconnoitered Freeman's Ford and found artillery and infantry of Milroy's brigade protecting the crossing. Although Stuart did not want to have a full-scale battle at Freeman's Ford he felt compelled to at least test Milroy's strength. Stuart ordered Capt. John Pelham's four guns to unlimber and fire at Milroy's command. Less than five minutes after Pelham's guns opened, Milroy deployed Capt. Aaron C. Johnson's 12th Ohio Battery.[45] Johnson's guns opened a furious fire against Pelham's guns and the Ohioan's tenacity in battle earned Johnson Milroy's eternal respect. In his report of the battle Milroy praised the artillerist: "Too much praise cannot be awarded the captain for the promptness and skill exhibited in bringing his battery into position.... [Johnson] had silenced their heaviest battery."[46]

Although Johnson's battery checked Pelham's four cannon, artillery on both sides belched forth iron shot and shell for nearly two hours. Finally, around 3:00 P.M., the enemy's guns stopped their fire. Uncertain of the cause of this immediate cessation of activity Milroy and about 150 of his cavalry crossed the ford and noticed the enemy withdrawing in the direction of Sulphur Springs. Soon the Confederate rear guard caught a glimpse of Milroy and his horsemen. The Confederates opened fire first and Milroy sent for his sharpshooters who engaged the Confederates, but seeing that a fight against the rear guard would yield little, Milroy pulled his men back. They remained at Freeman's Ford throughout the night.[47]

Despite Milroy's efforts to hold Freeman's Ford, one of Stonewall Jackson's brigades, under Gen. Jubal A. Early, slipped across the Rappahannock later that day. No other force would cross that day. Torrential rains swelled the river so that no one else could get across, and Early's men were isolated.[48] Also that night Confederate cavalry under J.E.B. Stuart attempted a raid on Catlett Station along the Orange and Alexandria Railroad. If Stuart's men could burn the bridge over Cedar Run at Catlett, Pope's supply line with Manassas Junction would be severed; fortuitously for Pope's army the rain-soaked bridge would not ignite and Stuart's men abandoned the mission.[49]

Weather had worked tremendously in Pope's favor on August 22 and presented him with an opportunity to corner at least a part of the Confederate army: Early's brigade, isolated on the Union side of the Rappahannock. Early on August 23, orders went out to commanders to concentrate in the vicinity of Rappahannock Station. However, Pope's army was spread out on a wide front and if he waited for all of his army to concentrate the opportunity would be lost. The corps closest to Rappahannock Station and in the best position to strike at the Confederates on the north side of the Rappahannock was Sigel's.[50]

At 7:00 A.M. on August 23, Milroy received orders to move out toward Sulphur Springs and secure the rear of the corps. As the corps moved out on the road from Rappahannock Station to Sulphur Springs Milroy received another message to take his brigade on a much rougher but shorter route to Sulphur Springs. After a march of several miles the road less traveled joined the main road from Rappahannock to Sulphur Springs and Milroy's brigade found itself in the advance of Sigel's sluggish corps. As Milroy's brigade approached Great Run, about one mile southeast of Sulphur Springs, Federal cavalry in the advance had attracted the attention of some Confederate artillery and a sharp little fight ensued until dusk. Early's skirmishers and artillery held the Federals in check. Near the end of the fight the main body of Sigel's corps arrived but did little to change the outcome of the fight.[51]

The following morning the pioneers began work on rebuilding the bridge over Great Run destroyed by the Confederates. At this point Milroy became impatient and instead of waiting for the bridge to be rebuilt marched his infantry across Great Run on the bridge's remnants and proceeded to Sulphur Springs. As the brigade neared Sulphur Springs it came under enemy artillery fire and suddenly found itself in the midst of a hornet's nest. Milroy remembered that "the woods and hills became alive with the enemy; the deserted batteries were suddenly manned, and a semicircle of guns nearly a mile around us commenced pouring a steady stream of shell and canister" upon Milroy's troops.[52]

While Confederates harassed Milroy's brigade the Gray Eagle received orders to lead Sigel's corps to Waterloo Bridge, about four miles northwest of Sulphur Springs. Around 5:00 P.M. Milroy arrived with his troops to find Confederate artillery and marksmen on the bluffs and woods near the bridge. Union artillery checked the Confederate guns and prevented them from crossing while Milroy sent his sharpshooters to "pick off the reble sharpshooters."[53] Throughout the night artillery sounded along both lines and skirmishing resumed in the morning.

Amid the pop of musketry and roar of cannon Milroy received orders during the late afternoon to burn Waterloo Bridge and move to Warrenton with the rest of Sigel's corps. With Confederates massing on the opposite side of Waterloo Bridge the task of firing the bridge would not be an easy one. Milroy's brigade along with another sent by Gen. Carl Schurz occupied the Confederates long enough while 15 men from the 82nd Ohio fired the bridge. After successfully igniting the oak structure Milroy's men marched to Warrenton.[54]

When Milroy's men arrived in Warrenton during the early morning of August 25, they received some welcome news—reinforcements from the

Army of the Potomac were arriving.⁵⁵ That same day, however, General Lee cut Jackson loose and sent him to destroy Pope's supply depot at Manassas Junction while Gen. James Longstreet's Confederates occupied Pope along the Rappahannock. Two days later Pope responded with a plan to destroy Jackson's wing. Pope marched his Army of Virginia to Manassas Junction and by nightfall of August 27, the lead elements of Pope's army were a mere five miles from Jackson and Manassas Junction.⁵⁶

Despite his success in destroying Pope's supply base Jackson knew that his situation could become perilous. Longstreet was in no position to quickly support Jackson and the Army of the Potomac was in the process of linking with Pope. If this happened Jackson would be annihilated. Instead of allowing the Federals to dictate the strategy, Jackson set the stage for battle on the fields where nearly one year earlier he earned his eternal sobriquet. As Pope's army closed in on Manassas Junction during the night of the 27th Jackson's men marched out of Manassas Junction and positioned themselves north of the Warrenton Turnpike in an unfinished railroad bed on the fields of the war's first great land battle.⁵⁷

The following day, August 28, Pope's men headed toward Manassas and in the distance could be heard the rumblings of battle. The small but bloody fight at Brawner's Farm signaled the opening of battle. Jackson had achieved his objective of drawing Pope into battle; all he needed now was the other half of Lee's army.

Not wanting to squander an opportunity to destroy Jackson's command, Pope ordered Sigel to attack Jackson early on August 29. When Sigel's line moved forward it encountered Brig. Gen. William Starke's brigade in Groveton Woods and drove it back. As Milroy's men huddled in Groveton Woods Confederate cannon from Maj. Lindsay M. Shumaker's artillery opened fire. Milroy along with General Shenck tried to answer Shumaker's guns with 20 cannon, but it did little to protect the Federals in Groveton Woods. Milroy knew that his men were becoming target practice for Shumaker's gunners and that the guns could be silenced only if taken by an infantry assault. Milroy prepared his men for a frontal assault, but he changed his mind when he heard the sharp report of musketry to his right. Fearing the right end of Sigel's line held by Gen. Carl Schurz was on the verge of destruction, Milroy without any reconnaissance of the situation blindly deployed two regiments—the 82nd Ohio and 5th Virginia—to support Schurz who was "hotly engaged." With the remaining half of his brigade Milroy planned to charge the Confederate artillery position, but the troops from Ohio and western Virginia sent to Schurz's aid were being destroyed by the fire from troops under Brig. Gen. A.R. Lawton.⁵⁸ Milroy's troops from Ohio and western Virginia attempted to crack the enemy position by making repeated charges, but as Milroy noted in his report of the battle they "were driven back each time with great loss."[59]

With half of his brigade in a perilous situation, Milroy sent the 2nd Virginia to support them. The reinforcement was futile. As three-fourths of his infantry regiments bore a tremendous brunt of the fire from Jackson's

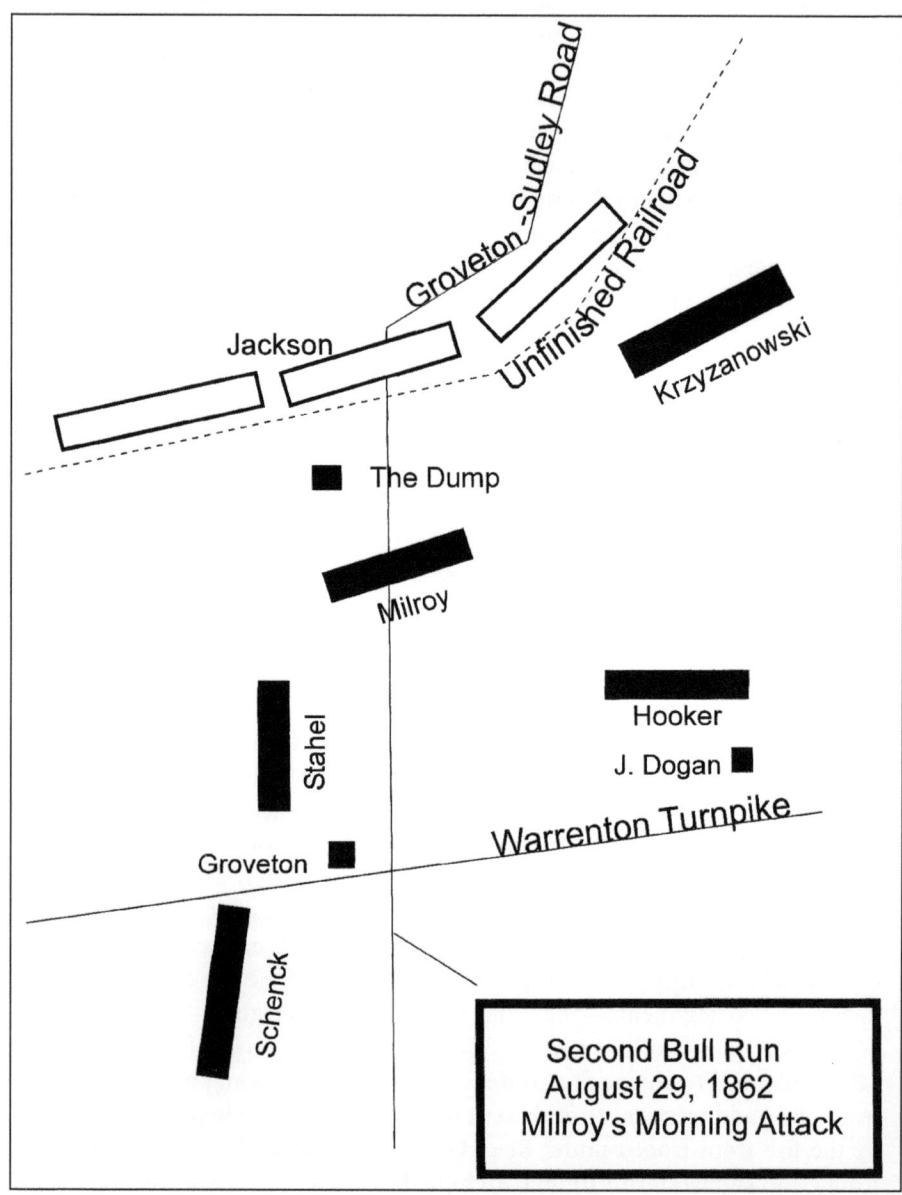

men, Schurz's bruised division withdrew from the field, leaving Milroy's brigade alone. Milroy employed artillery and his reserve regiment, the 3rd Virginia, in an attempt to hold his ground. When all seemed lost Brig. Gen. Julius Stahel, ordered by General Schenck to support the Gray Eagle's brigade, found Milroy on the field and asked Milroy where he should place his brigade. Milroy told him to his left, and Stahel hastily rode off to bring his brigade forward, but Confederate pressure on Stahel's brigade prevented the Hungarian from properly supporting Milroy. Throughout the afternoon Milroy maintained his position and fire against Jackson's line.[60]

During the afternoon Gen. Cuvier Grover's brigade of hearty New Englanders arrived on the field to strike Jackson's left. When Grover launched an attack against the enemy position Milroy prepared his men to take advantage of Grover's offensive, but Milroy's men were able to do little.

Also that afternoon, another brigade under command of Col. James Nagle marched onto the field to strike Jackson's center. Milroy watched Nagle's men advance from his position in the Groveton Woods. As Nagle's tide of blue surged forward Milroy became reenergized and decided to support the assault. Milroy took his 3rd Virginia, which out of all of his infantry regiments had seen the least action that day, and moved out against the Confederate center. As Milroy neared the Confederate line he noticed two Confederate brigades bearing down on his lone regiment and ordered them to pull back. Milroy's voice, however, was no match for the sound of battle and the 3rd Virginia withdrew only after suffering severe losses.[61]

As night descended upon the battlefield Milroy withdrew his men about three-fourths of a mile to the rear. The following day Milroy's brigade remained in reserve until around 4:00 P.M. when he threw it across the Warrenton Turnpike to halt the retreating men of Maj. Gen. Fitz-John Porter's V Corps. Porter launched a massive and savage attack against Jackson's line, but it proved futile. Milroy decided to halt the retreating troops under his own volition. "I saw that a *Second Bull Run* was commencing and thought I would stop a great tide of cowardly runaways," Milroy explained to his wife.[62] Initially Milroy thought he could rally Porter's fleeing troops at the point of his sword, but when the attempt proved useless he ordered his entire brigade to fix bayonets and stem the retreat. Some frantic soldiers could not be halted, but Milroy's men managed to halt a sizable number. As Milroy's brigade organized the troops to be sent back to their proper commands he received orders from General Sigel to move to the Union left on Henry House Hill.[63] The situation on Henry House Hill was serious — a gap had opened in the Union line. Milroy plugged it promptly by placing his troops into the Sudley Road cut. On his left were troops under Lt.

Col. William Chapman and on his right were the Pennsylvanians of Brig. Gen. John F. Reynolds.

Milroy's position in the Sudley Road was a good one. "The road in which my brigade was formed was worn and washed from 3 to 5 feet deep, affording a splendid cover for my men," recalled Milroy.[64] From their concealed position Milroy's men suffered little loss from the "perfect hurricane of balls" being fired by the Confederates.[65] Initially Milroy's men along with artillery from atop Henry House Hill delivered a destructive fire into the Confederates. As the battle raged the gunners became prime targets for Confederate marksmen. Suspecting that destruction in the gun crews might prompt them to retire prematurely Milroy rode to the guns and shouted words of encouragement. While cheering to bolster their courage Milroy's horse was shot in the head. As he searched for another mount he noticed that the troops to his left, Chapman's, were beginning to give way. Milroy rode to the left of his brigade to rally the troops, undoubtedly cheering perhaps his most favorite command — "Pitch in Boys: Pitch in" — but while he urged his men to fight he feared the artillery would withdraw.[66] Soon, the gunners began to do just that and the situation became chaotic.[67]

Fearing for the safety of his troops, Milroy searched for reinforcements. Milroy found General McDowell and "appealed to him in the most energetic Manner for a Bgd. telling him that that the crises of the battle and of the nation was at hand and that not a moment was to be lost."[68] According to Milroy McDowell cared nil about Milroy's plight and as Milroy remembered "answered me coldly and insultingly that he was not bound to help every body and that he was not going to help Gen. Sigel."[69] When Milroy told McDowell that he was not part of Sigel's command (Milroy did belong to Sigel's corps) McDowell apparently agreed to help and sent one brigade to the troubled spot.

McDowell remembered the incident differently and stated that he did not receive Milroy coldly; rather, McDowell claimed that he had some difficulty in ascertaining what Milroy wanted. In his report of the battle McDowell stated that Milroy "came riding up in a state of absolute frenzy, with his sword drawn, and gesticulating at some distance off…. His manner ... showed him as being in a state of mind as unfit to judge of events as to command men and as being away from his command, caused me to receive him coldly."[70] McDowell's report written two months after Milroy's claims that McDowell could not decipher what Milroy wanted. Only after McDowell received a message from Brig. Gen. George G. Meade did reinforcements move forward.[71]

The initial reinforcements sent forward were a brigade of United States Regulars under Lt. Col. Robert C. Buchanan. When Milroy tried to direct some of Buchanan's troops into line, Buchanan quickly put Milroy in his place. After the battle Buchanan wrote of Milroy's behavior: "General Milroy's manner was excited, so much as to the attract the especial attention of those present, and induced many to inquire who was rushing about so wildly and what he wanted."[72] Milroy complied with Buchanan's request and tended to his own men.

As the sun began to set the Confederates continued to pressure the Federal position and more reinforcements arrived. Col. Edward Ferrero's brigade reached the Union left that evening and as he led his men onto the field Milroy greeted him. A soldier in the 21st Massachusetts recalled that as they marched onto the field Milroy greeted them "frantic with joy ... and as we dressed our lines, rode along our front, shouting like a crazy man."[73] Ferrero asked Milroy to leave his command alone and again he complied. As night descended over the field, Milroy's men, nearly out of ammunition, pulled back. Around 8:00 P.M. Pope issued orders for a withdrawal and before midnight Pope's men were en route to Centreville.

Shocked at the order to withdraw from the field Milroy stated that had "an ice bolt shot through me, I could not have been more agonizingly shocked." Milroy sought Sigel and implored him to disregard Pope's order and fight. "I urged Gen. Sigel," Milroy wrote his wife, "for the sake of our Country and posterity and of all we had dear not to give up the field but to go back with the brave fellows that were still holding there." Amid the retreat Milroy explained to Sigel "that not only had all the good, treason labor and suffering of our Govt. and people since the beginning of the war had been thrown away and made a useless waste by that miserable cowardly order, but that it had also rendered all that was gained by the American Revolution a nullity by completing the destruction of the Union."[74] As much as Sigel might have wanted to remain he had orders to withdraw and his corps had suffered severe losses. Sigel explained to a furious Milroy that "it was a great wrong to leave the field, but that his own Corps was badly cut up and scattered and he had command of no other troops and that all had been ordered to fall back and had for some hours been on the move and that orders had been sent to the troops on the field to fall back and cover the rear."[75]

For Milroy the Second Battle of Bull Run foreshadowed disaster for the Union. After the battle he lamented in his official report: "I felt that all blood, treasure, and labor of our Government and people for the last year had been thrown away ... and that most probably the death-knell of our glorious Government had been sounded by it."[76] To his wife Milroy explained: "Up to this time I was buoyed with confidence in our glorious cause, but now I was entirely cast down [and] all appeared to be lost and the glorious inheritance won and transmitted to us by our fathers [was] gone forever."[77] Once again Milroy blamed the defeat on West Pointers. He condemned professional soldiers: "All this has been brought about by *West Pointers*— Soulless, brainless, Selfish Villains who having made their *Profession*— Care nothing for the country, so they can be hoisted into high places."[78]

Miserable and dejected Milroy believed that the Lincoln administration should "make a treaty with the traitors and get a king and stay the tide of blood and ruin and misery that was sweeping over the country."[79] The Gray Eagle firmly believed that after Second Bull Run there was no hope. "I see no hope," he explained to his wife, "Our Govt. is lost and we must bequeath war, misery, and anarchy to our children. I have about lost all hope—I have never had the blues so bad in my life."[80] As disgusted as he was with the leadership, or perceived lack of it, after Second Bull Run, Milroy thought his men, under the circumstances, performed admirably. "The highest praise," Milroy explained, "I can award to the officers and soldiers of my brigade, in all the hard service and fighting through which we have passed, is that they have bravely, cheerfully, patiently, and nobly performed their duty."[81]

The day following the withdrawal from Manassas, Milroy received a message from Sigel stating that he had not been feeling well and that Milroy needed to report to General Pope at once and assume command of Sigel's Corps. For the next three days Milroy remained in command of the corps, but on the evening of September 2, Sigel returned and Milroy's brigade moved out to Fairfax. By September 7, Milroy's brigade was encamped near Fort Ethan Allen—one of the capital's defenses.[82]

Within such close proximity to Washington, D.C., Milroy used the occasion to do some sightseeing. He also used the opportunity to have his photograph taken in Matthew Brady's gallery. Coaxed by his friends to have his image as a brigadier general captured, Milroy had two photographs taken—one a full length and another an upper-body shot. Milroy wanted to get some of the images so that his wife could give them to loved ones, but the demand for the images by his soldiers and the public was so great according to Milroy that Brady's gallery could not produce them fast enough.[83]

Milroy's frequent visits to the nation's capital involved more than photographs and wandering the streets. He used the time to speak with some of the nation's leaders—most notably Lincoln, Secretary of War Edwin Stanton, and General Halleck. On one occasion during September Milroy met with all three at the same time. Lincoln, Stanton, and Halleck treated Milroy cordially and as Milroy remembered: "They treated me with the most marked respect and friendship and flattered me so much about my fighting and bravery that it made me blush and feel awkward."[84] Once introduced to the three men, Milroy wasted no time in venting his frustration against Pope, a man whom Milroy identified as "an incompetent egotist vain braggadocio."[85] Milroy could still not reconcile, in his own mind, Pope's "cowardly order to retreat." The veteran general not only used the meeting to degrade Pope, but also used it to show the folly of using West Point–trained officers to run the army. According to Milroy's correspondence after the meeting he pulled President Lincoln aside and told Lincoln that if he "continued to let West Point rule in our armies that it would ensure the destruction of the Union beyond doubt." Lincoln gave no reply to Milroy's advice, he simply glared at the Gray Eagle.[86] Although Milroy would never see his wish for Lincoln to remove control of the armies from those who attended West Point, he would see Lincoln, on September 2, relieve Pope and give General McClellan command of the combined Army of Virginia and Army of the Potomac.

This image of Milroy as a brigadier general was taken in early September 1862 in Mathew Brady's gallery in Washington, D.C.

While Milroy exhibited his disgust against Pope and others who attended West Point to various officials in Washington, D.C., some of Milroy's western Virginia soldiers signed petitions and sent them to Lincoln and Stanton—they wanted to be sent back to western Virginia. These Virginians knew full well that by September 1862 much of the territory they had gained in the war's first year was mostly under Confederate control and Union sympathizers—the Virginia soldiers' families—stood at the mercy of Confederate soldiers and partisans. The soldiers also pleaded with the

Lincoln administration to promote Milroy to major general and give him command of troops in western Virginia. Undoubtedly the plea for promotion pleased Milroy, but the thought of returning to western Virginia did not. When he learned of the petition and also of a delegation from western Virginia who came to Washington to secure troops under Milroy's command for the defense of the region Milroy simply wrote his wife, "I have no desire to go back to Western Va. again." He would go under one condition — if he received a promotion to major general.[87]

On September 17, while the Army of Northern Virginia and the Army of the Potomac under Gen. McClellan locked in deadly combat near Sharpsburg, Maryland, Milroy received orders to prepare to move to western Virginia. He did not receive his promotion and despite his disgust with the war, lack of willingness to go to western Virginia, and desire to be with his family isolated on "some lone isle out in the ocean or in some secret secluded Mountain Valley of the Rocky Mountains," Milroy's sense of duty kept him in the field.[88] "I wish my stern sense of duty would permit me to quit and come home," Milroy explained to his wife, "but it wont and I must stay and stand by my country in this her darkest gloomiest hour till the ship sinks— I may get to you from the wreck."[89]

Despite his aversion to going to western Virginia he did believe that he could be of some use there as long as the War Department gave him a proper command and cut him loose to go after the Confederates. Milroy was already aware by mid-September that the Confederates had gained possession of the salt works on the Kanawha — something of vital importance for the production of gunpowder. The Gray Eagle wanted to go after the Confederates and complained: "If the War Department here, or rather the West Point Dynasty will consent to give me an adequate force and will leave me untrammeled by order and let me have my own way, I will insure to clear all Western Va., of rebles in forty days from the time I commence." Clearly, however, Milroy understood that he would not be allowed to act freely so he had to come to terms with the notion that he would be "trammeled and tied up so that I will have to spend another miserable Winter in Western Va. now made more miserable by the long desolation of war." Perhaps the only consolation that Milroy had as he would move his troops from the nation's capital to western Virginia was that he would pass through the area where his wife grew up in Pennsylvania and might have the chance to speak with her relatives. That was small comfort to a general who saw opportunities for crushing the rebellion and earning glory slip away.[90]

As September came to a close Milroy wrote his wife that his "connection with the Army of the Potomac is about to cease ... forever I hope." By October 3, Milroy's brigade reached Clarksburg, Virginia. Six days later it arrived in Point Pleasant. There Milroy assumed temporary command of approximately 12,000 troops.[91] Milroy's stay in Point Pleasant was short. On October 13, Maj. Gen. Jacob Cox arrived and took command. Cox sent Milroy with his brigade to Clarksburg to take command of 12 regiments, four artillery batteries and four companies of cavalry — in all about 10,000 troops. When Milroy arrived in Clarksburg area Unionists received him warmly. "I am surprised at the confidence the people of Western Va. have at my return. They come 20 to 30 miles to welcome me frequently with tears in their eyes," Milroy wrote. According to Milroy the loyal citizens told him that "they had not peace or security or safety since [he] left, but they feel perfectly safe since I have come and are sure that the country will soon be cleared of rebles and guerillas. They have the most unbounded confidence in me."[92]

In command of the Cheat Mountain Division, once again, Milroy's troops needed to push into the interior of western Virginia and drive the enemy out. The achievements Milroy and his men made in helping to secure western Virginia in the conflict's first year had been lost by the late summer of 1862. "Since I left there," Milroy wrote, "that portion of the state has been nearly over run by the rebles and will all have to be fought over again." Although a "vast undertaking," Milroy's "deep sense of duty to [his] Country" gave him the energy to perform the "dreaded task."[93] Milroy pushed his men through the end of October south from Clarksburg to the vicinity of Beverly. Again he was within sight of Cheat Mountain, the location of the dreadful winter of 1861–1862. Already in the middle of autumn, Milroy feared another winter in this unforgiving region. "I dread it so much that I would most gladly avoid it for the comfort of home did not stern duty forbid," penned Milroy.[94]

Various problems confronted Milroy's Cheat Mountain Division in the fall of 1862, but none was greater than Confederate partisans—most notably those under Col. John D. Imboden. Partisans were Milroy's greatest bane during the war's first year in western Virginia. Milroy tried conventional means to stop partisan activity in 1861, but a year later Milroy would be a bit more aggressive in trying to curb the activities of Confederate irregulars. Troops from Milroy's command marched out on a daily basis into Pocahontas, Bath, Highland, and Pendleton counties and rounded up Confederate sympathizers and partisans. Unionist families feared for life and property and every day a steady stream of civilians poured into Milroy's camps for protection. They had nothing but praise for the Gray Eagle. These Unionist civilians boosted Milroy's ego so much that he believed that if he ran for president he would "be unanimously elected ... by the Union men of Western Va."[95]

Although patrols scoured the countryside on a daily basis for Confederates it was not enough for Milroy. He felt that some act of retribution should be carried out against Confederate sympathizers for the losses of Unionist civilians. In early November 1862 Milroy issued an order that levied a fine on Confederate sympathizers to compensate for the loss of property and life of a Union sympathizer.[96] The destruction of Unionist property by irregular forces occurred on a frequent basis and as one of Milroy's subordinates wrote after the war: "The loyal citizens of that part of the state [western Virginia] were subjected to the most cruel persecutions by rebel guerillas; and it was not [an] infrequent occurrence for loyal citizens to be shot at their own door steps as they left their homes.... The dwellings of loyal citizens were burned, and their horses and other domestic animals stolen." These sorts of actions did not "appeal favorably to General Milroy, and in fact it stirred every drop of fighting blood with vindictive indignation."[97] Milroy directed his subordinates to follow his compensation law to the letter. In an order to Capt. Horace Kellogg, commanding the post at St. George, Virginia, Milroy stated: "If they fail to pay at the end of the time you have named their houses will be burned and themselves shot and their property all seized, and be sure that you carry out this threat rigidly and show them that you are not trifling or to be trifled with." Milroy also directed Kellogg and other commanders in his post to make certain that people understood that they must also inform Federal troops when Confederates were near. Those citizens who refused risked having their houses burned and the men executed.[98]

Furthermore Milroy ordered that any civilian who did not take an oath of allegiance to the United States furnish provisions and quarter the troops under his command. Milroy's General Order No. 39 reminded the Confederate sympathizers of western Virginia: "While loyal men are obliged to leave their families and homes endure the hardships, take the risks of a soldier's life, and shed their blood in defense of the only truly Republican Government in the world Rebel sympathizers aiders and abetters seeking its destruction must be made to feel the strong arm of the government."[99]

Milroy's controversial order of levying fines against Confederate sympathizers came to Imboden's attention in early December after Job Parsons, a resident of Tucker County, Virginia, was assessed $14.25 and went to Imboden's camp to enlist.[100] Parsons also told Imboden of two other penalties levied by Milroy; one on Parsons' father for $300 and another on a relative for $700.[101] Perhaps no penalty infuriated Imboden more than the one issued against Adam Harper, a $285 fine. It was not the monetary amount that Imboden may have found intolerable; it was the physical condition of the man upon whom Milroy levied the charge. Over 80 years old, crippled and infirmed, Harper could neither read nor write.[102]

Upon learning of these cruel edicts—which became a hallmark of Milroy's style of military governance from this point forward—Imboden dispatched the information to Richmond. Imboden's letter reached Confederate president Jefferson Davis first. Davis then forwarded the correspondence to General Lee and directed him to send a note to General Halleck to investigate Milroy's actions. Halleck never reprimanded Milroy for issuing the order as Halleck "did not see proper to incur the odium of ordering its rescission."[103]

As Milroy developed his plan of retribution against the Confederate civilians of western Virginia, Imboden continued to plan operations and wreak havoc on Union supply lines in the region. In early November Imboden planned a raid into Tucker County, Virginia. At the same time Milroy considered a movement against Staunton to capture the strategic rail center—something he failed to achieve earlier that year. Confederate partisans reached the town of St. George in Tucker County, the home of Job Parsons, on November 9. There the Union garrison of a captain and 33 men surrendered to Imboden, who immediately paroled them. The Union garrison at St. George, however, would be the last of Milroy's troops that Imboden paroled. After learning of Milroy's harsh order in early December Imboden vowed never to parole any Union soldier until Milroy relented. When Milroy learned of Imboden's raid he abandoned his plan to strike Staunton and instead marched a force, about 2,000 strong, to intercept Imboden. Confederate partisans eluded Milroy's force and escaped safely.[104] The entire affair infuriated Milroy because not only did he fail to capture Imboden, but Imboden disrupted Milroy's Staunton operation.

The feud between Milroy and Imboden continued throughout the remainder of 1862. Imboden continued to hamper Union operations in the region throughout the first half of 1863. Occasionally Milroy ordered the execution of Confederate partisans and even the execution of two civilians near Philippi for failing to comply with his orders.[105] He also arrested 15 Confederate sympathizers after Imboden arrested a Union sheriff and sent him to Richmond. Milroy ordered the sheriff's immediate release. If Imboden failed to secure the sheriff's release Milroy was prepared to execute the prisoners. Imboden replied to Milroy's threat that if any Confederate civilians were killed, two of Milroy's men would die for every civilian. The Gray Eagle countered Imboden's warning by stating that he had far more Confederate prisoners than Imboden had Union detainees. Luckily, neither side executed any soldiers or civilians as a result of this particular affair.[106]

As Milroy continued his operations against Imboden he received a letter from his wife that informed him that Ben Summit—the runaway slave Milroy sent to Rensselaer in 1861—was becoming very complacent and did not want to work very much, even for Mrs. Milroy. "I was in hopes that Ben had too much sense to get spoiled," Milroy wrote his wife, but, "Slaves who have obtained their freedom are apt to run their freedom in excess if not restrained."[107]

Even though he must have worried about Ben's future his heart must have ached when his daughter Ella asked why her father could not come home "like the other officers do." Undoubtedly Milroy would have loved to come home, but he believed that it was his duty to remain at his post. Milroy wanted his wife to explain to Ella that "I cannot get my own consent to act the rascal because the other officers do it, for I consider that in these times when the fate of our country and the cause of free Government is at Stake, any officer or soldier who is able for duty and obtains leave of absence or furlough to go home, is a swindler for the time he is absent from duty." Milroy further explained to his daughter bluntly: "No officer or Soldier should go home while this war lasts, unless disabled by disease or wounds, or he can go by going home [to] relieve his family from distress and misery or save himself and them from great pecuniary loss."[108]

Sternness with his daughter did not mean he did not love her, rather it showed Milroy's fear for certain peril for the Union and intentness on doing whatever it took to bust up the Confederacy even if that mission strained a family. By mid-December as Milroy was somewhat disheartened over Ben's lax attitude and his daughter's longing for him, Milroy wondered what lay on the west side of the Blue Ridge in the Shenandoah Valley. He believed, correctly, that only a small force of Confederate cavalry was in the Valley and that it ought to be driven out and his force, at least part of it, should occupy the northern part of the Shenandoah. From here, Milroy believed, his command, along with other Federal forces in western Virginia and western Maryland, could better protect what remained of the Baltimore and Ohio Railroad. Curious, Milroy sent one of his brigades under Gen. Gustave P. Cluseret into the Valley. A native of France, Cluseret came to America in 1862 to fight for the Union. He was an experienced military officer, having served in the French army and the cause for Italian liberation in 1860. Although a capable leader, many Union officers including Milroy perceived Cluseret as a soldier of fortune.[109] Cluseret first marched to Strasburg and after a small skirmish in which Cluseret's men captured several Confederates he then decided to push north to Winchester. By Christmas Eve Cluseret's force of 3,000 occupied the strategically important town of Winchester.[110] When Cluseret's men entered Winchester they set up camp on the property of the colonial founder of Winchester, James Wood, and Winchester's Laura Lee could only write: "The wretched, horrible Yankees are here again!"[111]

Cluseret's first two days in Winchester were not without incident. On Christmas Day a small band of Confederate cavalry menaced Cluseret's command. According to his subordinates the Frenchman performed horribly. Officers in the brigade complained to Milroy that "there was so much confusion in his disposition of his forces and in his own understanding of that disposition that we find him ordering infantry to fire on his Cavalry whereby one horse was killed and the lives of men put in jeopardy at the hands of their friends." Complaints, such as this one, about Cluseret's ability would become fuel for Milroy to rid himself of the soldier of fortune.[112]

When Cluseret arrived in Winchester he sent a dispatch to General Kelley. Kelley understood the importance of Winchester and he at once ordered Cluseret to remain in Winchester and ordered the remainder of Milroy's division to proceed to Winchester.[113] Milroy approved of the idea as he preferred to be in the Valley for the winter. From here Milroy felt confident that his command could better protect the Baltimore and Ohio. From the northern Shenandoah Valley Milroy also believed he would have a better opportunity to enforce the Emancipation Proclamation, which would go into effect on January 1, 1863.

Winchester had not been occupied by Federal soldiers since September 2, 1862, when Union Gen. Julius White evacuated the town and fled to Harper's Ferry.[114] The following day the 5th Virginia Infantry, commanded by Lt. Col. John H.S. Funk, arrived in Winchester. Funk secured the town as a base of operations for Lee's invasion of Maryland, culminating in the Battle of Antietam on September 17, 1862. Following Antietam, Winchester remained in Confederate hands through mid-November 1862. By mid-November Maj. Gen. Ambrose Burnside's Army of the Potomac had replaced McClellan and Burnside's army was moving toward the Rappahannock River and Fredericksburg. Lee needed to concentrate his troops. Gen. James Longstreet's First Corps moved across the Blue Ridge in late October, but the Second Corps under Stonewall Jackson remained in Winchester. On November 22, with an ominous threat against Richmond from the north, Lee ordered Jackson from Winchester.

After Jackson's departure only a token Confederate force remained under the command of Brig. Gen. William "Grumble" Jones and troops of the Maryland Line under Brig. Gen. George H. Steuart.[115] This token force would not be enough to hold off any Federal attempts to capture the town. On December 3, Federal forces under command of Brig. Gen. John Geary occupied Winchester with little opposition from Confederate forces. This event probably more than any other had convinced Milroy that Federal troops could occupy the lower Shenandoah Valley. Geary's force remained in Winchester for only a few hours. Contrary to Milroy's assumption that

Geary had been ordered to withdraw from Winchester, news of a smallpox epidemic in town forced Geary to leave.[116] Confederate forces returned to Winchester after Geary's withdrawal, but on December 13, Jones withdrew his command south to Strasburg.[117] In the week and half that followed Winchester enjoyed a peaceful, unoccupied tranquility.

As 1862 came to a close Milroy's penchant for military fame and glory had transformed into a quest to end the rebellion and abolish the institution of slavery. Although always an ardent abolitionist Milroy believed that the causes of the Union's misfortunes in the East were directly linked to slavery. Regardless of the fact that he had been banished from the Presbyterian Church in 1861 as a result of being involved in a fight and questioning church doctrine, Milroy firmly believed in God.[118] After countless military setbacks, Milroy believed that, aside from removing West Pointers from command, the government needed to abolish slavery. He lamented to his wife that "our ill success still confirms me more and more in the opinion that Providence is not with us in this War until the 'Powers that be' removes and abolishes the great and mighty curse and cause of the War, *Slavery*. I have very great doubts of any permanent success in the Union cause until this is done."[119]

Enforcing emancipation would be one of Milroy's primary goals as he occupied a town that held connections to Judge Richard Parker, who presided over John Brown's momentous treason trial, and to Senator James Mason, author of the 1850 Fugitive Slave Law. Historical connections to slavery were important to Milroy as he prepared to move to Winchester. He knew the town was "a very aristocratic old town or rather city," and that it was the "residence of the infamous scoundrel Mason and Judge Parker who presided at the trial of Old John Brown." The town's ties to slavery's past provided Milroy with the perfect setting to enforce emancipation.

5

"To play the tyrant among these traitors"

Throughout the day on January 1, 1863, Milroy's division descended on Winchester from the west. As the long column of troops marched to Winchester, officers in the rear of the column heard shouts coming from the front. Curious as to the cause of the shouting, Col. Joseph Warren Keifer of the 110th Ohio rode to the head of the column to find Milroy. Keifer asked Milroy about the cause for the excitement. With a speech impediment he always had when excited Milroy exclaimed to Keifer: "Colonel don't you know this is Emancipation Day, when all slaves will be made free?"[1]

Throughout the march to Winchester Milroy rode up and down his lines, halted momentarily and delivered a short speech. Milroy proclaimed to his men: "This day President Lincoln will proclaim the freedom of four millions of human slaves, the most important event in the history of the world since Christ was born. Our boast that this is a land of liberty has been a flaunting lie. Henceforth it will be a veritable reality." Milroy explained to his men that God did not bless the army with success because "we waged a war to protect and perpetuate and to rivet firmer the chains of slavery." If Milroy's men enforced emancipation then he assured them that "the Lord God Almighty will fight on our side ... and the Union armies will triumph."[2] Milroy's speech may have been more than a simple attempt to exhibit joy over emancipation; it may have been an attempt to illustrate to his men, some of whom were from western Virginia, the ultimate importance of the abolition of slavery in the Union's effort to win the war. Undoubtedly Milroy was keenly aware of the problems that the preliminary proclamation created among the rank and file.[3] He did not want to deal with petitions condemning the measure, desertion, and other acts of disobedience.

As Milroy's men entered Winchester on New Year's Day their spirits were high. Buoyed by his men's reception of his speech about emancipation, Milroy's confidence in his mission to enforce Lincoln's proclamation soared as he viewed a bright sun burning in a cloudless sky as a sure sign "that President Lincoln's immortal Proclamation had enlisted God almighty on our side and that he will soon clear away the storms and tempests of war occasioned by that mighty curse, slavery."[4]

Without a doubt Milroy was the exception rather than the rule when it came to the Emancipation Proclamation. Many Federal officers did not approve of Lincoln's measure; yet at the time the final proclamation was issued many enlisted men began to see that abolishing slavery would be a valuable weapon in ending the rebellion.[5] Although the majority of Milroy's men were galvanized by his New Year's Day speech and actively enforced his policies in the lower Shenandoah Valley, a portion of his command did so begrudgingly. A member of the 87th Pennsylvania, Thomas Crowl, wrote his sister from Winchester that "our old General [Milroy] says that he thinks more of the Blacks than his soldiers, but if we get into Battle he will stand a good chance of getting his infernal old gray head shot off ... the war may go to hell for me, I never intend to stay here and risk my life for these damned niggers."[6] Crowl, unlike Milroy, believed that abolishing slavery would hurt the Union war effort. "This Nigrow freedom," Crowl penned, "is what is playing hell, this is a wrong thing, this will destroy our army we never enlisted to fight for Nigrows."[7]

When Milroy arrived in Winchester, his reputation preceded him. Winchester's townspeople already knew of Milroy's activities in western Virginia and feared they might suffer the same fate. His harsh treatment of the civilian population made many Confederates liken him to Union Maj. Gen. Benjamin F. Butler—noted for his boorish treatment of the affluent members of New Orleans society in the spring of 1862. Winchester resident Kate Sperry noted of Milroy in her diary: "He's a second Butler and $100,000 is the price the Confederacy (some people in the Confederacy) has placed on his head—I wish I could get it."[8]

Milroy's force at Winchester served as part of Gen. Robert Schenck's Middle Department. The Gray Eagle controlled the lower Shenandoah Valley with nearly 7,000 men while General Kelley controlled the Union defenses of the upper Potomac River with his headquarters at Harper's Ferry. From his position at Winchester, Milroy deployed detachments on a constant basis to contend with Confederate raiders threatening the Baltimore & Ohio.

While Milroy confronted many problems in the lower Valley, his first and one of his longest-lasting was disease. Smallpox, typhoid fever, and mumps plagued Milroy's division and some of the townspeople. Disease remained a constant threat to both armies during the war and claimed more lives than bullets on the battlefield. Throughout the occupation, smallpox cases were reported, but luckily never gained epidemic proportions. Milroy reassured his wife during the first week of the occupation that "the small pox is here but I think will not spread among the troops much. My health is excellent."[9] Typhoid also plagued the townspeople and soldiers in Milroy's command in April. In one regiment, the 110th Ohio, nearly 115 men contracted the disease. Colonel Keifer of the 110th lambasted the Union surgeons for not properly caring for the sick and even threatened to expose their ineptness to authorities in Washington, D.C.[10]

FREEDOM TO SLAVES!

Whereas, the President of the United States did, on the first day of the present month, issue his *Proclamation* declaring "that *all persons held as Slaves in certain designated States, and parts of States, are, and henceforward shall be free,*" and that the Executive Government of the United States, including the Military and Naval authorities thereof, would recognize and maintain the freedom of said persons. *And Whereas*, the county of Frederick is included in the territory designated by the Proclamation of the President, in which the *Slaves should become free*, I therefore hereby notify the citizens of the city of Winchester, and of said County, of said Proclamation, and of my intention to maintain and enforce the same.

I expect all citizens to yield a ready compliance with the Proclamation of the Chief Executive, and I admonish all persons disposed to resist its peaceful enforcement, that upon manifesting such disposition by acts, they will be regarded as rebels in arms against the lawful authority of the Federal Government and dealt with accordingly.

All persons liberated by said Proclamation are admonished to abstain from all violence, and immediately betake themselves to useful occupations.

The officers of this command are admonished and ordered to act in accordance with said proclamation and to yield their ready co-operation in its enforcement.

R. H. Milroy,
Brig. Gen'l Commanding.

Jan. 5th, 1863.

"Freedom to Slaves!" was perhaps Milroy's most famous decree. Issued on January 5, 1863, it informed the citizens of the lower Shanandoah Valley that Milroy was going to enforce President Lincoln's Emanciation Proclamation and anyone who interfered would be punished severely (Jasper County Public Library, Rensselaer, Indiana).

Aside from combating disease and protecting the remnants of the Baltimore & Ohio, Milroy's self-appointed duties in Winchester were to actively enforce Lincoln's Emancipation Proclamation, protect area Unionists, and do whatever was necessary to help bring about a speedy end to the war. The determined Hoosier would let no one stand in his way, Union or Confederate.

Three days after Milroy entered Winchester, he reportedly received a copy of the Emancipation Proclamation. Seeing that it encompassed his military district, Milroy issued his own decree — "Freedom to Slaves!" — to the citizens of Winchester and Frederick County the following day. The Gray Eagle's decree read in part: "I expect all citizens to yield a ready compliance with the Proclamation of the Chief Executive, and I admonish all persons disposed to resist its peaceful enforcement, that upon manifesting such disposition by acts, they will be regarded as rebels in arms against the lawful authority of the Federal government and dealt with accordingly."[11]

After he issued his order one of the greatest concerns of the residents of the lower Valley must have been that disgruntled former slaves might lash out violently against their former masters. In order to prevent such acts Milroy added a sentence to "Freedom to Slaves!" that directed "all persons liberated by said Proclamation are admonished to abstain from all violence, and immediately betake themselves to useful occupations."[12]

Federal troops immediately began to enforce Milroy's proclamation and throughout January and February scoured the countryside for slaves and free blacks who sought refuge. Some former slaves remained in the Winchester area and worked for Milroy's division, but a sizeable portion gathered their meager possessions, boarded trains, and headed north. Milroy actually preferred that the former slaves remained in Virginia. "I try to persuade them to remain in Va.," Milroy explained, "assuring them that they will remain free." Verbal assurances carried little weight among former slaves. Frequently the slaves who headed north told Milroy that they "would much rather remain among friends and neighbors with whom they were raised [and] if the war was over and they could be assured that the Proclamation ... would be enforced but considering the uncertainty of war and the certainty of slavery if the South should destroy the Union, they wish to make ... sure of their freedom while the way is open."[13] As hundreds of newly freed blacks boarded empty supply trains and emigrated north they were each given an image of John Brown. As the trains departed the Valley, those in Winchester could hear, coming from the cars, "songs of freedom and the religious hymns peculiar to the race with the universal but more cheerful music of the fiddle and banjo."[14] No riotous behavior occurred as former slaves left their masters; rather many departures were filled with tears. In the Valley, unlike other places throughout the slaveholding South, slaves were not treated brutally as slave and master worked side by side. "It must not be assumed," Colonel Keifer penned, "that the slave owners in the Valley were, in war times at least, cruel to their slaves; on the contrary, kindness and indulgence were the rule." Former masters offered tokens of remembrance to house servants, and compassion was reportedly expressed by both parties in numerous instances.[15]

Although Milroy's troops made concerted efforts to enforce emancipation his operations were often hampered, not by masters, but rather by Confederate partisans—a constant hindrance throughout Milroy's Civil War career. On February 9 "a negro came rushing into my quarters ... to tell me that a party of Reb Cavalry were gathering up the darkies in his neighborhood, about ten miles from town," Milroy wrote. The former slave explained to Milroy that the Confederate horsemen gathered as many slaves as they could find, including the unidentified slave's wife and children, and were sending them south. Alarmed, Milroy deployed the 13th Pennsylvania Cavalry several days later to disrupt the operation. The troopers from the Keystone State succeeded in stopping their foe and captured a Confederate lieutenant in the process. The slaves were once again emancipated and reunited with their families. Happily Milroy penned his wife: "It would do you good to see the poor creatures rejoice when they find they have liberty and their scattered families unite."[16]

While the lion's share of the area's Confederates looked upon emancipation with disdain so too did some of the town's Unionists—Milroy's local allies. One of Winchester's Unionists, Julia Chase, remarked on January 1: "According to the President's Proclamation, all the slaves are to be freed from today. This will give great dissatisfaction to Slaveholders but joy to the Negroes. I doubt whether they will be better off by having their freedom."[17] Chase, like many of the town's Unionists, did not approve of freeing the slaves and were angered over the matter. Their resistance to emancipation loosened after they realized the importance of emancipation to ending the conflict. "The only light," Chase wrote, "which I can see right is, that the slaves are in the way of putting down the rebellion in that they are tilling the soil while their masters are in the army fighting against the U.S. Government."[18]

News of Milroy's emancipation caused anxiety in Richmond. Officials in the Confederate government already knew about Milroy because of the Gray Eagle's harsh policies against civilians in western Virginia, in response to which the Senate of Virginia claimed Milroy's "acts and doings are contrary to the usages of civilized and honorable warfare."[19] Milroy's proclamation "Freedom to Slaves!" created a much greater hatred toward the

Hoosier general and prompted more legislative action by both the Commonwealth and the Confederacy.

Alexander R. Boteler, a member of Virginia's House of Delegates, received a copy of Milroy's decree shortly after it was issued. Boteler immediately forwarded the circular to Virginia's governor John Letcher.[20] "I have just received [a] ... copy of a Proclamation '*Freedom to Slaves*' recently issued by the notorious Milroy in the District which I have the honor to represent," Boteler wrote to Letcher. Boteler informed Letcher that "this man Milroy has announced his determination to enforce by arms on our devoted Valley the fiendish abolition policy which the infamous John Brown vainly attempted to inaugurate at Harpers Ferry and for which he received from ... Virginia the punishment he so richly deserved."[21]

When Letcher received Boteler's dispatch he was shocked and took immediate action. The governor sent a message to the Senate and House of Delegates the day following receipt of Boteler's message.[22] Letcher's communiqué lambasted both Milroy and President Lincoln for their proclamations of emancipation. In Letcher's eyes Milroy's policy was "brutal" and he also noted that "Lincoln had violated all principles of humanity."[23] He continued his tirade against Milroy: "He is in all respects a suitable tool, for the execution of so execrable a mark. He follows the lead of his master, and therefore promises to maintain the freedom of the slaves, urges a ready compliance with the Proclamation of Lincoln."[24] Not only did Virginia's governor view Milroy's and Lincoln's measures as attempts to abolish slavery, but he also saw them as efforts to incite slave insurrections.[25] In Letcher's eyes Milroy's emancipation "violates in the most positive manner, the provisions of our act of assembly, which declares if a free person advise or conspire with a slave to revolt or make insurrection, or with any person, to induce a slave to rebel or make insurrection he shall be punished with death."[26]

Milroy's policies toward the Confederate civilian population prompted Virginia and the Confederacy to combine resources to post a $100,000 reward for Milroy's capture. On January 10, Virginia's legislature offered a resolution in support of Governor Letcher declaring Milroy an outlaw. Both houses of the Virginia legislature recommended that Milroy be hung as he performed acts with a "barbarous and fiendish spirit which calls for the severest measures of repression."[27] No threat worried Milroy. He truly believed that since he was performing God's work the Almighty would protect him. Only an Old Testament–style scourge of the land, Milroy believed, could rid the country of slavery and end the rebellion. He expressed this fervent belief to his wife: "In ancient times the cry of a nation of slaves went up to a God out of Egypt and He heard them and sent Moses and

Aaron to reason with the slave holders and try to get them to emancipate their slaves, but all the arguments and reasoning ... were received by the slave holders with scorn and ridicule." Milroy continued that a "long bitter cry has went up to the same God from a nation of slaves in America. He has heard that cry and for many years been sending good men to reason with the slave holders ... but the slave holders have met all arguments ... with scorn." Since slaveholders met decades of compromises with derision, Milroy believed that only a bloody conflict could end slavery and reunite the country. "War, devastation, want, Misery, disease, terror and death are everywhere around them," Milroy explained to his wife, "but still they defy God and refuse to let their slaves go free.... Hell deserving iniquity until like the Pharaoh and his host, they will overwhelm in total destruction."[28]

While emancipation was a priority for Milroy, he could not neglect other military matters. During the first several weeks of his occupation of the lower Valley, Milroy felt vulnerable in Winchester. He received intelligence that Confederate cavalry under Generals "Grumble" Jones and Imboden roamed somewhere near Strasburg, south of Winchester. Perceiving the inevitability of a cavalry attack on his Winchester post Milroy pleaded with his superiors to be reinforced. He sent a message to Kelley at Harpers Ferry to send him the 13th Pennsylvania Cavalry.[29] Unexplainable delays kept the cavalry from arriving until February 13, more than one month after Milroy sent his request.[30]

In the meantime Milroy did everything he could to bolster his position in Winchester through military policy and physical labor. Milroy believed that he could garner the support of Winchester's townspeople by rewarding those who took the oath of allegiance to the United States with special privileges and withholding necessities from those who did not. Milroy had no cause to believe that this would not work. After all, during his tenure in Rappahannock County and western Virginia during 1862 he employed a similar practice and had decent success.[31] However, Winchester's Confederate population would not cave so easily.

Some of Milroy's subordinates supported him in this policy, but some did not—chief among them was General Cluseret. The French soldier of fortune did not see eye to eye with Milroy on a number of issues, including slavery and indecent treatment of civilians. Constant tension between the two prompted Milroy to push for Cluseret's dismissal during the first two weeks of the occupation of Winchester.[32] Winchester's Mary Lee, a staunch Confederate who would become one of Milroy's most baneful foes among the town's citizenry, noted of Clusert's disapproval of Milroy's practices: "He did not come here to fight for negroes, & to arrest women, & that it is contrary to the usages of war to refuse to feed prisoners."[33]

Even though Milroy never emphatically spelled out that the reason for the dismissal was Cluseret's lack of enthusiasm for Milroy's policies, Milroy generally described to his superior, General Schenck, why the Frenchman should be dismissed. "I have had trouble with Genl. Cluseret," Milroy wrote Schenck. "I ... observed that his harsh disrespectful and unfeeling course towards his officers and men, and the difficulty in their understanding him and him them, was making him very unpopular.... [Cluseret is] hasty tempered impatient insulting tyrannical & overbearing to those under him."[34] While Milroy forced Cluseret to relinquish his command during the second week of January, Cluseret did not officially resign until March 1863.[35] Driving people out of service who did not support Lincoln's emancipation policy was not something unique to Milroy. Other Federal officers, including Gen. Ulysses S. Grant, dismissed subordinates who failed to see the advantages that emancipation presented to the Union war effort.[36]

Regardless of Milroy's animosity toward Cluseret, at least nine officers of Cluseret's brigade had problems with the Frenchman. Two days after Milroy came to Winchester officers from Cluseret's brigade respectfully requested "that the Gen. [Cluseret] now in command of the Brigade should be relieved." The officers complained that he was a "foreigner unable to speak our language so as to be understood and he himself has some difficulty in understanding us hence our intercourse thus far has been nothing but a perplexing series of mutual blunders and mistakes."[37] They protested further: "He has shown the utmost disregard and contempt for the rights and feelings of officers ... below him in rank, repelling them with a tyrannical and despotic air when in the conscientious discharge of their duty to their commands they applied to him in a respectful manner for a redress of their grievances ... he is to play the tyrant over all who belong to his command." The angry officers closed their letter to Milroy by informing him that Cluseret should be dismissed because he simply was not one of them, he was a European. "He knows nothing of the genius of our institutions," the officers explained to Milroy, "or the spirit of our people and whilst he might do to command an army of European conscripts he can never command an army of American volunteers."[38]

Aside from contending with Cluseret during the first weeks of occupation, Milroy did everything to ensure the safety of his command. Throughout his time in the lower Valley, Milroy ordered frequent expeditions to Berryville, Strasburg, and Front Royal. Anywhere Milroy's command went, the inhabitants of that town felt his wrath. During Milroy's first 10 days in the Valley several regiments of his command made two raids into Berryville, several miles east of Winchester. Milroy's soldiers looted, pillaged, and also arrested at least six Confederate sympathizers.[39]

During a raid to Front Royal on January 12-13, Milroy's soldiers learned that many of the lower Valley's citizens held contempt for anyone in a blue uniform and were not afraid to exhibit their disdain. Five companies of the 110th Ohio marched to Front Royal and captured four Confederate soldiers during the expedition.[40] The Ohio troops seized mail, tobacco, and other luxury items. While the men of the 110th roamed Front Royal, the regimental officers arranged to have dinner at the home of a local Confederate sympathizer. Even though their host sympathized with the Confederacy, he treated the Federal officers cordially. As the officers ate they got their first taste of the defiant spirit of the Valley's Confederate women. In a parlor that adjoined the dining room several ladies gathered around a piano and sang Confederate tunes. This scornful display amused the officers.[41]

While small parties of Milroy's division reconnoitered on a frequent basis, Milroy kept the bulk of his command near Winchester to help him keep a tight reign on the civilian population and to strengthen the town's defenses. To contain the town Milroy established a line of pickets, three deep. All stood within calling distance of each other and had specific orders to not let anyone come into or leave town without a proper pass.[42] The Gray Eagle directed his men: "Before the Picket's Guard is posted they must be instructed in addition to their general duties that all citizens entering the lines must be halted at the outer Post and informed before passing in that they cannot return and pass out without taking the prescribed oath of allegiance." Despite his directive, some of Milroy's pickets did permit civilians to pass in and out of the lines without taking the oath of allegiance.[43]

Milroy also did everything in his power to reinforce the town's defenses. Federal troops rebuilt Fort Garibaldi in the northwestern portion of town and renamed it Fort Milroy. Union soldiers also strengthened West Fort, located northwest of town and constructed a new fortification, Star Fort, north of Winchester. Federal troops built Star Fort on the old site of Fort Alabama, a series of gun emplacements constructed earlier in the war by Stonewall Jackson's men.[44] Not only did Milroy gain a strong sense of security because of the forts, he was also gratified knowing that some of the materials used to build these defensive works came from the home of Senator James Mason, author of the 1850 Fugitive Slave Law.[45]

Work on the forts consumed one day per week for soldiers in Milroy's division throughout the nearly six-month occupation. The other days of the week involved three days of guard duty and three days dedicated to camp chores. The many tasks soldiers had to perform on a weekly basis included collecting firewood, gathering material to build winter quarters, and constructing fortifications.[46]

Since much of the wood supply had been exhausted by soldiers from earlier occupations, Milroy's men took any piece of wood they could find. Soldiers razed all of the wooden houses, barns, fences, and stables on the outskirts of town during the opening weeks of the occupation. Federal troops also demolished a number of buildings within the town limits, including the Winchester Academy and the Quaker Church.[47] Disgusted at these acts, Winchester's Portia Baldwin Baker wrote that Milroy and his men "are foot by foot and plank by plank destroying our property ... I am always wishing them in their homes."[48]

Even though Milroy's command destroyed considerable amounts of property during the occupation he did place some restrictions on his men. Milroy ordered his men, except those on guard duty in town, out by six o'clock in the evening.[49] He also forbade the possession of liquor among his troops. He allowed surgeons to use it only for medicinal purposes.[50] Furthermore, Milroy appointed a board of survey on several occasions to examine damage done to the property of Winchester's civilians.

While no evidence exists as to action taken on Milroy's part to reconcile property damage, evidence does exist to indicate that Milroy appointed these boards of survey to investigate destruction done to private property whose owners possessed Union sentiment. For example, Milroy appointed a commission to assess the damage done to Mary E. Hollingsworth's property on February 19, 1863.[51] Strong evidence suggests that Hollingsworth may have had Union sympathies and at one time swore allegiance to the United States. She filed a claim with the Southern Claims Commission in 1878 for damage done to her property during the war, perhaps the damage done during Milroy's occupation.[52] Hollingsworth must have been a Unionist, as only those loyal to the Union were allowed to file claims with the Southern Claims Commission.[53] Nevertheless, the commission denied her claim for compensation by stating that her property was destroyed as a result of the fortunes of war.[54]

The other boards of survey appointed by Milroy also stressed the importance of the victim's Unionist sentiment. If a victim did not have Unionist sentiment his likelihood of being compensated was nil. For example, in late March 1863 Milroy ordered a board of survey "to fix the damage done to the 'Taylor Hotel' in the town of Winchester ... by the troops of this Division, resulting from its use as a Hospital." The Taylor Hotel was constantly used as a hospital throughout the war by both armies, but the large numbers of sick men in Milroy's division housed in the Taylor Hotel had evidently created some damage. Milroy directed the board to not only assess the damage, but to determine whether or not the owners of the Taylor Hotel "are loyal to the United States, and what evidence they have of such loyalty." Nothing suggests that the Taylor Hotel or any other person who filed a claim with Milroy received any compensation for damages done to their property during Milroy's occupation.[55]

As Milroy continued his daily activities in the lower Valley throughout January, General Lee prepared a plan to dislodge Milroy from Winchester. Lee worried about the lack of provisions available to his troops. In a letter to President Jefferson Davis in late January Lee wrote: "The want of supplies for the troops ... causes me the greatest uneasiness."[56] The Shenandoah Valley, the Confederacy's breadbasket, was a major source of provender for the Army of Northern Virginia. Lee knew that as long as Milroy's force remained in the northern end of the Valley, Confederate farmers' crops could not easily reach Confederate soldiers in the field. Lee devised a plan to dislodge the Hoosier's garrison.

On February 2, Lee directed Gen. Grumble Jones to prepare and collect supplies for an additional 2,000 men. Lee informed Jones that if the Army of the Potomac, under command of Maj. Gen. Joseph Hooker, did not move, now would be the time to strike Milroy.[57] Lee planned to dispatch nearly 2,000 men to the Valley from Maj. Gen. J.E.B. Stuart's cavalry to join Jones in the Valley. On February 13, Lee ordered Stuart to deploy Brig. Gen. Fitzhugh Lee's cavalry brigade to Upperville, enter the Shenandoah Valley via Snickersville, and rendezvous with Jones near New Market.[58] Lee also informed Stuart that if he could afford the loss of extra men to detach a portion of Brig. Gen. Wade Hampton's cavalry brigade to join the effort.[59] Lee's plan was short-lived. On February 15, two days after Lee set in motion his plan, he informed Stuart that a Union corps was massing near Newport News, Virginia. The plan would have to be abandoned.[60]

Even though Lee abandoned his plan to reinforce Jones, Grumble continued to gather supplies in preparation for an offensive against Milroy. Throughout the second week of February, Milroy received information that Jones had been replaced and that Jones' former command had been reinforced by infantry and Imboden's cavalry. The reports about command change and reinforcements turned out to be erroneous, but they nonetheless created some apprehension with Milroy in Winchester.[61] Uncertain of Confederate intentions, Milroy wrote to General Schenck on February 17 and asked for reinforcements. Milroy requested that Schenck send the nearly 1,400 troops under command of Col. James Washburn, garrisoned near Romney, to Winchester.[62]

Milroy had further reason to request reinforcements and fear an attack. Twice in January Imboden's troops raided the railroad between Winchester and Martinsburg. The Gray Eagle wanted badly to aggressively pursue his nemesis from western Virginia, yet his superiors would not let him.[63] Throughout his tenure in Winchester, Milroy made constant pleas with

Schenck to turn him loose, as Frémont had done early in the spring of 1862. Milroy wrote Schenck: "The season for action operations is at hand and I am very desirous of breaking the forces and unwelcome torpor of Winter. I have not had the pleasure of meeting the Rebs since our waltz with them at Bull Run and I am anxious to do something towards wiping out the unpleasant recollection of that affair." Milroy implored his superior: "You will do me a very great favor if you will get the embargo on my movements removed and let me be free to act pro bono."[64] Schenck never lifted the "embargo."

As Milroy pleaded with his superiors to cut him loose and allow his command to go after the Confederates, Jones prepared to strike. Early in the morning of February 26, a small force of about 150 troopers attacked Milroy's cavalry pickets on the southern edge of Winchester along Cedar Creek Grade.[65] The assault soon turned into an embarrassing defeat for Milroy's cavalry. About half an hour after the attack commenced, Milroy ordered the 13th Pennsylvania Cavalry to drive the enemy. The Pennsylvanians, known for their lax behavior, did not begin their pursuit until 6:00 A.M., nearly an hour and a half after Milroy issued the order. Eventually the 1st New York Cavalry reinforced the 13th Pennsylvania and both began the pursuit of their Rebel counterparts.

The Federal horsemen followed their foe for nearly 30 miles to Woodstock. At Woodstock two of Jones' regiments—the 7th and 11th Virginia Cavalry—met the Federal troopers. Milroy's cavalry did not put up much of a fight against the Virginia horsemen and withdrew in a hasty and confused manner. Disgusted, Milroy wrote that the behavior of the troopers "was disgraceful and cowardly."[66] Milroy tried to do everything in his power to punish the officers of the 13th Pennsylvania. While he took no immediate action, two of the regiment's officers—Capt. Samuel Speese and Maj. Martin Byrne—were discharged from the service later that year for reasons unknown.[67]

Less than a week after the disastrous retreat of Milroy's cavalry from Woodstock, Imboden proposed a plan to Lee to destroy the bridges and trestles of the Baltimore & Ohio from Oakland to Grafton, west of Winchester. Imboden wanted Grumble Jones to move out of the Shenandoah Valley and capture Romney, New Creek, and Cumberland. Lee liked the idea because he felt that it would force Milroy from Winchester, as Lee knew one of Milroy's main goals was to protect the Baltimore & Ohio; the plan would also leave the door open for Confederates to seize the remaining horses and cattle from the Shenandoah Valley. Lee approved the plan and ordered J.E.B. Stuart to make a diversion east of the Blue Ridge to distract Milroy.[68]

Nearly a month and a half passed before the famed Jones-Imboden raid commenced. The raid lasted from April 20-May 27, 1863.[69] During the raid, reinforcements were sent to the Federals in western Virginia from Milroy's command. While Milroy's aggregate strength was depleted momentarily during the raid, he did not pull out of Winchester or at all become shaken by it.

While Confederate forces planned operations to distract Milroy, his superiors kept a tight rein on his movements in the Valley but did nothing to control his occupation. For nearly half a year Milroy kept a firm grip on the inhabitants of Winchester. Milroy established martial law and boasted to his wife, "I can now realize something of the weighty and unpleasant responsibility that rests on a king ... my will is absolute law — none dare contradict or dispute my slightest word or wish ... both male and female tremble when they come into my presence ... I feel a strong disposition to play the tyrant among these traitors."[70]

Even though Milroy treated the civilians of Winchester harshly, and some of his officers may have viewed his practices as improper, Milroy actually may have partially justified his policies based on recommendations that had come from Halleck and Quartermaster General Montgomery C. Meigs. Meigs' year-end report for 1862 stressed the need for occupying forces to live off of the land and to forage while in enemy territory.[71] Halleck's and Meigs' recommendations that occupying forces live off the land was ambiguous. The vagueness of the order was not defined until April 1863 when General Order No. 100 (more commonly referred to as Lieber's Code) was issued. It clearly pointed out that property could be confiscated only for military necessity and that churches and schools ought to be protected. While the code helped clear up some uncertainties, it still left some, among them how to deal with disloyal civilians.[72]

Milroy passed numerous edicts to make life difficult for the civilian population. Anytime they wanted a favor, they had to make a trip to his office. In several instances Milroy behaved rather civilly toward the townspeople, but only in matters that did not present a security threat to his operations or to those people who were unquestionably Unionist.

One of the most common practices in a town under martial law was mail censorship. Provost clerks read all mail going out or coming in to Winchester.[73] Numerous examples exist of Milroy arresting or exiling citizens, mainly women, for carrying letters with the slightest anti-Union rhetoric. During the first week of Milroy's tenure, Lal Dinkle was exiled from Winchester for carrying letters with Confederate sentiment.[74] Even though Milroy's provost clerks censored all letters, some were smuggled through the lines. To intercept these defiant civilians, Milroy hired several professional detectives.[75]

Milroy also established a military court headed by Colonel Keifer. Numerous cases ranging from petty theft to espionage were brought before Keifer's court. It also held trials for civilians of Winchester and the surrounding area who had violated the oath of allegiance in some manner or had attempted to purchase goods from a sutler without a proper permit.[76] One of the cases brought before the court involved George W. Kitchen, a citizen of Frederick County charged with entering a Federal camp as a spy.[77] Milroy wanted the man convicted, however, Keifer's court found Kitchen not guilty.[78]

Espionage and other major crimes were not Milroy's biggest problem in Winchester so far as the townspeople were concerned. His chief dilemma centered around how to deal with civilians, mainly women, constantly insulting his troops. While Union officers in occupied areas dealt with similar troubles, they addressed them differently. When General Butler occupied New Orleans in May 1862 he dealt with a feisty female population by issuing his famous "Woman Order," which stated that any woman who insulted a Union soldier would be treated "as a woman of the town plying her avocation."[79] Milroy dealt with women differently. Punishment for insulting a Union soldier was either imprisonment or exile, depending on Milroy's mood.[80] According to the diary of the staunch Confederate Mary Lee, conditions under imprisonment may have been akin to treatment accorded by Milroy to Confederate prisoners of war — little or no food and horrid living conditions.[81]

Milroy continued to play the role of tyrant when he refused to allow farmers from outside of town to sell their produce. Winchester's Mary Lee simply remarked of the cruel edict: "Milroy is trying to starve us out."[82] Later during the occupation, he forbade sutlers who received any supplies from the North from selling goods to any man, woman, or child without their first taking the oath and also securing a permit from the provost. Milroy's Special Order No. 4 stated: "The Sutlers, non-resident Dealers, and those resident Dealers who are receiving supplies from the North, are hereby prohibited from selling any article whatever, to men, (not soldiers) women, or child." Milroy vowed that any violator of the law would have all of his goods confiscated and be imprisoned.[83]

The prohibition of selling farm produce to the civilians without permits was not only an attempt to force the Confederate civilian population to take the oath, but also a means by which Milroy could help deplete any existing supplies of livestock in the area. Milroy knew that if he did this, and later was driven form the Valley, there would not be much livestock available to the Confederate army. Livestock died daily from starvation because their owners could not obtain enough grain to feed them.

One day Winchester resident Emma Cassandra Riely went to Milroy's office to plead with him to get feed for her livestock. As she sat in a waiting room, she heard yelling coming from Milroy's office. Milroy was shouting at a woman who had come there for the same purpose. Riely heard Milroy exclaim: "You all brought on this devilish rebellion and ought to be crushed and deserve to starve with the cows!"[84] Knowing her plea would fall on deaf ears, Riely left the general's office without speaking to him.

The martial law Milroy implemented also made it difficult for civilians to move about town. He placed a curfew on all residents — 8:00 P.M. except Sunday when the curfew was extended one hour.[85] He also forbade inhabitants from gathering in groups of two or more in the streets. In many instances even groups of schoolgirls were disbanded if there were more than two in one area.[86]

Milroy ruled without prejudice. Even children were subject to punishment. Winchester had passed through a terrible winter; even by mid–March snow still blanketed the ground. One day a group of young boys were playfully throwing snowballs in the streets and one accidentally struck a Federal officer. Seeing this as an insult the Federal officer arrested Harry McDonald, who happened to be holding a snowball at the moment and whose father was an officer in the Confederate cavalry. The boy was released from jail later that night at the request of the quartermaster, who boarded at the McDonald home.[87]

Even though many of the civilians held strong Confederate convictions, some of them had no choice but to beg Milroy for a permit for food. More often than not Milroy expressed no sympathy to the townspeople. Cornelia McDonald went to Milroy in late February to obtain such permission.[88] Naturally Milroy asked her if she was loyal to the Union. McDonald replied that she was not. She added that the generals previous to him did not require the oath of allegiance as a prerequisite for purchasing food and other necessities.[89] Milroy did not care what his predecessors had done. He repeatedly stated: "The way of the transgressor is hard and that if they could not afford to renounce treason they must suffer on as they need expect no favor."[90]

After listening to McDonald's plea he informed her that he felt a need to be harsh on the women of the Confederacy as he firmly believed that had it not been for them, the men in the field would have come home.[91] Milroy's supposition has some credence as many historians today place a tremendous amount of importance on the role of Confederate women in keeping soldiers in the field.[92] In particular, women who stood firm in the face of adversity at the hands of Union occupiers seemed to embolden many Confederate soldiers to remain on the front lines. Recognizing the importance of women to the Confederate war effort Milroy explained: "The young ladies, most of whom have brothers and lovers in the Reb Army are especially bitter against me, but I have given orders that any ... female Reb who utters a disrespectful word against or to an officer or soldier shall be instantly trotted into the guard house."[93] After Milroy completed his rant about Confederate women he calmed down and handed McDonald a piece of paper. He told her to present the paper to his adjutant in the next room. When the adjutant asked if she was loyal, she replied that she was not and walked out of the room, unable to purchase any goods. McDonald, as well as many other women in Winchester, felt it more important to hold onto their pride rather than submit to Milroy.

Time and again Milroy heard pleas similar to McDonald's, but his response was always the same — a personal declaration of loyalty to the Union would allow anyone to get what they needed. Regardless of how hard Milroy tried to get people to take the oath, he could really do nothing to break the impenetrable spirit of Winchester's Confederates. A survey of the identifiable oaths of allegiance form the Middle Department reveals that no new oaths were taken at Winchester during Milroy's occupation.[94] Some of Winchester's staunch Confederate women had too much pride even to attempt to ask Milroy for a permit to purchase food. "I will do without," declared Mary Lee in her diary, "as I have never asked a personal favour from a Yankee."[95] Even though Lee benefited from friends who obtained permits, without Milroy's knowledge, from sympathetic soldiers in the provost office, she looked down upon the act of asking any Federal soldier for a favor as undignified.[96]

The townspeople found various means through which to obtain food and other necessities. Some smuggled food through Union lines. Others played on the sympathies of Union soldiers. Troops traded meat, sugar, and coffee with Winchester's women in exchange for fresh baked bread or flour. Even officers on Milroy's staff gave some food to the civilians and let some of them take a few pieces of wood a day for fuel.[97] Some sutlers also sold goods on the side to civilians. Once Milroy found out about this black market, he threatened to close any sutler who sold goods to civilians without a permit. Secret detectives roamed the town and arrested anyone who defied the order. Many sutlers complied; nevertheless, some continued to defy the order.

Even though Milroy's men aided the civilians it did not reflect a lack of respect for him. Without a doubt, Milroy was beloved by his men — except a few such as Thomas O. Crowl of the 87th Pennsylvania. Crowl despised the Gray Eagle, African Americans, and everything that Milroy did in Winchester. In a letter to his sister in late January, Crowl wrote: "Our old General says that he thinks more of the Blacks than his soldiers, but if we get into Battle he will stand a good chance of getting his infernal old gray head shot off."[98]

While Crowl did not like Milroy, some of the contempt expressed for him may have resulted from the fact that many of his men had not been paid in nearly six months.[99] Milroy knew that his men desperately needed pay and he did everything within his power to see that his men received proper care. He recognized the poor morale among his troops and wrote to Schenck: "The tales of anguish and misery that come to me from my poor soldiers, whose helpless families are depending upon their scant pay ... is very damaging to the morale of the army ... and creating deep discontent and hatred of the service.... This evil should be promptly remedied."[100]

While some soldiers may have had contempt for Milroy, strong evidence suggests that the majority of Milroy's command adored the Gray Eagle because on many occasions he took their best interests into consideration. After the war a Union officer who served with Milroy reminisced: "He lived on a footing of very democratic comradeship with his men. The most extraordinary stories were told of his discussing with his subordinates what was to be done, of his permitting them to take amazing liberties with the orders to be executed ... he ... was respected and liked by all."[101] Not only did Milroy know that many of his men respected him, he also knew that a handful of citizens in the region approved of his policies.

Despite the fact that most lower Valley residents held Confederate sympathies, Milroy knew that part of the population, albeit a small one, held Union loyalties. As spring approached, Milroy informed Schenck that he needed money to establish a home guard defense of local Unionists. Milroy hoped that this local defense could help him stave off incursions by small enemy detachments on the outskirts of Winchester.[102] He lamented to Schenck that a number of residents from Shenandoah and Frederick counties wanted to form a home guard.[103] Milroy thought that government money and arms ought to be furnished for the purpose of establishing this unit. "I think it is an important movement & that it ought to be encouraged," Milroy wrote.[104]

Great difficulty exists in determining the size of the Unionist population in Milroy's area of control; however, a petition from the loyal population in the area under Milroy's command slightly illuminates its size. Approximately two months after Milroy's loss at Second Winchester in June 1863, a group of Unionist citizens from Winchester and Frederick County sent President Lincoln a petition asking that Milroy be restored to command. Sixty-five male residents of the area signed the appeal. It read in part: "Have him restored to his command, and forwarded to Winchester for the protection of the interest of the Union cause, for which we consider him fully competent and what is almost the wish of all citizens."[105]

Even though Milroy reveled at having a small portion of the population with Union sentiment, the majority of the area's citizens maintained Confederate loyalties and contempt for Union troops. Area Confederates hated Milroy and he knew it. "The Reb citizens in this place are very hostile to me, call me a modern Nero, and other hard names."[106] They showed disdain for Milroy on a daily basis, but several of Winchester's women exhibited their contempt for him in a unique way. A couple of days prior to Valentine's Day, Cornelia McDonald and several other women proposed they send a card to Milroy as result of the rude treatment of Mrs. Robert Baldwin. During a visit to Milroy's headquarters, Mrs. Baldwin had been shown out of the room so that two black women might speak with Milroy. McDonald painted Milroy sitting down, greeting two free black women and throwing out a white lady who was wearing a dress of red and white stripes.[107] McDonald also made several copies of the valentine, one of which

This "valentine" drawn by Cornelia McDonald of Winchester, Virginia, was sent to Milroy on February 14, 1863, in response to the supposed boorish treatment of Mrs. Robert Baldwin. Baldwin was apparently thrown out of Milroy's office when two free black women came to speak with Milroy. Milroy never found out who drew the valentine. Although enraged with Winchester's citizens, he took a more light-hearted tone about the affair with his staff and family. McDonald made several copies, this is the original that Milroy received (Jasper County Public Library, Rensselaer, Indiana).

was given to Fanny J. Barton.[108] When Milroy received the card he immediately ordered the search of all homes and the immediate prosecution of the artist.[109] Luckily for McDonald, Milroy's men could not find any copies.

Although Milroy took action against the civilian population in searching for the offender he had a more lighthearted tone about the affair with his staff and family. Milroy enclosed the card in a letter to his wife. "You see they have made me very amiable looking," he explained, "while I am ordering one of the secesh misses out of the room and politely inviting two negro wenches to be seated near me. It is pretty well got up and has made considerable fun for my staff.... How do you like my looks? Ain't I getting Handsome?"[110]

Mary Lee, Cornelia McDonald, and other women did all they could to exhibit

Cornelia McDonald was one among many of the female population of Winchester, Virginia, who loathed Milroy and his policies. She drew the "valentine" that several of Winchester's women agreed to send the Gray Eagle in response to the rude treatment of Mrs. Robert Baldwin (Handley Regional Library Archives, Winchester).

their Confederate pride. On George Washington's birthday Milroy held a celebration in honor of the nation's father. Activities included a parade, speeches, and a cannon salute. As the parade of Milroy's division passed through town many of Winchester's staunch Confederates stood on their porches "hurrahing for Jeff Davis, the Southern Confederacy, Washington, the first Virginia rebel." Very few of Milroy's men heard the anti–Union cheers, but one soldier who did remarked simply, "Those are the damndest women I ever saw."[111]

The town's Confederate civilians did whatever they could to show their disdain for their Union occupiers. Milroy's many rules implemented to curb Rebel enthusiasm did not work. Mary Lee noted that it "aggravates them to see how fearless we are & that they cannot subjugate us." While acts of contempt ranged from a prankish card to shouting at Union soldiers and smuggling things through the lines, many of the staunch Confederate women sewed garments and gathered supplies for Confederate soldiers, which was perhaps their ultimate form of resistance.[112]

While Milroy carried out many policies to break the will of the people, perhaps one of the most troublesome was his employment of Jessie Scouts. He utilized these Union soldiers dressed as Confederates to entrap the southern population. On numerous occasions Milroy's Jessie Scouts went about town at night, knocked on doors, and portrayed themselves as war-weary Confederate soldiers asking for food and shelter. When the people opened their doors and expressed sympathy to what they thought was a beleaguered Confederate soldier they were placed under arrest or exiled.[113]

As if Milroy's deception was not bad enough, Milroy's detectives entered homes dressed in civilian clothes. They passed themselves off as ordinary civilians who slipped through Milroy's lines. When they entered homes, they tried to identify anyone who spoke positively about the Confederacy and to see if children played with Confederate flags.[114] While a presence of the detectives always existed, Milroy increased their use as spring approached. They also monitored stores—waiting for someone to buy an item without a permit.[115]

Even though Milroy's system of espionage may not have been characteristic for military manner at the time (the extremes Milroy went to were never practiced in Winchester prior to his occupation and were not as vigorous in succeeding Federal occupations), his system was undoubtedly supported by his immediate superior. General Schenck sent Milroy at least $500 "to prefer a system of espionage on the Rebs."[116]

As the spring campaign season approached, Milroy seemed to tighten his grip on the civilian population. The search of homes for contraband items continued. In mid-March, Milroy issued orders for the enlisted men to occupy houses that had no one living in them. Furthermore he ordered the officers in his division to quarter themselves in the homes of the town's Confederate population — if they had not already done so.[117] In early April, Milroy directed that sutlers refrain from selling anything to citizens whether loyal or disloyal.[118] Milroy put this order in place because he feared that some of the loyal civilians might be selling goods to Confederate sympathizers who were not simply taking goods to feed their families, but rather might have been stowing supplies for Confederate troops.

Aside from tightening his rein over the civilian population, in the spring Milroy deployed Col. Andrew T. McReynolds' brigade east to Berryville. He wanted McReynolds to act as an advance outpost, keeping a keen eye on the passes of the Blue Ridge and the fords of the Shenandoah. He also ordered McReynolds to keep an open line of communication with General Kelley's force at Harper's Ferry.[119] McReynolds remained near Berryville until the approach of Confederate forces on June 13.[120]

As spring approached Milroy received some welcome news—he had been promoted to major general.[121] No doubt jubilant over earning his second star, he lamented over why it took him so long to get it. According to Milroy, Halleck's disdain for the Gray Eagle was the sole reason for the delay.[122] President Lincoln nominated Milroy for promotion near the end of 1862, but Halleck struck Milroy's name because of the orders Milroy issued regarding the civilian population of western Virginia.[123] He exhibited his disgust to his wife: "It has now been so long and so unjustly held from me, and so many others, with little or no merit, have been promoted over me, that I attach no honor to it, and look upon it as valueless, and were it not that it unshackled me and gives me wide field of action I would reject it with scorn."[124] Although bitter over the length of time it took to receive his promotion, Milroy relished in his "complete triumph over old Halleck."[125]

Unionist civilians and Milroy's men celebrated the promotion. Several civilians and officers sent Milroy congratulatory letters. The surveyor of customs for Wheeling, West Virginia, sent his best wishes and informed Milroy that his promotion was well-earned and that had there been other generals like Milroy "this *damnable slaveholding rebellion* would soon *be crushed.*"[126] The adjutant of the 116th Ohio Infantry, H.L. Sibley, joined in the adulation: "It is a glorious victory over the stupid prejudice, and the 'scientific' bigotry of 'book-worm' warriors."[127]

To celebrate Milroy's promotion, all of the officers of the division collected money from the men in the ranks for the purchase of an elaborate presentation sword. This sign of adoration was perhaps the highest honor that any commander could be given by his men. He received this honor a second time in Winchester when one of his Ohio regiments presented him with a sword in early May.[128]

The officers of his command presented him an ornate sword, manufactured by Jerre McLene of Indianapolis, on April 4, in honor of his second star. The ceremony began with a parade through Winchester's streets and concluded on a plain northeast of town where Milroy held a grand review of the entire division.[129] Col. W.H. Ball of the 122nd Ohio made the official presentation and undoubtedly Milroy was moved by the sword's inscription: "To Gen. Robert H. Milroy, A true Patriot and Hero. A man who loves his country and race, A Soldier who acts fearlessly and promptly, A chiefton to honor and follow."[130] Before he gave Milroy the sword Ball addressed Milroy and the onlookers. "By the sword," Ball proclaimed, "our forefathers established our independence, by the sword we are now enforcing that Constitution which they ordained for the Government of this people.... A rebellion surpassing in magnitude any such the human race ever witnessed before, now rends our free and once happy country." With admiration Ball stated: "The Officers of your command have observed alike with pride and pleasure, your devotion to your government, your heroism in its service.... Some of [your troops] ... have seen your indomitable courage inspire your command, have seen the enemy driven." The ornate weapon was truly a token of the appreciation of all of the men for Milroy's service and Ball made it a point to let his commander know how the men Milroy led truly felt about him. "Desiring to express their high regard to you as a friend, a patriot and a soldier, so that your posterity and theirs, and your country may know the esteem in which you are held by those who serve with you, who know you, who love you, your command tender you this offering." Near the end of his speech Ball called Milroy to come and accept the sword. Looking Milroy square in the face Ball proclaimed: "Accept this sword, beautiful and appropriate, and may the God of battles protect you, that you may [for] years enjoy the blessings of the free, peaceful and benign Government, which you so contribute to Maintain."[131]

After he accepted the sword Milroy addressed his division and a contingent of the area's Unionists. "The capacity of man for self government is now on trial before this civilized world," Milroy proclaimed, "Our Fathers in founding the institutions under which we have prospered as a nation, performed their mission. It is the mission of this generation to demonstrate the practicability of those institutions."[132] Throughout the first part of his response Milroy tried to instill a sense of urgency in his command that if they failed to carry out emancipation and defeat the Confederacy any hope of a unified country, a nation created in the American Revolution would be lost forever. "The cause of the free government hangs trembling in the balance," Milroy stated, "and must abide the issue of the struggle which now deluges our country in blood." Milroy received very few signs of gratitude for his service to the Union, but the sword bolstered Milroy's resolve to continue the work he had undertaken knowing that his men, many of whom had been with him "since the beginning of this causeless and wicked rebellion," appreciated his "humble efforts." After Milroy finished his speech his entire command filled the air with cheers and shouts "that would deafen any one but soldiers."[133] Apparently Milroy cherished this sword more than any other because he demanded that it be buried with him. His request was granted upon his death in 1890.[134]

Several days after the sword presentation Milroy's already tenuous

The Logan house in Winchester, Virginia, at Braddock and Piccadilly streets, served as Milroy's headquarters. When Mrs. Milroy arrived in town in April 1863, General Milroy expelled the Logans from their home and exiled them from town. His treatment of the Logan family did nothing to improve relations with the citizens of this Shenandoah Valley community and caused some of Milroy's staff to resign their commissions (Winchester-Frederick County Historical Society).

relationship with the area's Confederate population became even weaker. Shortly after his arrival in Winchester, Milroy established his headquarters in the home of Mrs. Lloyd Logan. Situated at the corner of Braddock and Piccadilly streets, the Logan residence was (and still is) one of Winchester's more architecturally pleasing homes. Generals previous to Milroy made it their headquarters as well as commanders who succeeded Milroy, including Maj. Gen. Philip H. Sheridan. Union officers such as Gen. John P. Hatch used the home prior to Milroy's arrival, but still allowed the Logans to remain. Milroy extended the same courtesy to the family until his wife came to town during the first week of April.[135]

Mrs. Milroy's arrival unleashed a chain of events that severed an already weak connection with the townspeople. Milroy evicted the Logans from their home and exiled them from town. While many of Winchester's residents felt the Logans had been banished on account of Mrs. Milroy's desire to have the house all to herself, Milroy gave another reason. In his eyes the exile of the Logan family was retaliation for the ill-treatment of a

Jessie Scout. Winchester's Mary Lee recorded that the Logans "collared him, shook him and threw him out of the house."[136] Milroy's act conformed to his policy to punish anyone who mistreated a Union soldier.

Milroy did not allow the Logan family to gather any clothing or any other items. One of the Mrs. Logan's daughters, afflicted with erysipelas (a severe type of skin infection), was not even allowed to take medicine with her.[137] As the Logans walked out of their house for the last time and prepared to board a wagon that would carry them south, about seven miles to Newtown, Mrs. Milroy sat in a wagon and as Kate Sperry recalled, "viewed their removal with the utmost complacency."[138] The Logans boarded the wagon and as it drove off one of the Logan girls pointed her finger at a Union soldier in a mad rage and shouted: "There is a man whose brains I could blow out."[139]

The eviction of the Logan family not only unleashed greater hatred for Milroy, it also created some dissent among the officer corps of Milroy's division. The Union officer who escorted the Logans beyond the Federal lines was reportedly dishonorably discharged by Milroy for extending sympathy to the family.[140] Other Federal officers threatened to resign their commissions. One disgruntled junior officer reportedly tore off his shoulder straps and threw them down at Milroy's feet in disgust.[141]

The Logans were not the first to feel Milroy's wrath and they certainly would not be the last. While Milroy exiled people during the winter months he banished secessionists from town far more frequently as the spring campaign season approached. Perhaps he did this to protect his security so that individuals would not inform the Confederates as to Milroy's position and strength. On April 10, three days after the exile of the Logans, Milroy sent 10 more people south beyond the Federal lines.[142] Among those banished was a schoolteacher. Milroy expelled her from Winchester because his secret detectives intercepted a note from her with negative comments about the Union occupiers. Even though the school where she taught had not broken any rules, Milroy closed it down the same day.[143] Other exiles soon followed and continued regularly until the Second Battle of Winchester in mid–June.[144]

The departure of Milroy's wife in early May for Indiana could not have helped his attitude toward the town's secessionists. Milroy sulked in his wife's absence. "My room was painfully lonely after you left," he wrote, "and I kept out of it and absorbed in business as much as possible. Your visit was a bright beam amid the darkened gloom of war, a delightful oasis amid the darkened gloom of the desert of widowhood and banishment from home."[145]

Milroy continued to try to break the spirit of Winchester's Confederate inhabitants throughout the spring, but nothing could have dampened their spirits more than devastating news from eastern Virginia — Stonewall Jackson was dead. On the evening of May 2, 1863, after a spectacular flanking maneuver against the Union XI Corps at the Battle of Chancellorsville, Jackson and his staff had gone out to reconnoiter the Federal position. Upon returning to Confederate lines, a North Carolina regiment mistakenly opened fire. Three bullets struck Jackson. Dr. Hunter Holmes McGuire, a Winchester native and Jackson's medical director, amputated Jackson's left arm. For the next several days Jackson appeared to be healing, but his condition took a turn for the worse and he perished on May 10 from pneumonia.[146]

Winchester's Confederate women showed their adoration for Jackson, the first "liberator" of Winchester, by adorning themselves with mourning ribbons that contained a Virginia state seal in the center.[147] Milroy did not want these women walking around town displaying the seal of a state in rebellion so he ordered the women to replace the Virginia seal with an image of George Washington. He also issued an order forbidding anyone to wear the mourning ribbon for more than 30 days.[148] Mary Lee adored Jackson as much as she despised Milroy and could not believe the news. "I do not believe it," she confessed in her journal, "though the bare idea has given me a more hopeless feeling than any other event of the war."[149]

Arguably no town had a greater affinity for Jackson than Winchester and perhaps Jackson had no greater admiration for a town's people than Winchester's. Shortly after Milroy arrived in Winchester Jackson learned of the citizens' plight and he was appalled and often thought of the townspeople. "Though I have been relieved from command there," Jackson confided to his friend Alexander Boteler, "I feel deeply when I see the patriotic people of that region again under the heel of a hateful military despotism.... There are those who have so devotedly labored for the relief of our suffering, sick, and wounded soldiers."[150]

Following the Confederate victory at Chancellorsville and Lee's seizure of the strategic initiative Milroy feared an attack. His command had been involved in several skirmishes that month, yet the results were favorable for Milroy's division. Confident that his forces could defend Winchester against any attack, he boasted to General Schenck that Confederate forces "may come in sufficient numbers to surround me, but they will never capture me."[151]

After Chancellorsville, Milroy's Jessie Scouts (now commanded by Colonel Keifer), reported regularly to Milroy that Lee's army was on the move and that a portion of the Army of Northern Virginia might strike Winchester.[152] Keifer's scouts provided such detail about Lee's operations that Milroy ought to have given them more credence than he did. Milroy believed Lee would not detach a large portion of his army to dislodge him. Instead, the Gray Eagle thought that nothing more than small bodies of enemy cavalry would strike Winchester. Milroy informed Keifer that the Rebels had fabricated the story "to cause him to disgracefully abandon the Valley."[153]

Keifer and his scouts did not believe it was a ruse. The Ohioan tried to convince Milroy of the validity of the reports that a sizable body of Confederates would attack Winchester on June 10, but to no avail. Milroy refused to withdraw. Although adamant about not leaving the lower Valley, Milroy continued to strengthen his defenses in preparation for an attack.[154]

Although Milroy ignored his scouts' reports, General Halleck did not. The idea of an attack on Winchester had crossed Halleck's mind more than once during the spring. Even before reports surfaced of a possible Confederate assault on the town Halleck lambasted Milroy's immediate superior, General Schenck, for keeping Milroy's men in the vicinity of Winchester. At the end of April, Halleck reminded Schenck: "As I have often repeated to you verbally & in writing, that is no place to fight a battle. It is merely an outpost, which should not be exposed to an attack in force."[155] Despite messages like this to Schenck and Milroy throughout May both remained firm to hold Winchester.

As May drew to a close and Lee's Army of Northern Virginia was on the move, Halleck fretted over the safety of the Winchester garrison. His correspondence with Schenck and Milroy became ominous. "Forces at Harpers Ferry, the Shenandoah Valley, and western Va.," Halleck warned on May 29, "should be on the alert and prepared for an attack."[156]

With Lee's army on the march, Halleck and others in the War Department worried about the vulnerability of Milroy's position, yet Schenck and Milroy showed little apprehension. All Milroy felt he could do (and should do) was to continue strengthening his defenses and await June 10. Even though Milroy appeared largely complacent, his command was extremely active during the first week of June. Mary Lee noted on June 5: "The Yankees are in a panic; the horses are kept to the guns; no officers are permitted to come to town except on urgent business; the Sutlers are ready to go at any moment."[157] Regardless of how confident he felt about his defenses around Winchester and that no Confederate attack would come, Milroy did take the precaution of evacuating sick Union soldiers from the town.[158]

Milroy eagerly awaited June 10. The day came and went without incident. The absence of a Confederate attack buoyed Milroy's confidence that the Confederates would not strike Winchester. Furthermore Milroy surmised that if an attack did occur it would not be in any great force.[159] The

5. "To play the tyrant among these traitors"   105

Gray Eagle was mistaken. The reports from Keifer's scouts throughout May and early June proved genuine. The Confederates had planned to strike Winchester on June 10 but were delayed as a result of the advance of Union cavalry south of the Rappahannock River and subsequent Battle of Brandy Station on June 9.

While Milroy settled into his false state of security Lee set his invasion plan of the North into motion. Gen. Richard S. Ewell, commanding the Army of Northern Virginia's Second Corps, spearheaded the army's advance west of the Blue Ridge Mountains. Ewell knew the area well from campaigning with Stonewall Jackson in the Valley in 1862. Lee ordered Ewell to march to Winchester, dislodge Milroy, and then move north across the Potomac River.

On June 10, Ewell's corps, approximately 13,000 strong, departed Culpeper Court House. Meanwhile on June 10-11, Schenck sent his chief of staff, Lt. Col. Donn Piatt, to inspect Milroy's position.[160] Piatt wired Schenck from Winchester: "All looks fine. Can whip anything the rebels can fetch here."[161] For some reason, on his return trip to Baltimore, Piatt changed his mind about Milroy's ability to defend Winchester adequately. He dispatched Milroy from Martinsburg to take steps for an immediate withdrawal to Harper's Ferry.[162] While it is not entirely clear why Piatt altered his opinion of Winchester's defenses and Milroy's ability to guard against attack, it may have something to do with a telegram sent from Halleck to Piatt that same day. "Harpers Ferry is the important place," Halleck explained to Piatt, "Winchester is of no importance other than as a lookout."[163]

Infuriated over Piatt's sudden change of orders Milroy wired Schenck: "I think I have sufficient force to hold this place safely."[164] Schenck was not the only one who read Milroy's message. Piatt too looked at it and replied to Milroy's boldness: "The telegram received. It must be considered an order and obeyed accordingly. Take immediate steps."[165] Even though Halleck wanted Milroy out of Winchester, Schenck on June 12 gave Milroy clear orders. He informed Milroy to "make all the required preparation for withdrawing. But hold your position in the meantime. Be ready for the movement but await further orders."[166]

While the Union telegraph lines burned hot with messages on June 12, between Baltimore, Washington, and Winchester, Ewell's force marched to within 20 miles of Milroy's division. The following day, in a strategy previously employed by Jackson at Winchester in 1862, Ewell divided his force. Maj. Gen. Edward Johnson, Milroy's nemesis from earlier in the war, took his division and approached Winchester from the southeast via the Front Royal Road. Maj. Gen. Jubal A. Early's division advanced on Winchester from the south via the Valley Pike and Maj. Gen. Robert Rodes marched his division north to Berryville to drive out McReynolds' brigade. After driving McReynolds, Rodes was then to move north to Martinsburg to cut off a possible Union retreat.[167]

Milroy received the first intimation of a Confederate attack on June 12, when the van of Ewell's force appeared about 15 miles south of Winchester near Middletown. Ewell's lead elements under Capt. W.L. Rasin, consisting of the 1st Maryland Infantry and the 14th Virginia Cavalry, encountered some of Milroy's men near Middletown. Elements of the 87th Pennsylvania Infantry, 13th Pennsylvania Cavalry, and 5th U.S. Artillery commanded by the 87th's Col. John W. Schall engaged the token Confederate force and easily drove them from the field. Schall's detachment suffered no casualties, but inflicted 87 on the enemy.[168]

Also that day Milroy ordered McReynolds' brigade to pull back from Berryville to Winchester. He also told McReynolds to send all of his wagons to Martinsburg. McReynolds did as ordered and sent his troops west to Winchester and his wagon trains north to Martinsburg. During the course of the removal of McReynolds' wagon trains to Martinsburg they stopped near Bunker Hill to rest the teams. As they rested approximately 300 troops detached from the 87th Pennsylvania and 116th Ohio received word that nearly 1,500 Confederate cavalry were thundering down on their position. Heavily outnumbered, the Federals took cover in area buildings and fired at the Confederates. The fighting lasted into the evening when the Confederates withdrew. Sensing an opportunity to escape, the Federal soldiers withdrew to Winchester.[169]

The following day, June 13, Ewell continued the advance to Winchester. Around noon Ewell's lead elements found a formidable opponent near Kernstown, several miles south of Winchester. Fearing an attack that day from the south, Milroy deployed five infantry regiments, one cavalry, and an artillery battery to meet the impending threat.[170] Pickets from the 2nd Virginia engaged Milroy's pickets and drove them north.[171] As the musketry fire intensified south of Winchester so too did the curiosity of the townspeople increase. Many disregarded personal safety and climbed to rooftops to catch a glimpse of the men who came to deliver them from "Milroy's tyranny."

As citizens peered toward the battle, Johnson's division moved on the Front Royal Road and Early's division marched in strength on the Valley Pike to reinforce the lead elements of his command that had already engaged the Federals. As Early approached Kernstown he noticed several infantry regiments and one artillery battery perched atop Pritchard's Hill—a commanding rise slightly west of the Valley Pike. Early marched his men across the field at Kernstown, where Jackson had met defeat in March 1862, to take the heights.[172] Union troops defending the hill staved off Early's advance for a considerable time, but "Old Jube's" repeated attacks on the Union right cracked the line and sent the Federals reeling north as far as Cedar Creek Grade. There the Federals halted Early's advance. Meanwhile, southeast of Winchester, Johnson marched his division, unopposed, to the intersection of the Front Royal Road and Millwood Pike.[173]

Milroy's men fought ably against a formidable opponent, but Schenck grew uneasy about Milroy's situation and ordered him to retreat to Harper's Ferry.[174] The Gray Eagle did not fall back because he never received Schenck's order. Milroy claimed after the Second Battle of Winchester that he lost all communication with his superiors around noon on Saturday, June 13.[175] The last message that Milroy sent was received by Lieutenant Colonel Piatt, Schenck's chief of staff. It stated simply: "Enemy approaching in strong force. Infantry and artillery on Strasburg pike. [Brig. Gen. Washington] Elliott pitching into them. An extra star in the way; ought to be there myself. Will get them, if Elliott falls back."[176] After this Milroy sent no more messages to Schenck because the lines were down. Schenck became alarmed and sent two messages to Milroy later that day, but received no response. Whether or not Milroy made any attempts to repair the downed telegraph lines is unclear. According to the telegraph operator at Harper's Ferry there was a "slight current from the Winchester battery, which proves the wire is not broken. It is probably on the ground." Even if Milroy ordered the line to be repaired it would have been nearly impossible. A terrible storm swept through the area during the night of June 13-14 and would have wreaked further havoc on the telegraph lines.[177]

While the "artillery of heaven shook the earth" around Winchester that night the telegraph lines between Halleck, Lincoln, and Schenck buzzed with messages.[178] President Lincoln, concerned over Milroy's situation and the impending movement of the Army of Northern Virginia, wired Schenck: "Get Milroy from Winchester to Harpers Ferry if possible. He will be 'gobbled up' if he remains, if he is not already past salvation."[179]

Heavy rain during the night of June 13-14 and no communication with his superiors did not dampen Milroy's resolve to fight. The town bustled with activity as Union soldiers made last-minute preparations to defend against Ewell's attack. Winchester's inhabitants had mixed emotions about the immediate future. Excited at the prospect of liberation Mary Lee penned: "I have everything in nice order for the Confederates."[180] On the other hand Winchester's Unionists feared a Confederate victory. Julia Chase, one of Winchester's Unionists, lamented in her diary that "the town is all in an uproar, wagons lining the streets ... cavalry & infantry passing by, the secessionists very joyful flocking to the sutlers, buying up all they can for their friends.... God in his mercy, grant that Winchester may not be given up to the Rebels."[181]

Now certain that Ewell's entire force would attack en masse on June 14, Milroy ordered his command to take refuge in the three fortifications they had spent nearly six months strengthening. Throughout the day on June 14, Milroy went from fort to fort looking for any movement from Ewell. One of Milroy's staff officers noted of the Gray Eagle's vigilance: "All day, under the burning sun did General Milroy keep his position in the lookout, and with a glass anxiously scan the surrounding country."[182] Milroy knew an attack loomed. Throughout the morning Union troops skirmished briskly with Ewell's men in Winchester's streets, but by noon the skirmishing had stopped. The streets were quiet, and Milroy's men waited in the perceived security of their fortifications northwest of town.[183]

While Milroy eagerly waited for an attack, Ewell and Early met atop Bowers Hill, located slightly southwest of Winchester and discussed their options. After surveying the situation Ewell decided to attack Milroy from the west. Gen. John B. Gordon's brigade, the Maryland Line, and two artillery batteries would guard Bowers Hill, while Early would march west before turning north to strike West Fort. Ewell decided to attack West Fort, the smallest of Milroy's fortifications, because its artillery commanded Star Fort, and the guns in Fort Milroy commanded the approach to Star Fort.[184] If West Fort could be silenced, Ewell surmised, the other two forts could easily be taken by his troops.

With the aid of local guides,

Confederate General Jubal A. Early, an 1837 West Point graduate, commanded one of General Ewell's divisions at the Second Battle of Winchester. On June 14, 1863, Early led his men on a flank attack around the northwestern corner of Winchester and then struck Union troops in West Fort, beginning the erosion of Milroy's grip on Winchester. Slightly more than one year later, on September 19, 1864, Early would suffer defeat at the Third Battle of Winchester (*Battles and Leaders*).

Early took his men on a 10-mile flanking march. His men marched from Bowers Hill, circled around to the southeast and marched north across Cedar Creek Grade. After crossing there Early's division marched north and halted between the Romney and Pughtown roads on the west side of West Fort.

By 5:00 P.M. Early had completed his march and placed 20 guns on the reverse slope of the ridge west of West Fort. While Early made his flanking maneuver, Ewell directed artillery fire at West Fort from atop Bowers Hill. Recognizing this as a prelude to attack, Milroy bolstered West Fort with additional infantry and two guns from the 5th U.S. Artillery.[185] Defending the fort were the 110th Ohio, one company of the 116th Ohio, and six guns.[186]

Around 6:00 P.M. Early's guns opened on West Fort. Artillery poured iron shot and shell into West Fort for 45 minutes. After the artillery slackened, Brig. Gen. Harry T. Hays' Louisiana Brigade spearheaded the attack. More than a year had passed since the same brigade turned the tide at First Winchester. The Federals attempted to make a stand. The Union troops in West Fort fought stubbornly. "My men stood well to their work," remembered Colonel Keifer after the war. Keifer continued in praise: "There was stubborn fighting over the low breastworks, and some fighting inside of them, but not until our flanks were attacked did I order a retreat."[187] When Keifer ordered the retreat from West Fort to the safety of Fort Milroy speed was essential and the guns inside of West Fort had to be abandoned.[188]

Even though West Fort fell to Early's division, Milroy did not intend to give up yet. For several hours in the evening, Milroy's large guns in Fort Milroy and Star Fort fired on the Confederates. They had little effect.[189] It soon became apparent that Milroy's force could not defend against Ewell's command.

Around 9:00 P.M. Milroy held a council of war with his brigade commanders. At the meeting Milroy did not ask his officers for their opinions as to what they believed should be done. Regardless the officers at the council knew that their situation was perilous and they understood that Milroy had three options. First, he could remain and fight. Second, he could surrender. Third, he could withdraw to Harper's Ferry. By nightfall on June 14 Milroy knew that he could not stay and fight. Surrender was seen by some as an option, however, Colonel Keifer would not hear of it. Keifer informed Milroy that if he contemplated surrender he would take his infantry regiment and others who wanted to flee on an escape march out of Winchester north to Pennsylvania.[190] Surrender, however, was not in Milroy's vocabulary, nor was it part of his military nature. Now Milroy looked to his third option — evacuation. When General Elliott heard Milroy's idea to withdraw to Harper's Ferry he cautioned Milroy that perhaps

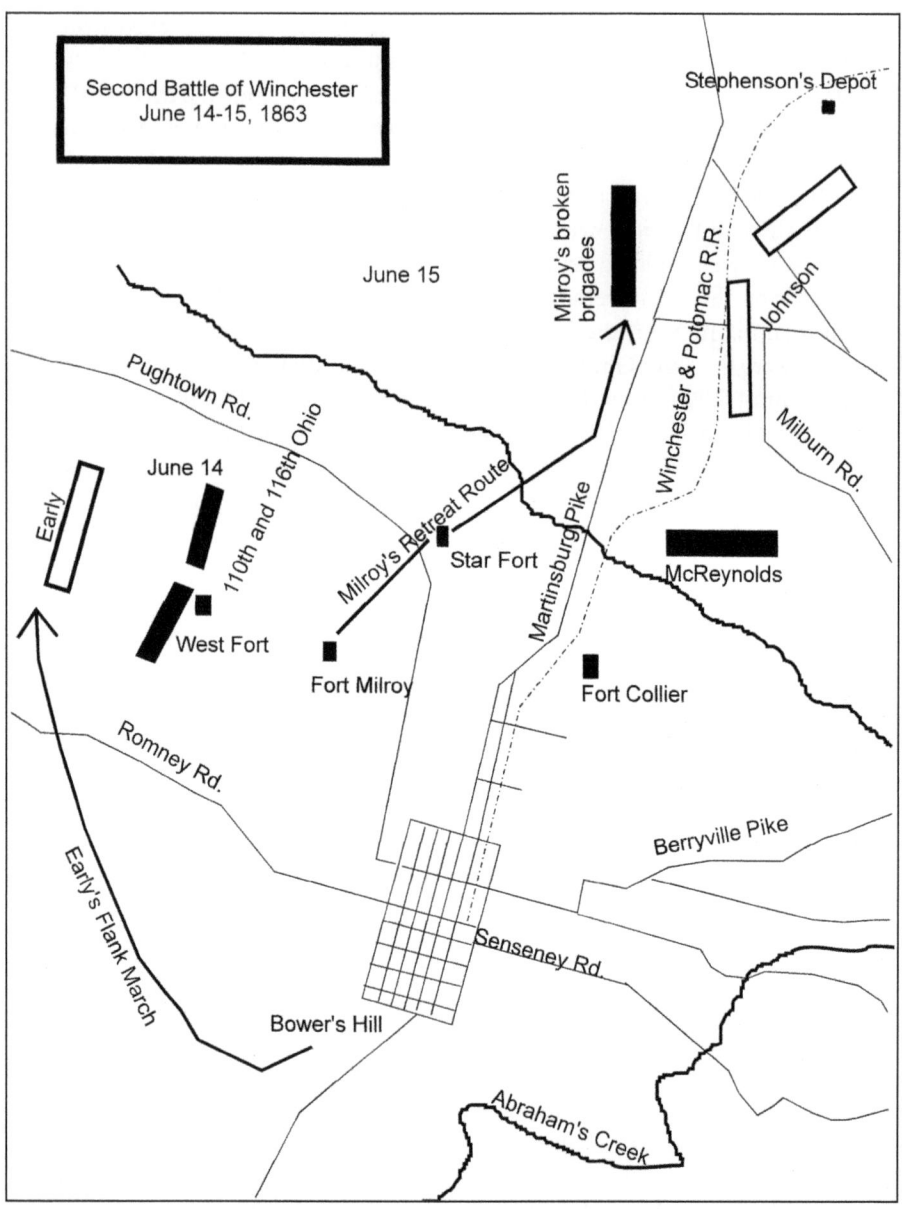

he should wait for a positive answer from Schenck "as it would be throwing the entire responsibility on" Milroy. While this might have been true, Milroy had no communications and with the full weight of Ewell's corps Milroy could not stay in Winchester another moment.[191] With rations low and the artillery ammunition nearly exhausted, coupled with the threat of another Confederate attack the following day, Milroy and his subordinates agreed to withdraw from Winchester.[192] The guns were spiked, supplies abandoned, and by 3:00 A.M. on June 15, the Federals were en route to Harper's Ferry.[193] As Milroy's men withdrew, Mary Lee wrote: "For the first time in six months, the air is not polluted by their immediate presence."[194] Another of Winchester's inhabitants described the town after Milroy's withdrawal "as still as death."[195]

Sensing that Milroy might withdraw north under cover of darkness, Ewell ordered Johnson's division north toward Stephenson's Depot to cut off a possible retreat route. As the early morning darkness hid the ground at Stephenson's Depot, Johnson's men heard the thud of marching feet. It was Milroy's command.

A soldier in the 87th Pennsylvania recalled: "We expected to be attacked in the rear by Confederate cavalry. We never for one moment expected any trouble in front."[196] Johnson had the element of surprise and as one Federal soldier noted: "The wily enemy, however, by a rapid flank movement, succeeded in throwing a heavy force of artillery and infantry in our front at Carter's Woods." Still, Johnson was not wholly confident that his line could hold if the Federals organized. Initially Johnson feared an attack against his left being held by Brig. Gen. George Steuart's brigade, but he quickly remedied that by placing the 2nd and 10th Louisiana perpendicular to the main Confederate line.

While he bolstered the left, Johnson anchored the center of his line at a bridge spanning a railroad cut with the artillery of Col. R.S. Snowden Andrews. The Confederate artillerists performed admirably during this fight although losses in the gun crews were high—13 out of 16 men had been killed or wounded, but the center held.[197] To protect his right he deployed the Stonewall Brigade under Brig. Gen. James Walker. Johnson's line was strong and Milroy's command would soon find that out.

The first two brigades of Milroy's division, Elliott's and Ely's, tried to face their men to meet Johnson's Confederates and then attack, however, confusion ran rampant and no coordinated attacks could be made. The 110th Ohio's Colonel Keifer wrote simply "there was no concert of action in the conduct of the battle."[198]

Milroy and his officers made numerous attempts to reorganize the broken Union ranks, but frightened teamsters and sutlers trying to escape complicated the situation. Fleeing sutlers and teamsters did more to break up Colonel McReynolds' third brigade than did Johnson's Confederates. The sutlers also sent Milroy's cavalry into a panic. One survivor of the battle wrote after the war: "The cavalry became panic-stricken and, commingling with the mules and horses on which teamsters and others were mounted, all in great disorder took wildly to the hills and mountains to the northwest ... the mules brayed, the horses neighed, the teamsters and riders indulged in much vigorous profanity."[199] Regiments not broken up made ill-fated attempts to crack the Confederate position. Frantic, Milroy did all he could to rally his men and when he could not he sought to command individual regiments, or what was left of one. He tried desperately to rally the soldiers of the 87th Pennsylvania and lead them in a charge, but his efforts were thwarted when his horse was shot out from under him.[200] There was no way that Milroy could rally his command. The surprise had been too great and as a survivor penned to the *New York Herald:* "Instead of finding a weak body of rebels, as they expected, they found at least a full division, well posted and drawn up in line of battle. When our troops reached the enemy's position they were met by a terrible shower of missiles and were forced to fall back."[201]

As the confusion intensified among the Federal soldiers, Johnson decided to go after his old nemesis, Milroy. With a band of several horsemen Johnson watched Milroy and his staff trying to escape. He noticed Milroy and his band fleeing northwest to the fords on the Opequon. He followed the Gray Eagle to the Opeqoun, but as he pursued down the creek's banks and into the water Johnson's steed got stuck in the muddy bottom and threw Johnson into the Opequon. His opportunity to capture Milroy and possibly get the reward the Confederate government had placed on Milroy's head had been squandered, but Johnson had defeated Milroy once again.[202]

Johnson had put the finishing touches on a well-orchestrated plan. Milroy had

Confederate Lt. Gen. Richard S. Ewell commanded the Second Corps Army of Northern Virginia which spearheaded Gen. Robert E. Lee's invasion of the North in 1863. Ewell's victory over Milroy at Winchester cleared a path for the Confederates to cross the Potomac River. Approximately two weeks after Winchester, Confederate fortunes were reversed at the Battle of Gettysburg (*Battles and Leaders*).

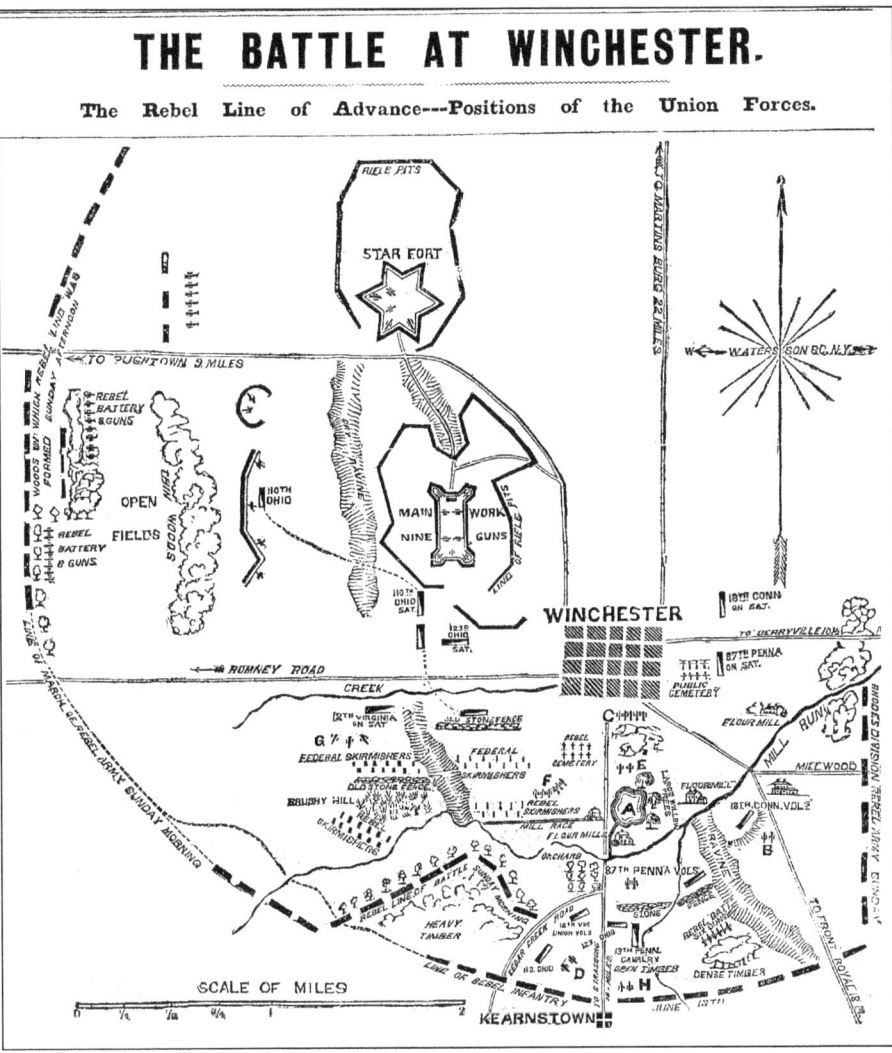

This map of the Second Battle of Winchester appeared in the June 22, 1863, edition of the *New York Herald*. This map is the only known depiction of the battle drawn by a Union eyewitness.

suffered a disastrous defeat. While approximately 3,900 men escaped, Milroy's losses far exceeded the men he retained: 4,443 men were lost in the fight. Among the casualties were 95 killed and 318 wounded.[203] Ewell lost little of his strength — 47 killed and 219 wounded — less than 5 percent of his total command.[204] Milroy also lost a tremendous amount of supplies. Confederate soldiers reveled at the amount of luxury items Milroy's division left behind. One Confederate soldier wrote home, on captured letterhead that bore an image of Milroy, and told his family that he ate so much "of Milroy's good things till it made me feel bad and sick."[205] Confederate soldiers also looted the sutlers' stores left behind. A comical scene erupted after Second Winchester when Confederate soldiers ransacked the stockpiles of women's clothing and shoes to send home to loved ones. "For days after the retreat you could see the Confederate soldiers going in every direction with ladies' dresses, ladies' and children's shoes, and even hoopskirts tied on to their trappings," remembered Winchester's Emma Cassandra Riely.[206]

Winchester's inhabitants reveled at their great victory over the Gray Eagle. The women who had endured so much took part in various festivities to commemorate the recent victory. The celebrations included the raising of a Confederate flag over the Union prisoners in Fort Jackson, formerly Fort Milroy.[207] A Confederate artillerist recounted the joy of Winchester's Confederate population: "The citizens seemed perfectly wild with joy, many old ladies and gentlemen rushing out on their porches in their night clothes, while children and young girls shouted and hurrahed until their strength failed them."[208] Winchester's Ann Carey Randolph Jones simply exclaimed to a friend after Ewell's victory that "*We Are Free.*"[209]

While the town's Confederates beamed with happiness at Ewell's victory,

Milroy patriotic envelope. Soldiers in Milroy's command frequently wrote letters home on stationery containing the image of their commander. After the Second Battle of Winchester in June 1863 a number of Confederate soldiers wrote letters home to their families on captured Milroy stationery.

Winchester's Unionists despaired at Milroy's loss. An area Unionist remarked of the Confederate capture of Winchester, "We are now in Dixie, oh what a sad, sad day, this has been to us." Unionists were not only saddened by Milroy's loss, but enraged at the amount of military supplies Milroy abandoned and left for the Confederates. To "have so much captured, it is outrageous," grumbled Julia Chase. "The Federal Government have from the commencement of the War fed, clothed & supplied with Arms the whole Southern Army. Is this state of things to continue to forever? If so, much better have Peace now than to go, sacrificing men & property," Chase concluded.[210]

The joy of Winchester's Confederate citizens at their victory over Milroy's force was short lived. Lee's Army of Northern Virginia met defeat at the Battle of Gettysburg, July 1-3, 1863, and the hopes of the Valley's citizens plummeted once more. In the weeks that followed Gettysburg, Winchester transformed into a vast military hospital for the wounded of Lee's army. The demoralized Confederate citizens aided in caring for the wounded. The Army of Northern Virginia pulled out of Winchester on July 25, leaving the door wide open to another Federal occupation. The following day blue-clad troops marched into Winchester.

By the end of July Winchester's Confederates were in the same situation they were in during the first half of 1863, but Milroy's situation was very different. His division's defeat and withdrawal from Winchester was abysmal. For that reason Milroy would spend the next several months on the defensive — not militarily, but rather with pen and paper trying to convince his superiors in Washington that he was not wrong for remaining in Winchester and that his actions were anything but cowardly. Second Winchester had become and would continue to be the central point in Milroy's life until his death in 1890.

6

"Halleck hates me without cause"

While Winchester's inhabitants remained joyous following Milroy's defeat, things turned worse for Milroy. On the night of Milroy's defeat, President Lincoln met with Halleck and Secretary of the Navy Gideon Welles to discuss the Winchester disaster. Halleck concluded that someone ought to be blamed. Naturally Schenck or Milroy would be responsible for the loss. Initially the fingers pointed to Schenck. Halleck had wired Schenck on June 14: "I have so repeatedly urged you to withdraw your main forces from Winchester and so recently [the 11th] directed it, that I cannot understand how Milroy could have been left there to be invested."[1] Even though Halleck expressed contempt toward Schenck for not pulling Milroy out of Winchester earlier, Milroy would initially shoulder the lion's share of blame for the defeat. Milroy would become, Secretary Welles wrote following the Winchester debacle, "the scapegoat, and blamed for the stupid blunders, neglects, and mistakes of those who should have warned and advised him."[2]

Foremost among Milroy's concerns following the battle was not who would be blamed for the defeat, but rather how could he reorganize his men. Following Second Winchester Milroy's division, what was left of it, was scattered throughout Maryland, Pennsylvania, and Virginia, and was in very poor condition. A soldier who escaped to Harper's Ferry described the condition of Milroy's troops: "Not a soldier of the command has a change of clothing — except [what] he has brought here.... A very large portion of the command are without tents or blankets, as the quartermaster's department at this point was not overstocked when they arrived."[3] Officers of the beleaguered troops also feared for the safety of their commands and the loved ones that may have been left behind in Winchester.

Throughout Milroy's occupation he permitted officers' wives in Winchester. Some of them, such as Mary Milroy, left Winchester several weeks prior to the battle. *The New York Herald* reported: "Many of the poor bearers of shoulder straps are going around with exceedingly long faces, moaning ... for their other selves, whom the exigencies of the occasion prevented them from taking away. Quite a large number of officers had had their wives with them." The *Herald* stated that many of those "unfortunate ladies are still in Winchester (if they have not been sent to Richmond), not knowing whether their husbands are dead or alive, prisoners or safe among their companions in camp."[4] After the battle, Secretary of War Stanton became alarmed when he read a report from the *Richmond Dispatch* that "11 Yankee ladies were taken from Winchester and are imprisoned in Castle Thunder." When Stanton heard this he asked for confirmation from Schenck. He informed Stanton that at least five or six wives were reported missing."[5]

On June 17, while officers worried about their men and safety of loved ones, Schenck ordered Milroy to move from Baltimore to take command of the troops at Bloody Run, Pennsylvania, and prepare them for an offensive against Confederate troops that might threaten Chambersburg, Pennsylvania. After dealing with the possible threat to Chambersburg, Schenck then wanted Milroy to proceed to Harrisburg to see if Maj. Gen. Darius N. Couch, commander of the Department of the Susquehanna, needed any assistance in defending the Keystone State's capital.[6] Nearly a week after his defeat at Winchester, Milroy arrived in Bloody Run and took command of his troops. When he arrived the men, who believed Milroy had either been captured or killed at Winchester, were ecstatic. "They all thought I had been killed," Milroy wrote his wife, "and when they saw me they shouted and yelled and were almost crazy with joy as they crowded around to shake hands with me." After the excitement subsided Milroy assessed his command's condition. It was deplorable. Men were without supplies and many men had improper footwear. Sadly Milroy explained: "Nearly all the infantry had their feet badly blistered. In some cases their boots and shoes which they had not had off for over a week were filled with blood and matter." Despite the wretched condition of the troops in Bloody Run, Schenck ordered Milroy's force to Chambersburg and then Harrisburg. Milroy had to make immediate preparations.

Although Schenck wanted Milroy to protect Chambersburg and march to Harrisburg, Milroy, after thinking over Schenck's order, did not believe it was the best decision. Milroy wanted Schenck to allow him to first organize the fragments of his command and have them reunite around Harper's Ferry. From Harper's Ferry Milroy informed Schenck that he wanted "to go back to Winchester for many reasons." Milroy did not explain the specific reasons, rather he simply informed Schenck that "I have learned a worth of experience in the Valley and would like to have a chance to make use of it."[7] After making an appeal to reenter the Valley, Milroy lambasted General Kelley, who had apparently treated the elements of Milroy's command that made it to the vicinity of Harper's Ferry as "cowards and skedaddlers." Milroy also condemned Kelley, who according to some soldiers "cursed them."

As Milroy's scattered command began to assemble in the vicinity of Bloody Run his ranks were also bolstered by approximately 2,000 Pennsylvania militiamen. Initially Milroy welcomed the reinforcements but he soon began to look for ways to rid himself of the militiamen from the Keystone State. "They are mostly a wild undisciplined mob, and a greater curse and terror to the people of the country than the rebels. They ... plunder and steal as they go and come and go and do about as they please," Milroy complained to Schenck.

Despite Milroy's pleas to enter the Valley and rid his command of the militia Schenck would not relent and the Gray Eagle did as ordered. Soon, however, Milroy realized that his biggest concern should not be the location of his command, but rather trying to keep his command. Milroy's military career continued down a slippery slope on June 26, when Couch ordered Milroy to relinquish command of the troops at Bloody Run. The Gray Eagle obliged and turned over command to Col. L.B. Pierce of the 12th Pennsylvania Cavalry.[8]

Pierce took command reluctantly and exhibited his unwillingness in a broadside that was distributed to his command. He began: "In obedience to [orders] I assume the command of the forces now here. I am aware that you in having your General taken from you, have met with an irreparable loss. That loss no one feels or regrets more than myself."[9] Pierce proceeded to let his command know he felt his tenure as commander would be temporary and that the separation between Milroy and the troops at Bloody Run "will not be final." Regardless of the ill feelings that Pierce and those under him might have felt as a result of Milroy's departure, Pierce instilled in his command a sense of duty and informed them that the future of the nation hung in the balance. "In assuming command of you at this time, I do it with great delicacy," Pierce explained, "rendered more so by the confused condition in which we are at present placed.... Should we come into contact soon again with the invaders of this state [Pennsylvania], I only ask you to give me that support which in times past you have given to your favorite chief, now absent from you. I feel assured you will maintain that reputation for ... courage and bravery." Even though the men under his command had a fair reputation in combat, he recognized discontent in the ranks and some unruly behavior. Pierce closed his statement to his men: "Let discipline be restored, order prevail ... and stout hearts will amply avenge the death of our fallen brothers in arms, and wipe out even the memory of our recent reverses." While Pierce smoothed things over with his new command and Milroy lamented the loss of his command to a captain, the following day Halleck put Milroy's military career on hold. On June 27, Halleck sent orders to arrest Milroy and hold him at Baltimore for the debacle at Winchester.[10]

The day after his arrest Milroy began a fierce letter-writing campaign to Federal officials to secure his release. He first wrote to Secretary of the Interior John P. Usher, also a fellow Hoosier. "Try to procure my release from the grasp of an incompetent unprincipled tyrant," Milroy pleaded.[11] He wanted Usher to pass on the letter to President Lincoln as soon as possible. Milroy used the letters written the day after his arrest as his first opportunity to defend his actions at Winchester. He explained that he had no orders to evacuate Winchester and was doing what Schenck ordered. Furthermore Milroy used these letters to convince Usher that the only reason that Halleck arrested him was because Milroy was not a West Point graduate. "No volunteer Gen[era]l," Milroy complained, "can have any justice with Halleck."[12] While Milroy felt Halleck held general prejudices toward volunteer generals he also believed that Halleck hated Milroy specifically. Milroy explained: "Halleck hates me without cause ... with the blind unreasoning hatred of an Indian & I can ask or expect nothing but injustice from him."[13]

Aside from defending his actions and explaining that Halleck would do anything to ruin him militarily, Milroy also used the letter to illustrate his strong sense of patriotism and duty. "I love my country & the Union dearer than life," Milroy confessed to Usher, "suspend my arrest only temporarily, during the present terrible crisis, and give me something to do.... If permitted I would freely resign my present commission, & take any command, or go into the ranks as a private."[14] Willing to put his life on the line to return to the field he explained to Usher that if allowed to fight, once the war ended "Halleck may have me tried to his hearts content and hang me if he can."[15]

Secretary Usher delivered the letter promptly to Lincoln. The president responded the following day. Lincoln explained to Milroy that he did not doubt his devotion to the Stars and Stripes, but he could not return him to command because he had just lost a division and that "*prima facie* the fault is upon you."[16] Lincoln's letter also lambasted Milroy for accusing Halleck of possessing contempt for the Gray Eagle. Lincoln curtly responded to the accusation: "You hate West Point generally, and General Halleck particularly; but I do know that it is not his fault that you were at Winchester on the 13th, 14th, and the morning of the 15th — the days of your disaster."[17]

During the first week of July, Milroy begged Halleck to be released and sent into the field. Milroy reminded Halleck of his prior service to the Union: "I love my country dearer than life or wife or children and since the beginning of this war have devoted every faculty of my soul and body to the salvation of the Union."[18] He used the opportunity to present Halleck with his version of the story, rather than just the one that he and others were reading in newspapers. Many northern papers portrayed Milroy as a bumbling, inept coward. To this charge Milroy reminded Halleck that he had "never avoided danger when duty called."[19] Truly, Milroy was not trying to find a way out of trouble; he was looking for an opportunity to command on the battlefield. "Place me in the 'fore front' of the battle," Milroy pleaded, "even in Hell itself rather than this position of disgraceful inactivity during the present terrible crisis of my country. After the crisis is passed I would court demand and defy the most rigid scrutiny into my conduct."[20]

Milroy's pleas with both Halleck and Lincoln during the end of June and first three days of July fell on deaf ears as Lee's Army of Northern Virginia battled with the Army of the Potomac in Gettysburg. Undoubtedly keenly aware of military events in Pennsylvania, Milroy during the end of June and beginning of July completed his report of the Second Battle of Winchester. After forwarding the report to General Schenck, Milroy implored Lincoln to "look at my report. My destiny is in your hands. I ask nothing but justice. Having been denied the privilege of participating in the glorious battle of Gettysburg and that which will complete the destruction of Lee's army, adequate justice cannot now be done me."[21]

Patiently Milroy waited as the days of July passed. By July 20, Milroy demanded action from Lincoln — at least the right to publish his report and clear his name. He informed Lincoln that the *New York Herald* and *New York Tribune* portrayed him "as a coward and as guilty of the most outrageous misconduct."[22] Milroy wanted the opportunity to clear his name, yet none was forthcoming — for the time being.

Even though Milroy appeared strong-willed in his official correspondence to politicians in Washington, the letters he wrote to his wife had a decidedly different tone, revealing his unhappiness and possible suicidal feelings. On June 30, he expressed his disgruntled attitude: "I have never in my life been so entirely wretched and miserable. Life has never had many attractions for me and were it not for you and for the children would not long endure in its agony."[23]

As July passed and Milroy waited for the opportunity either to clear his name or garner support for another command, many judged his actions at Winchester. An Ohio correspondent identified clandestinely as A.B.M. recorded: "The unaccountable defeat of Milroy, and his disorderly retreat in which he lost more than half of his command, is still shrouded in deep mystery to us in the West. We think it smacks of cowardice." The journalist clearly believed that the person responsible for the defeat was Milroy. "I do not believe the fault lies with the soldiers, those soldiers, were as brave as any other soldiers, anywhere. The fault lies with the commanding officer.... Some gain fame, and lose it because it was not well gained, and I fear that little Gen. Milroy had was of this character."[24] The correspondent thought that Milroy was a coward stating, "all accord him too much bravery, too much daring." The newspaperman opened himself up to much criticism.

When a soldier in the 116th Ohio read the article in late August he lambasted the cowardly correspondent who hid behind initials. The Ohioan defended Milroy's bravery: "No one who knows Milroy will ever call him a coward. And no one will make this charge a second time in the hearing of any of the men in his old Division.... Was it cowardly to save 4,000 men at the very last moment they could be saved?" The soldier further lambasted the journalist: "Was it cowardly to check the advance of Lee's army for three days, and thus give the Potomac army time...? Was it cowardly of him because he did not remain ... to be shelled by a hundred guns of the enemy, and have his command all killed or, captured?" Confident that the newspaperman would be proved wrong the enraged soldier from the 116th closed his letter: "General Milroy will come from under this cloud pure and undefiled, notwithstanding ... the jealousy of West Point Generals. Mark this."[25]

While some newspapers may have branded Milroy a coward and placed the lion's share of blame for the defeat on Milroy's shoulders not all of the papers did. *The Evening Gazette,* an Indiana paper, sought to solve the "strange mystery" as to why "Gen. Milroy was permitted to be attacked by the rebel army under Ewell, and then, because he retreated, was arraigned for misconduct."[26] The paper's Washington correspondent concluded that the only reason Milroy was arrested after Second Winchester was that Milroy "did not possess that sure pass port under the present General-in-Chief's regime, to military preferment, *A West Point Coat of Varnish!*"[27]

Indiana newspapers were not the only ones to come to Milroy's defense. Some of the soldiers who escaped supported the Gray Eagle. A soldier of the 116th Ohio defended Milroy's actions in an Ohio newspaper: "Somebody is responsible for the Winchester disaster, but *it is not Gen. Milroy.*"[28] The soldier went on to proclaim that "Gen. Milroy's men and officers love him. They honor him, they revere his very name."[29] The same soldier recognized that the ill treatment received after Second Winchester was the result of a West Point conspiracy against Milroy — an argument that Milroy himself would have believed. The Ohio soldier wrote: "The enemies of General Milroy now saw the fruition of their long looked for opportunity to cloud his [Milroy's] bright military record and at once proceeded to take advantage of it."[30]

Other soldiers sent letters to Lincoln that summer to show support for their commander. A contingent of officers from Milroy's division penned several paragraphs to President Lincoln from "Camp Milroy" in Sharpsburg, Maryland. "We feel that we would rather fight under the leadership of this veteran soldier than that of any other commander; and no other man living can inspire the officers and men of this Division with the same amount of courage, zeal and enthusiasm in the work of crushing out this infamous rebellion."[31]

Another regiment, the 122nd Ohio, wrote directly to Milroy from Sharpsburg and stated their admiration for him and desire for him to be back in command. The officers of the regiment informed Milroy on July 21 that they were "going to work energetically — and apply or petition the proper authorities that be and see if we can once more have you restored to us." The Ohioans boosted Milroy's broken spirit: "We want no other commander than Genl. Milroy and so far as your old d[ivision] is concerned this feeling I do know to be unanimous."[32]

Politicians from West Virginia also sent Milroy conciliatory letters and did everything in their power to have him restored to command in their state.[33] Samuel Young, a member of the West Virginia Senate, wrote Milroy in late July 1863: "I feel sorry and indignant [at] the way you have been treated, by the pompous officials at Washington. But you can console yourself that you have the confidence of all the soldiers who have fought and toiled with you from time to time. I have seen great numbers of them, all of whom are anxious to be in the service of their country with you again." Senator Young told Milroy that he should be buoyed in his confidence as "you have the confidence and applause; love and respect; of all the good union men of the nation." Young also gave Milroy some hope that he might be back in command soon in western Virginia. Although that would not be the case, Young informed Milroy that "I moved a resolution in the Senate, that you be called to command the military department of West Virginia, but the department has yet been formed." Urging Milroy to take action to promote the creation of the Department of West Virginia Young implored the Gray Eagle: "Abraham Lincoln, is your personal friend, write to him asking him to appoint you to the West Va. department. If you will come and take charge ... I will quit the Legislature and join you in driving the rebels beyond the Alleghany Mountains ... we have never had any protection since you left."[34]

While politicians and soldiers defended Milroy, some argued that his decision to remain in Winchester played an integral role in the success of the Army of the Potomac at the Battle of Gettysburg. After the war ended one soldier went so far as to say that had the Confederates "met with no resistance at Winchester their march would have been unopposed. They could have gone into Harrisburg, Philadelphia and perhaps the Capitol itself, levying a tribute to the rich country through which they passed."[35] While this soldier's remark may be a bit far-fetched, it nonetheless proves the point that many of Milroy's men defended his courage and decision to remain and fight at Winchester. Some soldiers even went so far as to defend Milroy on the grounds that Winchester was indefensible by nature and that no commander who attempted to defend the town ever held on to it.

Historians have the advantage of hindsight and know that the proclamations soldiers made about Winchester's indefensibility hold true. In the three battles of Winchester no defending force ever held off an attack. An officer of the 122nd Ohio related Winchester's permeable nature to attack to his family less than two weeks after Milroy's defeat: "Winchester is situated in the Shenandoah Valley in a very pretty place with elevations all around and presents no front to the enemy but can be approached from any or every direction."[36] The officer continued: "If I was going to fight the Rebels there again I would rather be on the out side and undertake to take the place from them than to be on the inside and try to defend it. It will take more men to defend the place than it will to take it. It can be surrounded as we were at anytime and all communications cut off."[37]

Not all of Milroy's men came to his defense, especially those captured at Winchester. Some prisoners from Milroy's division lambasted him for the mean treatment of the population of Winchester and the "cowardly" behavior exhibited during the battle.[38] A Confederate artilleryman who listened to the grumblings of some of Milroy's men disagreed with the opinions of the prisoners. He stated that Milroy "could have done his men no possible good by remaining with them.... I think he acted right."[39]

Clearly the detractors among his former command were in the minority. Not only did soldiers defend his conduct, so too did a portion of the lower Shenandoah Valley's Unionists. Loyal civilians of Winchester and Frederick County organized a petition and sent it to President Lincoln. Sixty-five male residents signed the document that stated in part: "Believing him to be an able, faithful, and efficient Servant to the cause of the Union and those who advocate the cause of good government ... take into consideration at the earliest opportunity Maj. Genl Milroy's case in a favorable manner."[40]

Pressure from Milroy, soldiers, politicians, and southern Unionists prompted Lincoln to take action and appoint a court of inquiry to meet in Washington on August 7.[41] The order required the court to "report whether the orders of the General-in-Chief [Halleck] in regard to the evacuation of Winchester were complied with; and, if not, by whom they were disobeyed." While finding who was to blame for the disastrous defeat at Winchester was the court's preeminent concern it was not its only charge. The War Department also ordered the court to "report whether the retreat of the command was properly conducted, and the public property suitably cared for; and if not, what officer or officers were in fault."[42] The War Department appointed Maj. Gen. E.A. Hitchcock and Brig. Gens. W.F. Barry and J.J. Abercrombie, and Capt. Robert N. Scott served as judge-advocate.

When Milroy received word that the court of inquiry was finally going to convene he must have been elated, but he was not overjoyed that he had no time to prepare and find proper legal counsel for the inquiry. Milroy needed to delay the court. It was set to convene at noon on August 7 in Washington; however, no suitable rooms were provided for the court and it adjourned to meet the following day. On the second day of the court Milroy arrived more than an hour late and when he finally made it he requested more time to prepare for the court and find counsel. The court granted Milroy's request and ordered him to be prepared on August 10. He agreed. The day came and Milroy requested yet another one day delay which the court graciously granted. Finally on August 11 Milroy was ready, but now the court was not. One of the court's officers, General Hitchcock, failed to show. What the members of the court did not know at the time was that Hitchcock had been removed from the court and replaced with Brig. Gen. G.A. DeRussy. The setback caused the court to delay once again, until August 13, to allow General DeRussy enough time to prepare; however, he did not show on August 13. Finally on August 14, one week after the court was ordered to convene, it was ready to hear testimony.[43]

When court opened Milroy announced to the court that his lawyer would be Mr. John Jolliffe. The court approved and Milroy made his first protest. He complained that none of the officers on the court were his peers, all being inferior to him in rank.[44] He implored the court "to appoint one or more major generals to examine this case, and ... to defer proceedings until this application shall have been acted upon."[45] The court carefully considered Milroy's appeal. The court adjourned until the following day.

When court convened on the morning of August 15, it denied Milroy's request to add a major general to the court. The court was correct in the decision. Milroy had no legal grounds to protest the members of the court being inferior to him in rank. According to the United States Army Regulations for 1863 courts of inquiry did not have to consist of men of equal or higher rank. Courts of inquiry needed only to "consist of one or more officers, not exceeding three, and a judge advocate."[46] After informing Milroy that he had no legal basis for making such a complaint they entered into evidence nine telegraph messages from Halleck to Schenck ranging in date from January 5 to June 15, 1863. These messages would become perhaps the most important evidence in the court's deliberation as they determined whether or not Milroy was at fault for the defeat. Following the admission of evidence the court adjourned. It would convene on Monday morning, August 17, and begin calling witnesses. Milroy would be the first of 17 to receive a bombardment of queries.

When the court convened on August 17, Milroy was sworn in and immediately began answering questions. Initially the court's questioning centered on understanding why Milroy remained in Winchester. Milroy informed the panel that even though the first intimation of an attack occurred on June 12, he did not feel threatened. "I supposed that with my fortifications," Milroy told the court, "I was able to stand some two or three times my own force." Furthermore Milroy thought that his command would be reinforced on June 14. Even though Milroy thought that General Hooker might send reinforcements to Milroy's aid, no messages indicate any certainty of additional troops being sent to Winchester.[47]

Furthermore Milroy decided to remain in Winchester and block the Confederacy's advance because he believed that the Shenandoah Valley was a place of strategic importance for the Union war effort. In late May 1863 Milroy explained to Schenck that "every dictate of military science, prudence and economy requires that this Valley should be occupied to Staunton at as early a day as possible.... This Valley is the key to the B&O.R.R. and to W.Va. and if occupied to Staunton both would be safe."[48] During the court of inquiry Milroy echoed this firm belief in the Valley's importance.

Admitted into evidence at the court of inquiry was a message Milroy sent to Schenck on June 12, reiterating Milroy's position on why he felt duty bound to remain in Winchester. First he explained: "This place is the key to the Baltimore and Ohio Railroad. Let this point be abandoned, and our forces withdrawn to Harpers Ferry, and no force that it would be practicable for our Government to place at Harpers Ferry, and at points along the Baltimore and Ohio Railroad west of that place, would or could secure it against raids from the enemy." Looking back on Winchester's history during the first two years of the war Milroy correctly observed: "That railroad has not been nor never can be kept from destruction while this place is occupied by the rebels."[49]

Milroy argued further that he was obligated to hold his position in Winchester because the "Union men and women of this and adjoining counties have been so often disappointed and abandoned to the demons of treason, that they had become very timid and doubtful, but our six months' occupation here has begun to give them confidence in, and many of them have come out and taken a decided stand for, the Union." Falsely Milroy buoyed this stance by stating that "the leading influential secessionists of this place, in private counsel among themselves, have determined, upon the first serious reverse to their cause in Virginia, to come out boldly and take the stump for reconstruction."[50]

Although the protection of the area's rail lines and Unionists were two excellent reasons for Milroy wanting to remain in Winchester there was another — one that would be recognized by Union generals Ulysses S. Grant and Philip H. Sheridan in the fall of 1864 — the importance of the Valley as a food source for the Confederacy. "There is a large amount of wheat in this and the surrounding counties," Milroy stated, "of the last two years' crops, still unthreshed, which the rebs would get, if we abandoned the country to them." Firmly Milroy told Schenck and subsequently the court that "every dictate of interest, policy, humanity, patriotism, and bravery requires that we should not yield a foot of this country up to the traitors again."[51]

After satisfying the first line of questions the court turned its attention to the retreat. The court wanted to know that if all the supplies Milroy left behind were properly destroyed and if the retreat was conducted accordingly. Milroy assured the court that he had given proper orders to destroy the military stores and artillery that could not be taken on the retreat. "I had everything loaded upon wagons, ready to bring away," Milroy explained, "but, not dreaming of being surrounded by such a heavy force, and supposing I would receive orders, I supposed I could take my trains back to Harpers Ferry ... we felt that if we moved a wheel or made the least noise the enemy would fall upon us in overwhelming numbers ... we knew that our safety was in moving quietly." Milroy believed, justifiably so, the best chance for a speedy escape was if he left the Union wagons and artillery in enemy hands.[52] He also told the court that the retreat was made in "as good as possible" order.[53] The first day of Milroy's testimony ended that afternoon and Milroy must have been absolutely spent over answering a barrage of questions. He answered them well and never wavered in his position that he did nothing wrong in defending Winchester.

That night Milroy reflected on his testimony and although he felt somewhat confident that his answers were adequate he wanted to make it clear to the court that he was only obeying orders to remain in Winchester. He decided that as soon as court convened the following day, on August 18, he would deliver a statement to the court. The court convened at 11:00 A.M. and before Milroy answered any more questions he made a formal statement.

"I never received orders to withdraw from there," the Gray Eagle stated. He continued, "If I had left there without fighting, I would have disobeyed General Schenck's positive orders. If I had withdrawn without demonstrating the fact that I could not stay there, it would have been disobedience to my orders." Milroy also told the court that he believed he was partly responsible for the Army of the Potomac's victory at Gettysburg during the first three days of July. "I checked the advance of Lee's army three days," Milroy boasted, "that was certainly doing something for the country. If they had been allowed to go on, they would have had three days longer for pillage and robbery in Pennsylvania, and probably ten times as much property as I lost would have been destroyed in that time."[54]

Following Milroy's statement the court asked him several more questions regarding the geographical limits of his area of operations and from whom he received instructions. After the additional questions ended the court asked Milroy to step down and then called other witnesses to the stand. The 16 witnesses who followed Milroy would either corroborate or refute the Gray Eagle's ability at Winchester.

From August 18 until September 7 the court listened to the testimony of officers from Milroy's command. The court asked them similar questions about Milroy's ability and whether or not he conducted the retreat properly. All of the officers agreed that Milroy conducted the retreat as well as possible and that he was on the field trying to control the fight. The witnesses also testified that Milroy was a courageous officer and carried himself as such throughout the evacuation of Winchester. Brig. Gen. Washington Elliott, one of Milroy's brigade commanders, testified of Milroy's bravery: "I saw no want of courage on the part of General Milroy. In fact, I thought he was too rash sometimes ... I saw nothing that would cause me to question his bravery." Although Elliott did not witness a lack of courage in Milroy he slightly damaged Milroy's position when he stated he thought Milroy "put his forces too far from their supports."[55]

The only real damaging testimony to Milroy's character came from Col. Andrew T. McReynolds, commander of Milroy's Third Brigade. McReynolds delivered a number of hurtful blows to Milroy. He informed the court that Milroy was not seen anywhere on the field during the withdrawal and that Milroy did not communicate any orders to him. "I thought it very strange that I received no orders from General Milroy during the progress of the fighting, as orders should have been sent to me.... I should have received orders."[56] Although McReynolds stated that Milroy gave him no orders at all during the fight he contradicted himself earlier during his testimony on August 20, when he testified: "The only orders I received from General Milroy, or from any other person, either directly or indirectly, was simply the verbal one from General Milroy in person when he was passing me: 'Hurry up your brigade; they are fighting in front.' From that time until I saw General Milroy at Harpers Ferry, on the same day, I had no communication with him."[57] Other officers who testified all suggested that Milroy, during the retreat, was on the field directing the troops as best as he could under the circumstances. For example, Milroy's assistant quartermaster, Capt. W.L. DeMotte, stated that he "did receive orders on the retreat.... He also ordered me to stay at the front of my column."[58]

McReynolds did further damage to Milroy's character when he began to criticize Milroy for the defeat, for remaining in Winchester, and for recalling his command from Berryville to Winchester. When the court asked McReynolds as to who should be held responsible for the loss McReynolds replied simply: "I suppose the commanding officer [Milroy] is held responsible."[59] Furthermore McReynolds supported Halleck's opinion that Winchester was of no importance other than as an outpost. When asked the purpose of Milroy's command in Winchester, McReynolds stated: "It was generally understood to be a 'running command.' It was viewed generally as a position to run from, if attacked by a heavy force with artillery; one not to be held obstinately. I have heard General Milroy speak of his dissatisfaction in not being allowed to make advances when he thought it advisable and that he was to run ... at the approach of ... the enemy."[60] Lastly McReynolds informed the court that he thought Milroy made a mistake in recalling his brigade from Berryville to Winchester. "I should have gone to Harpers Ferry," McReynolds claimed. But his command comprised nearly one-quarter of Milroy's division, and as Milroy had no positive orders to withdraw from Winchester and a fervent desire to hold onto the town, Milroy needed to concentrate his forces.[61] Although McReynolds' testimony was the most negative against Milroy his statements should be taken with caution.

More than likely McReynolds had a personal vendetta against Milroy and used the court of inquiry as an opportunity to damage the Gray Eagle's reputation. The two men did not see eye to eye on military policy in the lower Shenandoah Valley, specifically regarding the oath of allegiance and the zealous enforcement of Lincoln's Emancipation Proclamation. In early June Milroy sent a request to General Schenck asking to remove McReynolds from brigade command. McReynolds "drinks too much whisky and permits it to be drank freely in his command," Milroy wrote to Schenck on June 9. He continued his tirade: "He is very popular with the ... rebels and furnishes many of them with guards at their houses and allows them to pass in and out of his lines and purchase goods [from] his sutlers without [the] oath of allegiance in violation of my orders." Regarding slaves Milroy complained:

"He allows slaveholders in and around his lines to hold and enforce slavery."[62] More than likely Milroy's attempt to remove McReynolds from command embittered the brigade commander. Regardless of McReynolds' negative tone, the other officers found little fault with Milroy's conduct.

With similar testimony from 14 out of 15 of Milroy's subordinates, the court decided to call General Schenck. They believed, and justifiably so, that the key to the Winchester debacle rested with him. The court summoned Schenck on September 1. The following day the War Department amended the wording of Special Orders No. 346 that convened the court of inquiry. The role of the court was no longer to find out if the orders of the "General-in-Chief in regard to the evacuation of Winchester were complied with [and] ... whether the retreat of the command was properly conducted, and the public property suitably cared for," rather the court's purpose was now to "inquire into, and report the facts and circumstances in regard to the evacuation of Winchester."[63] This altered the mission of the court for now they were not supposed to determine anyone's guilt or innocence, but rather compile the facts for President Lincoln's review.

Earlier that day the War Department also informed the judge advocate that General Schenck should be relieved "from attendance before the court ... as soon as practicable."[64] Finally, on September 4, Schenck was ready to testify. Milroy must have been elated that Schenck was to be called as a witness, because he could corroborate Milroy's story, but Schenck

Maj. Gen. Robert C. Schenck, a politician from Ohio before the Civil War, was Milroy's immediate superior in 1863 as commander of the Middle Department. Schenck supported Milroy's decision to remain in Winchester in the days leading up to the Second Battle of Winchester. After Milroy's court of inquiry, many government officials in Washington, D.C., placed a sizeable portion of the blame for the Winchester disaster on Schenck's shoulders (*Battles and Leaders*).

approached the court of inquiry with a degree of trepidation. He knew that since he was Milroy's commander he could be held responsible for the defeat. Fearing that his testimony as a witness could turn into another court of inquiry, Schenck addressed the court before he was sworn in. He told the court that since the court of inquiry would be inquiring into the facts of Winchester and then awaiting President Lincoln's consideration he wanted to have the right to call other witnesses. Schenck implored the court: "I therefore respectfully request ... that besides testifying myself, I shall be permitted, as my right, to have such other witnesses as I may indicate summoned and examined, and especially Maj. Gen. H.W. Halleck ... and Maj. Gen. Joseph Hooker, and that I have the right also to cross-examine any of the witnesses."[65] The court denied his request.

When Schenck began to testify, he immediately informed the court that he differed with Halleck on the importance of Winchester. Schenck, as did Milroy, believed it to be vital to the defense of the Baltimore and Ohio Railroad. "One of the principal duties assigned to me was the protection of the Baltimore and Ohio Railroad," Schenck explained. "I did not believe that any number of pickets stationed immediately on and scattered along the road itself would insure its protection, and especially against cavalry raids, which we had most and constantly to apprehend ... I thought ... Winchester should be occupied." Schenck continued in his defense of Milroy remaining in Winchester: "Winchester" was one of the "keys to the approaches north."[66] Furthermore Schenck informed the court that treating Winchester as an outpost and occupying it with a small number of troops would make those troops vulnerable. Schenck continued in his testimony and stated that at no time did he consider the language of Halleck's messages to be an order to evacuate Winchester; rather he saw Halleck's messages as cautionary notes about the vulnerability of the place. The court specifically addressed a message sent by Halleck to Schenck on June 11, that stated: "If you have not executed my orders to concentrate your forces at Harpers Ferry, you will do so immediately." Schenck told the court "that is the only communication from him [Halleck] in which he refers to Harpers Ferry or any other place as a point of concentration in case Winchester should be abandoned. But I do not admit that that telegram contains an order, but only advises a partial evacuation of Winchester."[67]

Much of Schenck's early testimony helped Milroy's position, however Schenck's final statements only boosted Milroy's chances for being exonerated. When the court asked Schenck, "Do you know of any instance in which General Milroy disobeyed by neglect or otherwise any order from you relating to the evacuation of Winchester?" Schenck sternly replied "No." Milroy must have been relieved to hear him say that and the Gray Eagle's position appeared stronger when Schenck told the panel of officers that if he had had proper intelligence and enough time he would have "concentrated at Winchester, where I believe I could have held Lee's army in front or outside of the fortifications until Hooker could come up."[68]

Schenck's testimony bolstered Milroy's position, but did nothing to help Schenck's. After nearly one month of testimony the court compiled the facts that would ultimately be sent to President Lincoln for consideration and then sent the proceedings to Judge Advocate General Joseph Holt. Holt reviewed the testimony and evidence and prepared a summary of the court of inquiry that would be used for President Lincoln's consideration. He submitted his findings on September 17. Holt divided up the findings into five categories. First: "The circumstances and character of the occupation of Winchester before the attack"; second: "The orders given by General Milroy in reference to the evacuation"; third: "The circumstances of the attack"; fourth: "The evacuation (June 15)"; and fifth: "The retreat."[69]

Regarding the first item, Holt recommended that Schenck was entirely to blame. He recognized that Halleck and Schenck were at odds over the importance of Winchester, but Holt stated that the language of messages from Halleck after June 11 should have been regarded by Schenck as an order and Schenck in turn should have ordered Milroy to withdraw. The judge advocate general concluded that the "directions of the General-in-Chief, though sometimes not urged as forcibly as at others, were certainly intended, at least on and after June 11, to be taken as military orders, and to be executed as such, and therefore the view of General Schenck ... that the abandonment of Winchester was never ordered ... is an erroneous one."[70] Holt further lambasted Schenck by stating that "up to the time of the evacuation, General Milroy was under orders from his commanding officer, General Schenck, not to retreat at once, but to hold his post until further orders, which further orders had not been received up to the time of the evacuation, though telegraphed for by General Milroy." Regardless of Holt's certainty that Schenck should ultimately be held responsible for Milroy remaining in Winchester he did recognize that Schenck was heavily influenced by Milroy's confidence "to hold the post against a large force of the enemy."[71]

Concerning the second item, regarding the orders given to Milroy about preparing for evacuation, Holt determined they had been carried out to a certain extent. While the original directive from Lieutenant Colonel Piatt, Schenck's chief of staff, ordered Milroy to "send back your heavy guns, surplus ammunition, and subsistence," Milroy rid himself only of surplus items. On June 11, Milroy ordered 114 wagons to be loaded with the military stores and sent to Harpers Ferry. "General Milroy," Holt recorded, "did commence to make the preparations indicated for evacuation." The wagons arrived safely in Harpers Ferry.[72] Holt also noted that Milroy had made preparations for further evacuation of items, however, Schenck suspended the order until further notice.[73]

The third item—"circumstances of the attack"—served as an opportunity for Holt to outline the military action for President Lincoln. Nothing in that summary of Winchester suggests Milroy was at fault. If anything it suggests that faulty intelligence was to blame for the surprise attack. According to Holt, Schenck did not have proper notice of the Army of Northern Virginia's advance until late in the evening of June 13, and by the time a message could be sent to Milroy the "wires between Winchester and Martinsburg" were "cut by the enemy."[74] Despite the fact that the intelligence from the War Department, Schenck, and Hooker's command may have been inadequate, Milroy did receive word from his own scouts that an attack in force was imminent. Even though Milroy trusted the commander of the scouts, Colonel Keifer, he discounted the reports as erroneous because the War Department and Hooker were never able to corroborate the intelligence.[75]

Pertaining to the evacuation of Winchester, Holt concluded that since all of the officers on Milroy's staff, except Colonel McReynolds, felt that Milroy made the proper decision to withdraw and did the proper thing in abandoning artillery and the remaining stores, Milroy could have done no more. Speed and secrecy were the primary concerns during Milroy's withdrawal. Wagons and artillery would only have slowed down the column and could have caused Milroy's entire command to be captured. "A question is raised in the testimony whether the light batteries ... could have been brought off with safety," Holt wrote in his summary. He concluded "that though the batteries would have been very useful in the retreat in the engagement of the 15th, yet their removal would have occasioned so much noise as probably to have attracted the attention of the enemy in front, and advised them of the movement, and further that the roughness of the road might have seriously delayed the artillery."[76] The language of the conclusion finds no fault with Milroy's handling of the evacuation and what his command left behind in order to promote speed and secrecy during the withdrawal.

Holt's final category—"the retreat"—again found little fault with Milroy, stating that Milroy's conduct and that of his officers was appropriate.[77] Holt concluded that "the evacuation of Winchester by General Milroy was as well ordered as could have been expected under all the circumstances, and that the loss of most of the public property, which was abandoned, was inevitable." Holt did note that although the retreat was conducted as well as possible "the troops of General Milroy were not kept well in hand, but were very much dispersed." However, Holt did conclude that even though the troops were confused "this was in great part owing to the sudden attack made up on them in the darkness of the night, and to their being obliged to force their way through a body of troops superior in numbers."[78]

As an addendum to his opinion of the retreat Holt raised the question: "Whether, if General Milroy had evacuated at an earlier day, he might not have effected his retreat in good order, taking with him all his artillery and stores." Based on the inquiry's testimony Holt determined that he might have been able to do this if he "retreated either on the 12th or 13th." Even though it appeared that Holt might place some blame on Milroy for not withdrawing earlier he concluded that "the discussion of the question of whether the retreat was too long delayed is rendered much less important by the consideration that General Milroy was, during June 12, 13, and 14, under positive instructions from his superior officer to await further orders before retreating." Again the burden rested not upon Milroy's shoulders, but Schenck's.[79]

Ultimately Holt's conclusions exonerated Milroy for the defeat at Winchester and placed the lion's share of the blame on Schenck's shoulders. Holt, however, did not have the ultimate say in levying responsibility for the defeat. The final judgment would come from President Lincoln.

Even though Milroy had been cleared by Holt, he could not enjoy total success until Lincoln endorsed Holt's conclusion. As September closed and the days of October began to pass, Milroy became impatient with Lincoln. He unleashed another barrage of letters to the commander in chief. Perhaps, Milroy believed, the matter had escaped Lincoln's mind. He reminded the president on September 20: "There has not yet been any announcement, official or otherwise of any decision upon the evidence for the Court of Inquiry in which I was concerned. In the multiplicity of your duties this matter may have escaped your notice."[80] In the same letter Milroy also reminded Lincoln of the great injustice being done his reputation and the nation: "The treatment I have received from my Government by being suspended from command at the most important crisis of the country and placed in arrest and the continuance of that arrest for three months," Milroy lamented on September 20, "have occasioned me so much misery."[81] Six days later Milroy begged for a meeting with Lincoln and when he did not receive it continued his letter-writing campaign.[82]

Milroy's letters to Lincoln were not only laden with pleas for a decision on Lincoln's part concerning the court of inquiry, but were also filled with suggestions for how to better improve the army. For example on September 13, Milroy suggested to Lincoln that intoxicating liquors be prohibited for use by officers. "The use of intoxicating liquors in our army is enormous among the officers and drunkenness among them from the Genls. to the 2nd Lts. is very common and a very great evil to the service and should be reformed," Milroy suggested. In the same communiqué Milroy also suggested that measures should be taken to strengthen the Union's grip on the Shenandoah Valley.

Until the summer of 1864, Union military planners in Washington, D.C., had a limited view of the Valley's importance. They knew it was the "breadbasket of the Confederacy" but did very little to lay waste to the Valley, and were more concerned with using the Valley as a buffer zone between Confederate forces and the capital. It would not be until Gen. Philip Sheridan came to the Valley in 1864 that the destruction of the Confederacy's granary would be carried out. On September 13, 1863, more than one year prior to Sheridan's famous "Burning," Milroy pleaded with Lincoln, partly out of practicality and partly because he wanted a command: "Having been campaigning two years ... in the Valley and West Va. I know it is to be the Egypt of Va., from where ... the subsistence of Lee's army is drawn. It should be seized and held from Martinsburg to Staunton. A matter I would be pleased to do with a proper command."[83]

Amid the many letters he wrote to Lincoln and others asking for a final decision about the responsibility for defeat at Second Winchester and the possibility of a new command, Milroy spent some time writing to his wife and telling her about his situation and sadness. Undoubtedly Mary longed to be with her husband as she penned: "I well know your situation for some time has been a very sore and trying one to you, and your situation at Washington is truly a humiliating one to your brave and noble nature with all its sense conscious or innocence or any just cause for all this mental suffering." Although she sympathized with her husband, Mary did not want him to become too melancholy. "Why envelop yourself in the thick gloom of melancholy," she asked, "and refuse to be comforted by any of those cheering thoughts that ought to comfort you in this time your time of trouble. Will not History do you justice? Are not your friends innumerable?" Mary informed her husband that his friends would not think any less of him for what had been charged against him. She explained: "They do not think any less of you for Halleck's malice and petty jealousy—it is true he prevents you from laboring in the great cause of freedom. That cause which lies so near your heart, and that cause for which you so freely sacrifice your life." Mrs. Milroy then continued in her letter to her husband telling him that she was relieved to know that he would not be in a battle anytime soon: "I indeed dread to have you to go into battle after the Winchester disaster, for I know you would not be likely to come out of it alive. I do not think the time you spend at Washington so much like a prisoner ... have you not already obtained enough Glory enough for one life time. After all what is earthly honor?" Mary even suggested that her husband should be pleased with Halleck because he detained Milroy in Washington, D.C., out of harm's way. "And who knows," Mary explained to her disgusted husband, "but your enemy Halleck is the very man made use of in the providence of God to preserve your life for future usefulness." Using religion as a weapon, Mary informed her husband that it was more important to be a moral individual rather than be remembered as a gallant battlefield commander. She tried to boost her husband's morale: "I have always been more proud of your pure Moral life, than I could be of the Greatest Military Glory."[84]

While the letter may have made Milroy think, for a moment, about his position in life and made him feel somewhat better, his thoughts soon turned back to obtaining a military command. He overcame many obstacles to getting another command since his defeat at Winchester, however, there was one more hurdle — President Lincoln needed to make a final judgment on Holt's findings and endorse them. Finally on October 27, Lincoln addressed Milroy's court of inquiry.

John Hay, Lincoln's personal secretary, sent a page and a half letter from Lincoln to Milroy describing the chief executive's attitude toward the matter. Lincoln opened the letter with his own conclusions about whether or not Halleck had positively ordered Schenck to move Milroy from Winchester to Harper's Ferry. "It was very well known to General Halleck," Lincoln penned, "that it was of no service commensurate with the risk it incurred, and that it ought to be withdrawn; but although he more than once advised its withdrawal, he never positively ordered it." Lincoln also recognized the differences of opinion between Schenck and Halleck over Winchester's strategic importance. "Schenck," Lincoln explained, "believed the service of the force at Winchester was worth the hazard, and so did not positively order its withdrawal until it was so late that the enemy cut the wire and prevented the order reaching General Milroy." So far Lincoln's letter reiterated many of the points that Holt made, and Milroy must have been frustrated that Lincoln did not immediately come out and state Milroy's guilt or innocence. The end of the letter must have brought relief to Milroy when he read: "Some question can be made whether some of General Halleck's dispatches to General Schenck should not have been construed to be orders to withdraw the force, and obeyed accordingly; but no such question can be made against General Milroy." Lincoln concluded the communiqué: "Serious blame is not necessarily due to every serious disaster; and I can not say that in this case any of these officers is deserving of *serious blame*. No court-martial is deemed necessary or proper in the case."[85]

The court of inquiry and Lincoln had exonerated Milroy for the defeat at Winchester, but his military career remained in shambles. Milroy aimed to get even with the one man he believed was responsible for the demise of his military career — Halleck. The day following Holt's conclusion Milroy wrote a letter to Schenck explaining that he wanted to bring charges against Halleck.[86] First, Milroy proclaimed that Halleck had "maliciously & without probable cause ordered me to be deprived of command." Second, he declared that Halleck had not brought official charges against him in a proper period of time. Third, Milroy asserted that several telegrams sent to Schenck from Halleck from March through mid-June contained "false malicious & injurious expressions." Fourth, Halleck sent the aforementioned telegrams to be used as evidence at the court of inquiry. Fifth, Milroy claimed that Halleck tried to deny Milroy proper defense counsel at the inquiry, and finally Milroy accused Halleck of putting officers inferior to him in rank on the court when Milroy believed there to be at least 15 major generals not on any sort of active duty.[87] Probably at Schenck's urging, Milroy never carried out his campaign against Halleck. After all it had been quite clear that the judge advocate general placed blame on Schenck's shoulders and pressing charges against Halleck would only mean revisiting the Winchester issue and possibly putting Schenck's military career in jeopardy.

Milroy sat idly throughout the remainder of 1863. The only time that the monotony of the letter-writing campaign in Washington, D.C., was broken up was when he took a leave during the first half of November to see his wife and family in Indiana. When he returned to Indiana he was treated like a hero. In his native Jasper County, Milroy's arrival was advertised with broadsides emblazoned with the phrase "Hail to the Chief! Let our men, women and children turn out and meet the 'Old Grey Eagle' at the cars, and welcome him to the 'home of his childhood.' The Military will be out, and the first Flag that was fired into from Indiana." Milroy delivered a speech at the courthouse on November 11, 1863, before a crowd of admirers. His stay in Indiana was short and by the end of November Milroy was back in Washington continuing his efforts to secure a command.[88]

When Milroy returned to Washington, D.C., he hoped that Lincoln could obtain some sort of military post for him. Probably unbeknownst to Milroy, Lincoln tried, but the effort yielded nil. Even though Lincoln may have not possessed an affinity for Milroy he recognized the Gray Eagle as a stern abolitionist and patriot. Acknowledging these strong attributes Lincoln made an attempt to secure a command for Milroy. In December, Lincoln asked Gen. Ulysses S. Grant to see if he could find something for Milroy. "The Indiana delegation in Congress," Lincoln explained to Grant, "or at least a part of them, are very anxious that Majr. Gen. Milroy shall enter active service again, and I share this feeling." Lincoln continued, "He is not a difficult man to satisfy.... Believing in our cause, and wanting to fight in it, is the whole matter with him."[89] Grant, however, did not have the same feelings toward Milroy that Lincoln possessed. Regardless of how much the Indiana delegation in Congress or Lincoln wanted Milroy to have a command, Grant believed that there were other generals of equal or lesser rank who could do a better job than Milroy.[90]

As the new year of 1864 dawned, Milroy reflected on where he had been one year ago to the day — Winchester. Unknowing of the correspondence between Lincoln and Grant in late December, Milroy attempted to begin a campaign of persuasion with Lincoln. On January 1, 1864, Milroy took the opportunity to pen Lincoln a letter congratulating him on the one-year anniversary of the Emancipation Proclamation. "I could not permit this first anniversary of your glorious 'Proclamation of Freedom' to pass without making known to you my humble individual thanks and gratitude," Milroy explained, "a gratitude that is shared by every true friend of our country and of human rights."[91] Aside from congratulating Lincoln on the Proclamation's anniversary, the letter also had another purpose — to remind Lincoln that Milroy was among his greatest supporters and one of the first to actively enforce the Emancipation Proclamation. Milroy reiterated that when he came to Winchester he demanded that the people comply with the Emancipation Proclamation and should anyone refuse to obey they would suffer severe penalties. When he occupied the lower Valley, Milroy felt he "was on duty in the most righteous cause that man ever drew [a] sword in." He closed the letter by informing Lincoln that one year ago he was "a thousand more times happy than now."[92]

Unknown to Milroy, others wrote Lincoln on his behalf; 268 citizens of Martinsburg, West Virginia, sent a petition to Lincoln in December 1863 hoping to have Milroy restored to command in the region. They informed Lincoln that since Milroy left western Virginia many of them had been driven from their homes, leaving personal items and loved ones behind "to the cold and cruel mercies of Rebel iron rule." The citizens of Martinsburg, many of whom were actually displaced Unionists from the lower Shenandoah Valley, implored Lincoln to restore Milroy to command. "We desire hereby to show that while Gen. R.H. Milroy was in command in this Valley of Va. we had the most flattering prospect of the speedy restoration of the rights and privileges of the loyal citizens in that section, and Rebels were taught the importance of obedience." The citizens of Martinsburg pleaded with Lincoln to have Milroy, "that noble, brave, and fearless chieftain be put in command of the forces intended to operate in the Valley of Va."[93]

While Milroy, the Indiana delegation in Congress, and Unionist citizens of the Shenandoah Valley and West Virginia attempted to secure a field command for the Gray Eagle, Milroy remained in Washington and did nothing more than write about his campaigns and continue his letter-writing campaign. Milroy's disgust grew each day and compounding his problems was financial crisis at home. Three days before Christmas, Mary Milroy wrote her husband simply: "I am out of money but find that the demands on my purse do not cease." On New Year's Eve she informed her husband to fight the irresistible urge to send the children presents and rather send money as she was already buying foodstuffs on credit. She also informed her husband about the numerous bills, for items of necessity, which had mounted.[94] Financial problems coupled with his increased pessimism about being able to obtain a field command chipped away at Milroy's resolve to remain in the army and sit idly while his fellow comrades in blue suppressed the rebellion. He wrote his wife in early February: "If I see there is no chance for a command when the spring campaign opens, I will quit & come home."[95]

The year 1864 provided Milroy with some hope for command when he discovered that Lincoln needed a commander for the Department of West Virginia. Milroy no doubt felt qualified for the post because he had previously served in the region and knew it well. Others too believed Milroy best for the command. Governor Francis H. Pierpont, the leader of the movement to break West Virginia away from Virginia, implored Lincoln during the second week of January to have Milroy restored to command in the region. Pierpont explained to Lincoln that "I know of no man who would be so acceptable to Union men and soldiers as Gen. Milroy in that section."[96] Regardless of the amount of people trying to help Milroy get a command in West Virginia, the Gray Eagle never had "a very strong hope that the wishes of the Legislature of W.Va and the Loyal citizens and soldiers expressed by joint resolutions, petitions, etc. would prevail to get me the [command] of that Department where I know the country so well."[97]

Milroy's pessimism proved true and he did not receive the command. Instead Lincoln selected German-born Maj. Gen. Franz Sigel for the post. Milroy accused Lincoln of appointing Sigel because the president did not want to lose the German vote in the November presidential election.[98] "Old Abe," Milroy wrote his wife, "became alarmed about losing the German vote, and without consulting the wishes of the people of W. Va., or the good of the service, appointed Sigel."[99] Indeed Milroy's criticisms may have been warranted. Sigel was a leader in the German-American community and commanded their respect. In order to win reelection in November 1864 Lincoln needed their votes and so despite a military record that by no means exceeded Milroy's, Sigel received the command.[100]

The monotony of life in the nation's capital was broken in late January when Milroy was summoned to Cumberland, Maryland, as a witness at the court-martial of Col. George Latham of the 2nd West Virginia Infantry.[101] When Milroy arrived in Cumberland he was reunited with men he commanded earlier in the war. The opportunity to get out of Washington could have only lifted Milroy's morale, but undoubtedly his spirits grew enormously after he received a warm reception from the citizens of Cumberland "who expressed the strongest wishes for my return to command in W. Va." Perhaps nothing boosted his spirits more than a special song created for Milroy and sung to him by members of the 9th West Virginia Infantry on February 2. Milroy listened intently as the regiment's "opera troop" serenaded him with: "And gallant Milroy — brave and true, We'll try again — for he will do, Hurra — Hurra, Just now his stars are somewhat slighted, But the soldiers hope he will soon be righted, Hurra-Hurra."[102]

On his return trip to Washington, D.C., Milroy stopped in Martinsburg where the citizens greeted him in a way that, Milroy wrote, "was sufficient to satisfy the vanity of a King."[103] He spent several days in Martinsburg and according to Milroy the civilians and soldiers "crowded to ... see me and when ever I appeared I received the most hearty greetings and cheers." During his time in Martinsburg Milroy, "furnished with a horse and escort of some 30 or 40 officers," visited the various regimental camps. This was a sort of homecoming for Milroy as many of the regiments he visited had previously been under his command. After each inspection Milroy made "a few remarks." As he departed the camps, the soldiers cheered him: "Old Gray Eagle ... we want you back!"[104] One of the officers Milroy visited during his trip to Martinsburg was an officer in the 12th Pennsylvania Cavalry. The officer thanked Milroy for all he had done for the defense of the Keystone State. "He desired to thank me for the gallant defence I had made at Winchester by which Lees army had been checked three days— He said that the Citizens of Harrisburg felt and believed that that check of three days saved their citizens from capture and plunder by the enemy, and their State Capitol from destruction." The officer concluded that Milroy's stand at Winchester enabled "Meade to intercept the Reb Army at Gettysburg which wouldn't have been done if they had not stopped so long at Winchester." The officer's kind words and reaffirmation, in Milroy's mind, that the Gray Eagle's decision to remain in Winchester aided the Army of the Potomac was "very gratifying to me," Milroy penned.[105] He returned to the nation's capital somewhat energized from the cheerful receptions at Cumberland and Martinsburg and continued his attempts to get a command.

With the letters to Lincoln yielding no results, Milroy decided on a different approach during March — requesting a command from the new commander of Union armies, General Grant. Two weeks after Grant received his commission to lieutenant general, Milroy begged Grant: "I most respectfully ask General, that you will try me — try me where there is danger and hard fighting to be done, and if I fail have me shot.... I will gladly perform any duty to which you assign me ... I would prefer a cavalry com[man]d."[106] Grant knew little about Milroy's ability to command cavalry so he sent a message to Gen. George Meade to see if Milroy would be suited for such a post. Meade did not know Milroy personally, but he knew of him from reports of the Second Battle of Winchester and the extremely negative and sometimes unfair newspaper accounts of his courage under fire. "I should not judge him qualified to command a division of cavalry," Meade replied to Grant.[107] Grant trusted Meade's evaluation and did not assign Milroy to any post.

Undoubtedly exhausted by his efforts to secure a field command, Milroy's situation grew worse as winter came to a close when he was informed that his pay would be cut by $100. Congress passed a law that any officer who was off duty for over six months would have his pay reduced. This cut in pay only gave Milroy more worries. His wife needed money to care for the children, he needed money to pay the lawyers who provided services connected with the court of inquiry, and to top it off Milroy loaned $460 to an officer in Washington who took off without paying him back one cent. "I was never so taken in by any man in my life." The unidentified officer was reportedly "recommended by Gen. Grant and many other high officers, but turned out to be an infamous swindler.... It has given me the Blues most horrible."[108]

Things appeared abysmal for Milroy as the spring campaign season approached. He had little money, no command, and hundreds of miles separated him from his family. As winter closed Milroy simply wrote: "What a miserable world."[109] However, after nearly 10 months of inactivity and setbacks it appeared that during the first week of May, Milroy's fortunes might change for the better and he would get another opportunity to command troops in the field. On May 6, the War Department ordered Milroy to report to Nashville, Tennessee, and Maj. Gen. George H. Thomas, commander of the Army of the Cumberland.[110] When Milroy arrived in Nashville on May 20 he learned that Thomas had moved into Georgia. Milroy boarded a train in Nashville and headed to Thomas' headquarters near Two Run Creek.[111] On his way to meet with Thomas, Milroy stopped at the headquarters of Maj. Gen. William T. Sherman. Even though he had specific orders to meet Thomas, Milroy hoped to implore Sherman to give him a command in the field. Sherman did not grant Milroy's wish. He then proceeded to Thomas' headquarters.

When Milroy arrived at Thomas' camp, the Gray Eagle pleaded with Thomas to give him a battlefield command, but Thomas denied it. Thomas wanted Milroy to organize new regiments coming into Tennessee. Milroy was saddened by the news, but he was not the only one. Other individuals from Milroy's native Indiana felt the same way. An anonymous letter dated May 12, 1864, written from Indiana, reminded President Lincoln that in the spring of 1864 there were three major generals in the Union service from Indiana and none of them had a field command. Gen. Lew Wallace commanded troops in Baltimore and Gen. Joseph Reynolds commanded troops in New Orleans. Milroy, of course being the third, had command of nothing. This anonymous writer explained to Lincoln: "The last great campaign of the Great Rebellion is in full operation. Indiana has in this campaign over 100,000 men in the *field,* but *not one* Major General."[112] The individual also reminded Lincoln that there were 10 major generals and one lieutenant general (Grant) from Lincoln's home state of Illinois. "We Hoosiers think you are not giving Indiana a fair shake," the mysterious writer penned.[113] What others believed would be just treatment for Milroy and his reputation did not matter. The Gray Eagle would need to put his desire for a battlefield command aside and marshal his energies to command troops in Tennessee — a state plagued by Confederate irregulars and deep-seated disloyalty to the United States.

7

"Spreading death and fire"

Despite Milroy's efforts and those of others to secure him a field command, Thomas ordered Milroy to take charge of Sub-District No. 1, responsible for the defense of the Nashville and Chattanooga Railroad. The Gray Eagle replaced Gen. Alpheus Williams, who left that command to seek a field command, the one thing that Milroy wanted badly, but could not have. To defend this stretch of nearly 150 miles Milroy would have "100 day regiments" under his command — troops who had been veterans and reenlisted for easier duty and a shorter stint of service, as well as raw recruits.[1] Thomas first ordered Milroy to organize the units and then divide them into two brigades and send one to Bridgeport, Alabama, and another to Tullahoma, Tennessee.[2] Milroy would make his headquarters in Tullahoma.

Although somewhat melancholy over not being able to obtain command of troops in the field, the Gray Eagle must have felt a little joyous over being given any command at all. As Milroy departed Thomas' headquarters in Georgia for Tennessee, Milroy learned that his old regiment — the 9th Indiana — was encamped near Cassville, Georgia.[3] He went to their camp and accepted an invitation by the regimental chaplain to speak at church services that same day. Milroy spoke to his former regiment for about half an hour. The men frequently interrupted his remarks with cheers. This display of affection could have only boosted Milroy's melancholy spirit.[4]

After visiting with the 9th Indiana, Milroy took a train back to Nashville. During the several-hour journey, Milroy gazed out over the ground that passed him by and found a once-beautiful landscape destroyed by the ravages of war. Ten months on the shelf had done nothing to calm Milroy's fiery abolitionist spirit and hatred of Confederates. He firmly believed that the carnage, death, and desolation that surrounded him in Tennessee were well deserved. Had it not been for the slaveholders, Milroy believed, there would have been no secession crisis and no war, and since they had done nothing to bring about an end to the South's peculiar institution the devastation was earned. "In this favored and beautiful portion of God's creation 'man alone is vile,'" Milroy explained to his wife. He continued: "He has most Cruely apprised his fellow man.... Slavery had poisoned and deadened that enterprise."[5]

After he arrived in Nashville, Milroy then made his way to Tullahoma. When he arrived there on June 7, Milroy found much of the same destruction as he had in the country around Nashville. "This town is a little larger than Rensselaer," Milroy explained, "it was the headquarters of the rebel army for some time after the battle of Murfreesboro and was the headquarters of our army a while and has been occupied by troops so much that like Winchester it is badly used up. A large portion of it has been burnt and is a very cheerless place."[6] While he would have preferred to serve in Virginia "where hills or mountains [were] in sight" he was stuck to his new role.[7]

When he arrived in Tennessee one of the first generals he encountered was Brig. Gen. Eleazer Paine. Milroy knew that Paine was a West Pointer and that probably the two would clash; however, the two personalities meshed nicely. After speaking with Paine, Milroy learned he held the same

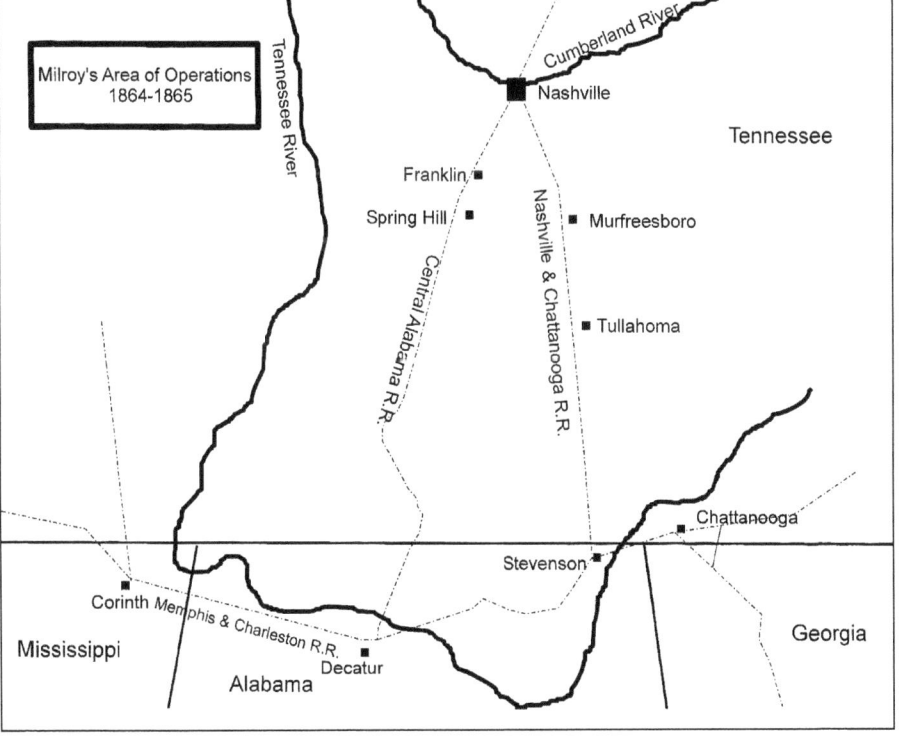

sort of disdain for many West Pointers that Milroy harbored. "I like Gen. Paine," Milroy informed his wife. He "is about my age — is a West Pointer but hates Halleck and West Pointers as generally as bad as I do. He says that Institution is a perfect hot head of aristocracy and is a curse to the nation and has dragged out and continued the war." Milroy identified with Paine. "He hates Halleck — Hates Slavery," Milroy explained, "and Treason and bushwhackers and guerillas." The Gray Eagle approved of Paine even more because he gave no quarter to Confederates — having many of them executed without a trial. Paine apparently also made it a regular practice to execute civilians at the mere suspicion of their being rebels. Of Paine's policies Milroy wrote: "He has had about 200 guerillas shot since he has been stationed here ... he orders [Confederate prisoners] quietly walked outside of the pickets and shot. I would not have known anything of it had I not happened on their dead bodies." Milroy, approvingly penned, "The Union citizens are greatly pleased with Paine's course and say he is the only man among the Union Generals who has done things right. No treatment of the Rebs is too severe and bloody for the Union citizens who have suffered so much." Milroy would follow similar guidelines for dealing with Confederates.[8]

In Tennessee Milroy had to perform the role of occupier and protector of Unionists — a task with which he was accustomed. During his first several weeks in Tennessee Milroy spent some time organizing his forces and touring the defenses along the Nashville & Chattanooga Railroad. Additionally he occupied his time touring battlefields in Tennessee. In early July he toured the Stones River battlefield with one of his subordinates, Brig. Gen. Horatio Van Cleve — a man Milroy described as "an excellent old man, and very pious and a West Pointer."[9]

In Tennessee Milroy confronted problems that he had dealt with in Virginia — disloyal citizens and Confederate guerillas. Milroy had a number of troops under his command to deal with these problems. The initial regiments he commanded were from Indiana, but as enlistments expired, new infantry would be rotated on a fairly regular basis.[10] Although the problems he confronted were the same as they had been in Virginia, the troops with which he had to deal with those problems were dissimilar, particularly his cavalry. The Tennessee troops under his command were rowdy and undoubtedly reminded him of the German immigrants who fought in the Union army in the Shenandoah Valley during the spring of 1862. "They are [a] wild, half civilized set of devils.... Most of the officers and nearly all the men get drunk — they have no discipline and do about as they please.... They ... rob, plunder and steal like a band of robbers." The Tennessee ruffians created some real problems for Milroy as at least on one occasion

Milroy and his staff atop Lookout Mountain, Tennessee, in the summer of 1864. Milroy is seated at right (Jasper County Public Library, Rensselaer, Indiana).

in June a group of drunken Tennesseans opened fire on Union infantry pickets, who returned fire. Fortunately no one was hurt during the friendly fire incident.[11] Despite their constant unruly behavior Milroy did little to restrain them because, as he explained to his wife, "they fight pretty well."[12]

The reason that they fought so well and were branded by Milroy as "splendid guerilla hunters" was because for them fighting bushwhackers was personal. Many of the Tennessee horsemen had family and friends who had suffered death and destruction at the hands of Confederate partisans. The Tennessee cavalry that Milroy had under his control treated captured Confederates boorishly — just as they had treated Union soldiers and civilians. Milroy explained to his wife, "Most of my Tennessee troops are refugees who have been driven from their homes, and all have wrongs to avenge so they take no prisoners."[13] Retribution and the black flag were Milroy's policy in Tennessee as he confessed: "No treatment of the Rebs is too severe and bloody for the Union citizens who have suffered so much."[14] Milroy turned a blind eye to his cavalry executing Confederate guerillas.

"This suits me exactly and they know it so I never see any guerrilla prisoners and frequently hear of them being killed and see their horses and arms."[15]

While Milroy undoubtedly turned a blind eye to the treatment of Confederate prisoners because he believed that they deserved it, he may have also done so for another reason — he did not want this command and wanted to be in the field. At the end of July, Milroy became disgusted with his situation and began another campaign to secure a field command from General Thomas. "I desire respectfully to remind you that I have not seen no flash or heard the sound of a hostile gun for near fourteen months," Milroy explained to Thomas. He continued, "I had been almost constantly in front and that sight and sound was my pleasure and my music. But without fault of mine I have been exiled from the front and condemned to inglorious *rear* service."[16] When Milroy closed the letter he made one last plea with Thomas and told him that he would take command in the field even with a lesser rank. "I will gladly waive any question of rank," Milroy implored Thomas in desperation, "and take any command you can give me if it is in front."[17]

The desperate plea fell on deaf ears and Thomas would not hear of it. Dejected, Milroy explained to his wife in August that "I see no prospect of being sent to the front or getting more honorable service. I am very sick of this lifeless monotonous service."[18] Milroy truly believed that his services could be better rendered, if not on the battlefield, in fighting copperheads in Indiana — people who were deemed disloyal to the Union and tried to block the Lincoln administration — than by remaining in command of the line of the Nashville & Chattanooga Railroad. [19]

Despite his failed attempt to convince Thomas to give him a better command, once again, Milroy would not relent to secure a more "honorable" assignment. In mid-September he petitioned General Sherman for command of troops on the front lines. Milroy heard rumors that Sherman was about to reorganize his command and Milroy deemed this a perfect opportunity to get back into the field. "From what I hear," Milroy penned Sherman, "you will soon reorganize your armies to some extent. If such should be the case, I respectfully ask that I may not be overlooked." Milroy firmly believed that his command in Tennessee was punishment and he informed Sherman, "I think I have done penance long enough in the rear to atone for all the sins of myself and masters.... The scattering R.R. guard I now command is barely a respectable [command] for a Brigadier. The R.R. is safe within the limits of my [command] and I am not needed here."[20]

After making his opening plea Milroy reminded Sherman that an active field command was the only way Milroy could restore his reputation which had been damaged at Winchester. "But having been educated as a soldier and seen some service in Mexico and since the beginning of the present war as a soldier," Milroy penned Sherman, "what little reputation I have as such is dear to me and I have some pride of character. My reputation has been blurred and blackened and my pride of character deeply wounded by a most unjust and causeless arrest."[21] Clearly Milroy's desire to have a field command was twofold: to be back in action, but also to have a chance to redeem his reputation that was greatly tarnished by the Second Battle of Winchester. "Give me a com[man]d in front," Milroy pleaded, "where I can have opportunity to wipe out to some extent the stigma of that arrest."[22] And just as he had done in his plea to General Thomas, Milroy informed Sherman that he would take a field command at a lesser rank.

After receiving no satisfaction from Sherman—who at the time was occupied in Georgia—Milroy sought the aid of President Lincoln. On September 22, one week after he wrote Sherman, Milroy sent a packet of letters to Lincoln. The documents were copies of all of Milroy's requests for a field command. He had written nearly a dozen generals, all of whom rejected his plea.[23] The "ring is closed against me," Milroy explained to Lincoln, "hopelessly unless you will open it ... after being kept in mortifying exile from duty for one year, as if found guilty, I was given an obscure scattered command ... where I can have no opportunity of doing anything towards wishing out the foul stigma of that arrest."[24] Four days later Milroy petitioned Lincoln again, this time for a command of troops in Texas. Milroy cited his brief stint as a citizen of the Texas Republic and knowledge of the geography as primary reasons why he would be a good candidate for such a post. He also reminded Lincoln that his current position guarding the Nashville & Chattanooga Railroad was a position unfit for a major general and could be "performed by a Brigadier, a Colonel, or even by an Inspecting Officer." Furthermore Milroy believed that if he was sent to Texas and given "permission to enlist white and colored troops there, I can in a short time reduce that state back to its former allegiance to the United States."[25]

Again the plea fell on deaf ears as Lincoln was more concerned with military operations and the upcoming election. Perhaps General Thomas best summed up the reason why so many generals refused to give Milroy a field command: "I regret that I cannot comply with your request to be assigned to a command in this army without by so doing, committing injustice to competent and worthy officers who by long service in the army deserve what advancement the incidents of the service may give them."[26]

Despite another active letter-writing campaign Milroy could not focus his attention solely on getting a better command as he had done in the 10 months following Second Winchester. He had command responsibilities and should he fail to carry them out he would lose that command and any hope of future advancement. Problems confronted him on a daily basis from dealing with Confederate partisans, disloyal civilians, and large numbers of former slaves seeking refuge behind Union lines.

Milroy dealt with former slaves in the same manner he had in Rappahannock County, Virginia, in 1862 and the Shenandoah Valley in 1863 — he treated them well, but put them to work. Freedmen found work in the quartermaster's department, railroad repair, lumber mills, and a host of other tasks including body servants to Union officers. Kind treatment, meals, and some security would not be enough for many of these former slaves. Although they had many wants and desires their largest demand and perhaps the most important was locating family and loved ones, especially their children. The freedmen were frightened at the prospect of returning to their former masters alone to claim their children. As a result Milroy received "daily applications from them to send for their children that they could not get away with them and they are afraid to go back for them."[27] Milroy recognized their heartache and created a special entity to deal with the issue of locating families.

Dealing with runaways was no easy task, but it paled in comparison to contending with disloyal civilians and Confederate guerillas. Among Milroy's nemeses in Tennessee was Robert Buchanan Blackwell — better known as "Capt. Bob Blackwell." Blackwell's boorish treatment of Union prisoners and Unionists was horrid.[28] Constant raids and executions by Blackwell's men infuriated Milroy. While news of Blackwell's activities enraged Milroy, perhaps no other episode incensed the Gray Eagle more than the execution of 10 Unionists — members of the Home Guard (Unionists who aided Federal soldiers in dealing with Confederate guerillas and helped in protecting local communities from raids) — executed by Blackwell in late September.[29] When word of the horrific act reached Milroy, he petitioned General Thomas for an immediate and proportional response. "Ten of the home guards captured at Shelbyville," Milroy reported to Thomas, "were taken out and near Fayetteville shot in cold blood." Milroy firmly believed that the event was unprovoked — yet in all fairness the same sort of horrid treatment was being conducted by both sides with Milroy turning a blind eye to the actions of his Tennessee cavalrymen — and that it should be answered by a "terrible retribution."[30] Milroy believed that capturing Blackwell's wife and all of the "secesh women" of Shelbyville, sending them through Confederate lines, and burning Blackwell's house would be an adequate response.[31]

As Milroy prepared to carry out his act of exile, as he had done so often in Winchester, he received a letter from four Tennessee Unionists.

The letter implored Milroy to not treat Mrs. Blackwell poorly and destroy her house because she apparently did not approve of her husband's actions. While at first glance it may appear that these Unionists defended Mrs. Blackwell on those grounds alone, they may have done so for another reason — fear of reprisal against their property and families by Confederates should Milroy carry out the order. Commonly Unionists throughout the South defended secessionists not because they were friendly with them or wanted to do the right thing; rather they believed that in times of a raid or Confederate occupation their properties and lives would be spared for having aided in the protection of Confederates during Federal occupations. Also, defending Confederate sympathizers was a means by which many Unionists ensured that should they ever be captured or be found in a similar situation, their Confederate neighbors would come to their aid.[32] Sometimes this worked and other times it did not, but doing nothing assured their demise at the hands of Confederate occupiers.

Undoubtedly knowing of Milroy's reputation, Mrs. Blackwell feared that he in fact might carry out the order, despite the support of local Unionists. Blackwell's wife and two children were sent through Union lines.[33] Blackwell continued to hamper Union efforts in the region for the remainder of the war. Even though Milroy failed to capture Blackwell, he did have a response for Blackwell's incessant activities aside from exile or execution. Harkening back to his days as commander of the Cheat Mountain Division in 1862, Milroy placed the burden of guerilla activity on the region's Confederate civilians. For each act of destruction or plunder Milroy assessed the area's Confederate sympathizers for the cost of the lost property. As he had in 1862, Milroy believed this would spur Confederate sympathizers to force partisans to halt their activities. It did not. Nonetheless Milroy actively pursued his reparation policy. His staff created a list of pro–Confederates and every time a Unionist had something taken away, the people on the list were held liable for the losses. As if to add insult to injury he also ordered that freedmen in the area should have their homes rebuilt, if damaged (by anything, not just Confederates), and the costs covered by local Confederates.[34]

Although Milroy longed for a field command, he had plenty to keep him busy. Part of his role as commander of Sub-District No. 1 was to prevent the formation of new units for Confederate service. In October, Milroy learned from scouts that nearly 200 men had formed three companies for Confederate service in Lincoln County. Wanting to thwart the companies before they created any havoc on Union forces in the area, Milroy deployed the 5th Tennessee Cavalry to Lincoln County to confirm the reports. When the horsemen corroborated the reports, Milroy gathered as much cavalry as he could spare and he also asked General Thomas to be allowed to send a "colored regiment" to aid in clearing out any Confederate recruits. Thomas agreed.[35]

Continually Milroy dealt with curbing the actions of new Confederate units and had to do everything in his power to break them up. As October closed Milroy petitioned his superiors for a leave of absence to return home to Indiana to vote in the November presidential election. He wanted to cast a ballot for Lincoln, but unfortunately the leave of absence came too late.[36] As November dawned Confederate activity increased in the region and Milroy would soon be commanding troops on the battlefield and would have an opportunity to redeem his reputation, forever tarnished at Winchester.

On November 22, nearly 40,000 Confederates under Gen. John Bell Hood marched into Tennessee from Alabama. Hood hoped to draw attention away from Sherman's operations in Georgia and to cripple the Union supply base in Tennessee. Hood's command marched north toward Franklin. On November 30, Hood's command engaged Maj. Gen. John M. Schofield's IV and XXIII corps. The fight had lasted all day and into the night. Shortly after midnight Schofield's army withdrew from the field, 18 miles north to Nashville to combine forces with Thomas. Although Hood claimed a tactical victory it was anything but, with more than 6,000 of his men killed and wounded. Sensing an opportunity after Franklin, Hood's Confederates pushed north to Nashville.[37]

After Franklin, Thomas, at Grant's urging, concentrated his forces so that they could protect Nashville and the supply bases in the region. Thomas ordered Milroy from Tullahoma to Murfreesboro on November 30 to help protect Fortress Rosecrans—a major supply depot and the largest Union fortress constructed during the war.[38] On the

Maj. Gen. Lovell Rousseau, a Kentucky native and successful lawyer before the Civil War, was Milroy's superior in Tennessee. After Milroy's victory near Murfreesboro in December 1864, Rousseau heaped praise on the Gray Eagle (*Battles and Leaders*).

march from Tullahoma to Murfreesboro Milroy's command, about 3,000 strong, faced minor opposition from a few bushwhackers who caused little damage to Milroy's column.[39] Milroy's men arrived in Murfreesboro on December 1 and combined forces with Maj. Gen. Lovell H. Rousseau. Rousseau's force of 8,000 had explicit orders from Thomas to do everything humanly possible to hold on to Murfreesboro.[40]

With Hood's army on the move, Rousseau's command around Murfreesboro on the Nashville & Chattanooga Railroad needed to keep in constant communication with Thomas in Nashville. On December 2, Hood's men severed the telegraph lines and Rousseau was left without any instructions from his superiors. The Federals in Murfreesboro and troops posted along the Nashville & Chattanooga Railroad kept a keen eye for Confederate movement.

The first signs of a Confederate advance came on December 4, when Maj. Gen. William B. Bate's division approached the railroad blockhouse at Overall's Creek, four and a half miles north of Murfreesboro. Bate initially met token resistance as he burned the blockhouses. Rousseau learned of Bate's actions and deployed Milroy with three infantry regiments and a section of artillery to drive off the division. Milroy had the opportunity he had waited for since his defeat at Winchester — a chance to command troops in battle and restore dignity to his reputation. The sun was beginning to set as Milroy's detachment of nearly 1,000 men reached Overall's Creek. He knew little of Bate's strength. When he arrived on the field he encountered the 13th Indiana Cavalry which had been deployed to Overall's Creek earlier in the day to investigate firing heard north of Murfreesboro. Immediately upon reaching the hot spot Milroy ordered the Hoosier horsemen to charge three enemy cannon. Obediently they surged forward. Confederate canister tore the command apart and now Milroy would have to rely on his infantry and artillery to break the resistance. His infantry plunged into the fight "furiously" and pushed the enemy from the field.[41] When the fight was over Milroy learned from 20 captured Confederates that he in fact had defeated Bate's division, about 3,000 strong. Better judgment prevailed after the sharp skirmish and Milroy did not pursue; instead he withdrew to the secure confines of Fortress Rosecrans.[42]

While Milroy reveled in his small victory, Bate joined forces with Maj. Gen. Nathan Bedford Forrest. Hood initially ordered Bate to move toward Nashville, but when Forrest arrived Hood altered the plan. Hood now wanted the two to combine forces and go on the offensive against Murfreesboro, drive the Federals from their position, and wreak havoc on the railroad. In order to damage the railroad successfully and carry out Hood's scheme Forrest knew Rosecrans had to be silenced, otherwise the Confederates would make easy targets for the 57 guns in the stronghold and the rifled muskets of the 8,000-man garrison.[43] Forrest knew that if they were going to have any success they needed to coax the Federals out of the fort and onto open ground.

On December 6, Confederate forces constructed breastworks of logs and earth across Wilkinson Pike, several miles northwest of Fortress Rosecrans. Rousseau knew that a sizable Confederate force roamed somewhere north of Murfreesboro, but he did not know precisely where. Rousseau deployed Milroy with seven infantry regiments, one artillery battery, and a cavalry detachment—a force that exceeded 3,000—to reconnoiter the enemy's position.[44] Milroy's command moved out around 8:00 A.M. on December 7.[45]

Confederate Maj. Gen. William B. Bate, a Tennessee native, lawyer, and Mexican War veteran, fought against Milroy at the action near Murfreesboro on December 7, 1864. Milroy's victory over Bate did little to improve the Gray Eagle's reputation, tarnished at Second Winchester (*Battles and Leaders*).

Forrest lured the Federals out of Rosecrans, but now he had to entice them to attack. Milroy never shirked from engaging the enemy. After several hours of marching, Milroy learned from the wife of a Mr. Spence, a local farmer, the complete disposition of the Confederate troops. She informed Milroy that Confederate cavalry was near Salem, and that troops under Generals Forrest and Bate were in position astride the Wilkinson Pike. Milroy deemed it best to strike Forrest and Bate.[46] Before he turned his column to the north he ordered one company to take "a drove of sixty fine, fat hogs," as Milroy feared they "would have fallen into the hands of rebels if left."[47]

When he first viewed the enemy position Milroy ordered his men to strike, but the attack failed. Furthermore Milroy's artillery and a Confederate battery exchanged shots for nearly an hour. The Federal artillery exhausted its ammunition while

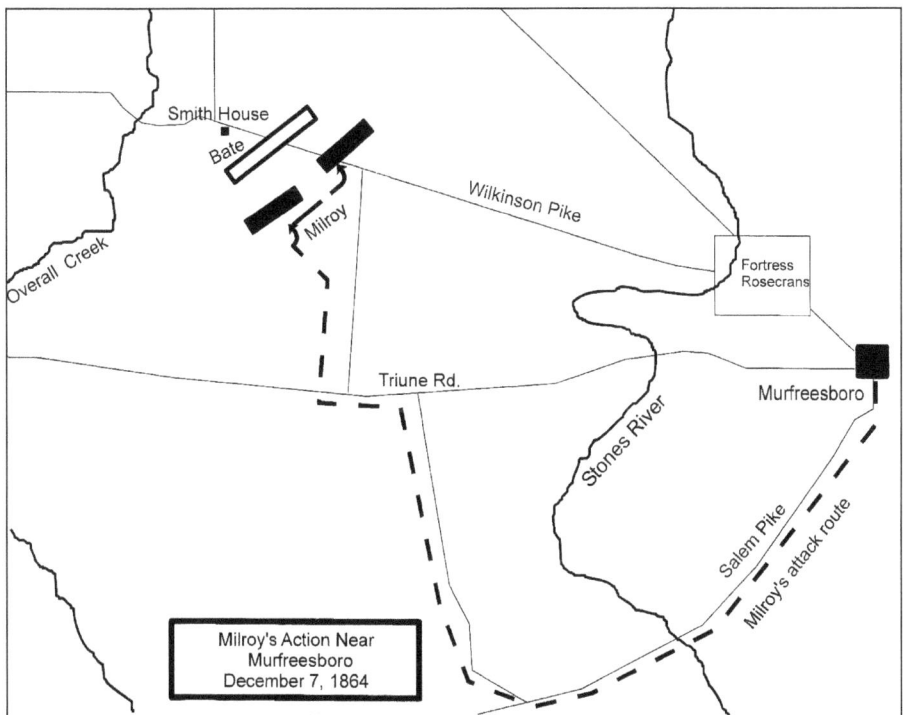

Milroy's Action Near Murfreesboro
December 7, 1864

the Confederate guns had some impact on Milroy's force. Reassessing the situation, Milroy decided it best to move his command to a position between the Confederates and Rosecrans—all the while making sure that the fortress was at his rear so that he could receive support from it.[48]

During the afternoon Milroy repositioned his troops, which placed them beyond the left flank of Forrest and Bate. When Milroy launched the attack the Confederates were caught completely by surprise and unable to organize any marked resistance. In a fight that lasted about half an hour Milroy's men drove them from the field. By 6:00 P.M. the engagement ended and Milroy had won.[49] No doubt joyous over the victory, Milroy's superior, Rousseau, penned his report of the fight: "The rout was complete, infantry and cavalry running in every direction. The fight was well-conducted by Major-General Milroy and the troops behaved most gallantly."[50]

Following the fight Milroy pursued his foe for approximately two miles, but darkness and the presence of another Confederate division compelled Milroy to withdraw to Murfreesboro. Milroy's men captured 207 soldiers, among them 30 officers. His men also seized two Confederate cannons. While no accurate numbers exist of Confederate dead and wounded from the battle, scores undoubtedly fell. Although it has the potential to be slightly embellished Milroy's letter to his wife after the engagement stated that his men killed a "large number among whom were two Cols."[51] The Federals too suffered casualties—25 killed and 187 wounded.[52] Some northern newspapers presented Milroy's role in the battle as nothing but heroic. The *Delhi Journal*, an Ohio newspaper, praised Milroy's action in the battle, stating that he led the charge and that Milroy "was the first man at the guns. His tall form and snowy head towered conspicuously in the fight, and his voice continually urged the men to redouble valor. He seemed inspired with the very genius of valor, and mindful only of defeating the enemy."[53] In the days that followed the fight, Milroy had the occasion to scrape with Forrest on Dec. 14 and 15 when he commanded a foraging party. Both times Milroy boasted to his wife that he "licked" Forrest.[54]

Milroy certainly enjoyed his time in combat, but it would be his last. Aside from small skirmishes with the enemy on foraging expeditions Milroy would never again see major action on the battlefield again. Milroy watched as Union forces defeated Hood's command at Nashville on December 15. In the wake of that defeat, the Confederate Army of Tennessee withdrew from the Volunteer State. With the threat of Confederate attack gone, Milroy returned to his previous post in Tullahoma.

Upon his return to Tullahoma the excitement of battle waned and he again dropped into a sense of bitterness at his position and reviled the people who had put him in this post—namely Halleck. Milroy truly believed that there was a conspiracy against him by the "West Point aristocracy." He felt that his popularity with the troops especially had made West Pointers view him "as a trespasser upon their special rights and the baleful eyes of the infamous Halleck were fixed on me." Every opportunity that Milroy had to gain fame on the battlefield, he believed, was squandered by West Pointers. "What little reputation I have acquired, is so small, so insignificant," he lamented to his wife on New Years Day 1865, "in comparison to what it would have been, had I been fairly delt [sic] by and justly treated, that I regard it as nothing—almost with contempt. I feel entirely hopeless and redress any of my wrongs."[55] That same day he confided to the pages of his diary: "I am ostracized from regular command and from all fields when laurels are or may be harvested. The infamous scoundrel Halleck knocked me out of the ring of all active and honorable service by most unjustly and brutally placing me in arrest and all the balance of the West Point tribe in high position, have assisted me in keeping me out." He even vented some anger against President Lincoln: "and the weak Lincoln, though acknowledging my merits and the injustice done me, only pities my case and is too cowardly to order any reparation of my great wrongs."[56]

While West Point animosity to Milroy may have existed on some level, it was never wholly apparent and was something that Milroy created in his own mind. Nonetheless the commands he held and the campaigns he was involved in, aside from his early days in western Virginia, were unsuccessful—partly because of the command choices of his superiors, but partly because of some of the decisions that he made on the field.

Regardless of his bitterness and perceived conspiracy of West Pointers against him, Milroy had a role to perform following his victory at Murfreesboro and he knew it. With the dawn of 1865 Milroy intensified his efforts to establish Home Guards around Tullahoma. Home Guards had been present in Tennessee since mid-September 1863, when Maj. Gen. Stephen A. Hurlburt authorized them as a means of dealing with Confederate guerillas, and Milroy in 1864 and 1865 used them to his advantage. Milroy had some experience with Home Guards as he attempted to organize a unit from loyal citizens of Frederick and Shenandoah counties in Virginia in 1863, but the size and success of the Home Guards in Tennessee towered above any Milroy presided over in Virginia.

The Home Guards around Tullahoma were extremely active during the war. They constantly dealt with Confederate bushwhackers and seized property from Confederate sympathizers. The fact that the Home Guards were native Unionists of the area made them huge targets for Confederate guerillas. Life expectancy was considerably shorter for Home Guard members, particularly for officers. Confederate bushwhackers not only targeted the leaders of the Home Guards and their men, but their families as well. Despite their role some viewed Home Guards as brutal and felt they ought to be disbanded. Some Union commanders, particularly in 1864, felt they were vital to neutralizing Confederates in the area.[57] Chief among the supporters was Milroy.

Constantly Milroy complained about the "brutal Murders by bushwhackers" which occurred on almost a daily basis.[58] By early 1865 Milroy believed he had developed a plan for dealing with "bushwhackers, horse thieves, and other lawless men." "I have fell on a plan," Milroy penned his wife, "to stir up the people against these monsters and to pitch in and help us clean the country out. Blood and fire is the medicine I use."[59] He continued in his explanation of military policy: "I shoot the men who are friendly with and harbour the bushwhackers and burn their houses. By spreading death and fire in a neighborhood where the bushwhackers have [a] friend, the survivors come rushing in demanding in terror 'What shall we do to be saved?' I tell them to organize companies." Milroy explained further to his wife in February 1865 that he told the frightened Unionists to "get guns—horse clubs or anything else and rush out after the bushwhackers—kill or capture them."[60]

This policy of blood and fire was Milroy's argument for the purpose of a Home Guard. He firmly believed in empowering area Unionists to deal with the enemy as the locals knew "where the hiding places and paths of the bushwhackers are."[61] On February 1, 1865, he issued a circular to citizens in eight Tennessee counties and one in Alabama ordering the creation of Home Guards. "All male residents from the age of fourteen years and upwards ... shall ... organize themselves into Home Guard Companies ... for the purpose of exterminating and driving out all Bushwhackers, Horse Thieves and other lawless Men and restoring law and order."[62] No male over the age of 14 was exempt from this conscription regardless of "age, infirmity or occupation." Everyone who fell into that broad category had something to offer in dealing with bushwhackers. "Those incapacitated from age, disease, or being cripples," Milroy ordered, "can give their influence, counsel, advice, send information, &c, &c."[63] Obviously Milroy did not expect cripples to take arms and fight Confederate sympathizers; only those who were able-bodied would actually take to the field in time of need. He did expect anyone who could not carry a rifle to alert him to any Confederate activity. Anyone who was infirmed and did not comply with this order, Milroy warned, would be "considered disloyal and treated accordingly."[64] Furthermore Milroy ordered that "Each neighborhood failing or refusing to organize a company within ten days after receiving or hearing of this order will be considered disloyal." Milroy believed correctly that the war was on the decline in early 1865 and that every bit of extra pressure on the Confederates would help bring the war to an end. "The time having come for all men to take sides," Milroy proclaimed, "and either show themselves [to be] active friends of the Union and of law and order, or openly join the enemy, inaction on the part of any one will be no longer tolerated."[65]

The companies organized in the weeks after he issued the order, and although Milroy was pleased to see area Unionists taking arms to defend themselves and protect their communities he must have approached this with a bit of trepidation because ultimately Milroy did not know who could be trusted. He recognized this shortcoming of the Home Guards and ordered that all company commanders had to first be approved by him.[66] In order to be confirmed, Milroy needed testimonials from loyal citizens that he knew and trusted.[67] Under Milroy's reign several Home Guard companies were organized and operated with a limited degree of success.[68] The Gray Eagle truly believed that these units would be the best defense against the enemy.[69]

While the Home Guards dealt with area Confederates, Milroy did not rely on them solely for the defense of his area. Patrols went out on a regular basis to hunt down bushwhackers and bring them to "justice." During the first half of February, for example, some of Milroy's Wisconsin troops seized two Confederate bushwhackers and brought them before Milroy. The two men that the Wisconsin soldiers seized had apparently been guilty of a number of crimes, but the most recent was the brutal murder of "two negroes after whipping them nearly to death mostly because they had been working for the Yankees."[70] Without any court, Milroy, the former judge and lawyer, wanted to hang both men at a public execution. Gallows were erected near the outskirts of Tullahoma and before an audience of 1,000 soldiers and scores of civilians Milroy wanted to execute the two lawless men. As the men stood atop the gallows and made speeches and bade their farewells Milroy received a dispatch from General Rousseau — to try the two men by military commission. "This was a great disappointment, especially to my Missouri troops, who are the greatest enemies to bushwhackers I have ever met," Milroy confessed to his wife. While it is unclear what happened to the two men, more than likely they were executed. "I can easily prove the villains guilty," Milroy wrote, "and will have the pleasure of hanging them yet."[71]

Duties in Tennessee did not detract from Milroy's ultimate objective as a soldier — to obtain a field command and clear his name. In February Milroy implored Secretary of War Stanton for command of African American troops. He implored Stanton: "I respectfully ask that a corps be organized of colored troops now in service, to which I may be assigned the command." Milroy recognized that there might be limitations on the amount of black troops in service and explained to Stanton: "If this is inexpedient, I would respectfully ask that a division of Colored Troops now in service be organized to which I may be assigned with the permission to recruit and organize two other Divisions." Although he did not explicitly state it in his communiqué to Stanton, one of the underlying motivations behind corps command would have been to get back into the field. Milroy probably knew full well that as the spring campaign season approached that an entire corps would not remain idle. Milroy did, however, give two explicit reasons why Stanton ought to grant the request. "First that Colored Troops," Milroy explained, "when properly disciplined and officered will fight as well as the best disciplined white troops." While his motives were good to prove that African American troops could fight, by February 1865 regiments of African Americans had proved themselves time and again on the battlefield as worthy soldiers. The second reason that Milroy felt he ought to be granted such a command was that it would give him the opportunity to prove that he was worthy of his rank of major general. Though "my education both civil and military was obtained at my own expense, and though left out of the ring of active service for near two years," Milroy wrote to Stanton, "I am not unworthy of my present rank."⁷² As the requests had scores of times before, this one too fell on deaf ears.

Although unable to get the field command that he hoped would redeem his reputation forever tarnished at Winchester (apparently he did not believe that his victory near Murfreesboro achieved redemption of his reputation), Milroy received a slight boost to his morale on February 22 when the citizens of Bedford County, Tennessee, presented him a splendid sword. The ceremony took place in Shelbyville and William H. Wisener presented the gift on behalf of the county's citizens. The gift was given to Milroy not only in commemoration of his victory near Murfreesboro the previous December, but in gratitude for the attempts that Milroy made to help area Unionists. Wisener's presentation speech could have only lifted Milroy's spirits. The Tennessee lawyer and Unionist opened his remarks: "It is my pleasant duty to present to you a memento...." The attorney recounted Milroy's earlier military service and patriotism: "When this rebellion broke out you were among the first to volunteer in defence of the country against domestic enemies in its mighty struggle for life, as you have been in former times

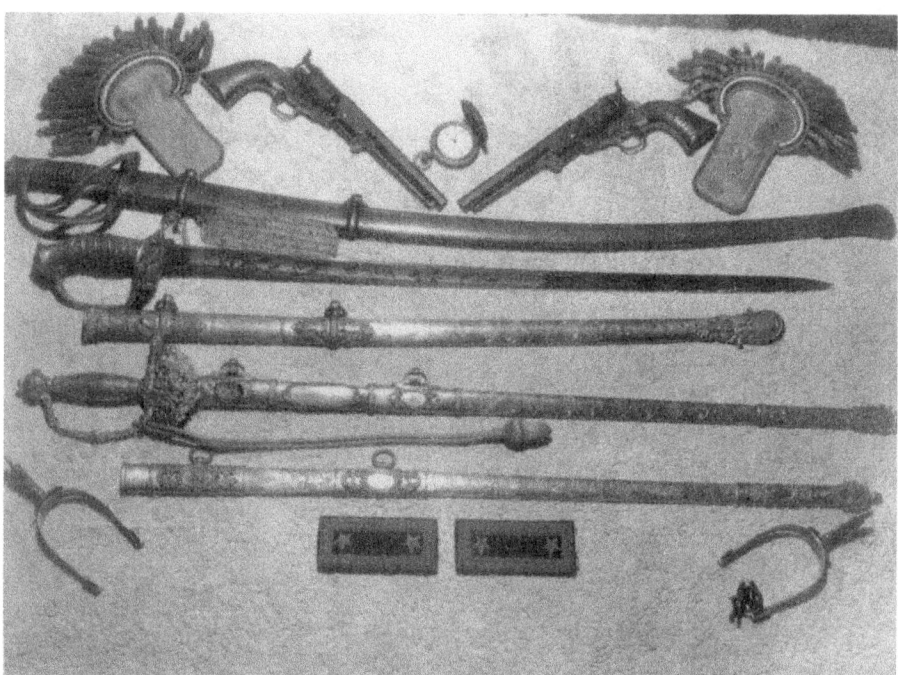

A collection of Milroy items: two presentation swords, a cavalry saber, two Colt revolvers, a pocket watch, spurs, epaulettes, and Milroy's major general shoulder straps (Jasper County Public Library, Rensselaer, Indiana).

in a war for National rights, with a foreign foe.... It is, perhaps, the most gigantic Civil War the World has ever witnessed." Wisener boosted Milroy's spirits further when he proclaimed: "In this mighty combat you have acted as a conspicuous part. By your gallantry in the field, you have won the admiration of this vast assemblage of your fellow citizens to whom, when this war commenced, you were a stranger ... you came among us, personally unknown to most of our countrymen ... but you have won imperishable renown." The presenter also made every effort to provide a glorious summary of Milroy's fight near Murfreesboro. "In the struggle around Murfreesboro ... where many who are joining in this ovation witnessed your gallantry, in the midst of danger there you were to be found, leading your brave troops to glory and victory." Inscribed on the sword's scabbard were the dates December 4 and 7, 1864, commemorating his action near Murfreesboro, as well as "Presented to Major General Milroy by the Union Citizens of Bedford County." The sword blade bore the inscription "Be Just and Fear Not." Wisener explained that this phrase was emblazoned on the sword "because it was in accordance with your past life. That you will 'be just,' they have the guarantee of a life devoted to principle. That in the execution of dangerous enterprises you will 'fear not,' they have been the assurance of a long, faithful and gallant service."[73]

Flattered by the presentation and kind words Milroy responded to the address: "I accept this beautiful badge of military authority and emblem of war [from] ... the patriotic citizens of Shelbyville and Bedford County, a County that has stood out like an oasis in the desert amid the dark tide of treason that swept into Middle Tennessee."[74] After thanking them for the elaborate gift, Milroy then took the opportunity to praise them, on the occasion of George Washington's birthday, that through the ballot box the loyal people of Tennessee had repudiated the act of secession and committed themselves to eliminating "that blighted, burning, degrading, disturbing curse, *Human Slavery*—the root cause of the rebellion."[75]

After thanking the citizens for the presentation sword he went off on a tangent exhibiting his disgust at his present command situation. "Very far from choice," Milroy told the crowd, "I am chained to a railroad, passing through your country as the commander of its stationary defences, and but few opportunities have been permitted me in your State, of meeting the armed enemies of our Government in the field."[76] He closed his remarks by telling the onlookers that the sword would be among his most valued possessions. "This sword," Milroy proclaimed, "your generous gift though obtained from me without price, shall ever be considered priceless, and be handed down as an heirloom to my children and posterity as a memento to them of Tennessee loyalty during the great Rebellion, and to teach them to love and venerate the Union."[77]

Feeling somewhat empowered after this event, Milroy made what appears to be his final plea for a field command. On March 15, 1865, Milroy wrote to Lincoln and asked him once again for a respectable post fitting to a major general. While he confided to his diary that Lincoln was weak and "though acknowledging my merits and the injustice done me, only pities my case and is too cowardly to order my reparation of my great wrongs," Milroy knew that as the Civil War neared an end Lincoln was his last hope to secure a field command and one last opportunity to bring "pride" to his "posterity."[78] "I feel very sure that had I been continued in the field and had fair play," Milroy penned Lincoln, "that I would have long since convinced your Excellency and the country that you made no mistake in elevating me to my present rank."[79] Milroy fervently believed that he deserved a command in the field because he had proved himself on it. True, Milroy had failures in the field, but no more than hosts of other Union generals. Experience, Milroy believed, was essential, and that should tower above any military education. Again conjuring this notion of West Point prejudice against him Milroy explained to the president: "Though had my education been attained at that place [West Point] I would have had no trouble in military matters, and like Grant, Sherman, Canby, Thomas, and others of that school have had, by acknowledged merit a position."[80] He continued his lamentation, "but history and my experience in this war, have proved to me the truth, that books and schools cannot make Generals, no more than they can Blacksmiths and Carpenters. Generals must learn their trade in the field, as the mechanic must at the anvil and the bench."[81]

While Milroy waited for Lincoln's reply, he noticed that the war was winding down and began to focus some of his attention on creating a postwar career. Six days after he wrote to Lincoln, Milroy organized the "Great South Western Oil and Mining Co." as he wanted to "try his luck in that business" when the war was over.[82] Despite any excitement he had over his future business endeavor, Milroy still had to make sure that he fulfilled his military duties. He continued to send out patrols throughout the spring to deal with bushwhackers, but preeminent on his mind was securing something worthwhile to do after the war ended.

Ten days after he made preliminary plans to organize an oil and mining company Milroy sent a letter to Don Matia Romero, Mexican minister to the United States. In the communiqué Milroy asked permission to correspond with him in the eventual hopes that Milroy at some point could be of some military assistance, either in combat or as an advisor, to help the Mexican government under President Benito Juárez — referred to by many as the "Abraham Lincoln of Mexico" — drive out the French army sent there by Napoleon III and depose the French-appointed Archduke Maximilian of Austria as the ruler of Mexico.

In his initial correspondence Milroy wrote that he wanted to help "our sister Republic, Mexico, now struggling against the efforts of a foreign invader to place the shackles of despotism on her."[83] Furthermore Milroy probably initiated the correspondence because he knew that as the war wound down and tensions heated in Mexico the United States might be forced to intervene on behalf of the Monroe Doctrine. "The triumph of Freedom," Milroy explained, "and the fast approaching peace in the United States, will soon disband our vast armies, and your brave patriotic President Juarez, can then have all the help he wants in driving out the invaders of Mexico." Undoubtedly Milroy saw this as another opportunity to create a heroic reputation for himself as he penned, "I desire to assist in that glorious work."[84] Less than a week after the initial letter Romero replied to Milroy: "Your favor ... informs me of the interest you feel in the struggle for Mexico against her invaders, as well as your desire of taking a part in the work of her salvation. I beg to acknowledge my gratitude for such noble feelings in behalf of my country."[85]

Throughout the next month and a half the two corresponded. It appears from Milroy's letters that he seriously considered joining the Mexican effort. On April 22, he asked Romero: "From what you know of the feeling of my Government towards Mexico, would there probably be any opposition to United States officers and soldiers, emigrating as citizens in large numbers, across the Rio Grande?" Milroy also informed Romero that he would keep any information he received in confidence, but he wanted Romero's permission "to communicate your views, and such information as I may receive from you to the officers and gentlemen who may be interested with me in this matter, that I may hear their views in arranging plans." As he had throughout the Civil War with his superiors he became testy when he did not receive a prompt reply to his questions. After nearly one month passed without hearing anything from Romero he penned him once more, in terse language, "I wrote to you on the 22nd ... making inquiries upon different points for information, which is necessary for enabling me to determine my course, and to be able to give information to others who desire to assist Mexico in expelling her foreign invaders." Milroy lambasted Romero: "Ample time has elapsed for me to have received a reply.... Thousands of veteran soldiers in this Dept. are awaiting the word to move to Mexico."[86] In the end Milroy did not serve in Mexico, nor provide any real assistance in the matter. While Milroy searched for something to do in the future, during the spring of 1865 the nightmare of the Civil War came to an end.

After four long years of war the first real sign that the conflict would soon be over was the surrender of Gen. Robert E. Lee's Army of Northern Virginia at Appomattox on April 9. Milroy received the "glorious news of the capture and surrender of Lee with the Reb Army" the following day and ordered a national salute at Tullahoma, Murfreesboro, and Stephenson. "So the head of the great rebellion is now off," Milroy reveled, "and the body of that vile serpent will not retain life much longer."[87]

Wonderful news of the war's end was darkened by news of the assassination of President Lincoln less than one week later. "O! God, what a calamity to my country and to the civilized world," Milroy lamented, "Why has an inscrutable overruling Providence permitted ... the political head of our Nation to be thus cut off? Has not the bloody Moloch of Treason yet had victims enough?"[88] Regardless of Lincoln's inability to obtain a field command for Milroy after the Winchester fiasco, Milroy admired the fallen leader, the "Great Emancipator," for his work in ending the vile institution of slavery. Mourning the death of the nation's president, Milroy penned in his diary: "The greatest and best man of our Nation and the most conspicuous of Earths Sons have now been sacrificed on this bloody altar."[89] He grieved further: "Great God! What an event in our nation and in Earth's history. Treason having failed to destroy the greatest and best Govt. on Earth has turned its defeated demonic assassin rage against the political head of our Govt. and having terribly shocked the nation, but not injured the Govt."[90]

Among Milroy's command, depression and sadness set in among the majority of troops, but not all mourned Lincoln's death. Two Illinois soldiers rejoiced at the news of Lincoln's assassination. When Milroy heard the news he ordered the "copperhead soldiers" arrested. Immediate preparations to try these two men were made as Milroy did not want "such monsters" in his command.[91] A short court-martial convened on the night of April 15 — the day Lincoln died. A commission of 13 field officers listened to testimony and by night's end the two men were found guilty. As punishment Milroy ordered their heads shaved, labeled as copperheads and had them paraded in front of the command.[92]

Although war had ended in Virginia and in the coming weeks the remaining Confederate forces in the field surrendered, Milroy, as did other Union commanders throughout the South, had to deal with irregular forces who simply refused to quit. As late as the first week of May bushwhackers were still wreaking havoc around Tullahoma. For example, on the night of May 6, Capt. Elijah Shasteen, who had served as a scout for Milroy, was killed and another unidentified man was murdered that night by pro–Confederate ruffians. Late that night Milroy sent out a cavalry patrol to round up the partisans. They found no one.[93] Union soldiers and citizens had hoped that by the first week of May the actions of lawless men would have ended, but they did not. Milroy wanted to be as relentless as the bushwhackers, but the orders of his superior, General Rousseau, would not allow it. Five days before the murder of Shasteen, Milroy received an order from his superior "to send flags of truce to all the armed bands of guerillas to surrender." "Have an abhorrence at sending flags of truce to those thieves and cut throats," Milroy penned.[94]

While Milroy dealt with the depression of Lincoln's death and roaming bands of Confederate partisans who refused to give up, several Unionist citizens of Tennessee informed Milroy that some people in Tennessee were devising a plan "to place [Milroy] in a false light with those who are unacquainted with the course you have pursued while in command of this portion of Tennessee." Milroy's faithful followers concluded the letter: "Although efforts may be made by unscrupulous parties from this State to detract from your well earned glory, and although unfair and undermining means may be used for that purpose we hope and pray their plans will be futile and that their machinations may recoil upon themselves and themselves be the worst sufferer for an attempt to injure [you]."[95]

Accustomed to character attacks Milroy paid little attention to the comments of his detractors. For the moment he was buoyed by the war's end and the constant good news about the crumbling of Confederate armies and capture of Confederate officials. Along with many other Unionists, Milroy reveled at the news of the capture of Jefferson Davis, "the arch traitor," in Georgia on May 10.[96] Several weeks later on June 5, Milroy learned that the Tennessee legislature approved the charter for the Great South Western Oil and Mining Co. In the following days the company was organized and preparations were made to start drilling.

Despite the good news and the prospects of a successful mining company, Milroy was not satisfied. His passion was to gain "military fame and renown as a general." On May 22, he petitioned President Andrew Johnson for another military command. "You would do me a great favor by giving me some active duty to perform before returning to private life (Which I suppose I will have to do soon, not being a West Pointer)," Milroy explained to Johnson. Milroy requested two possible posts—the border with Mexico or the military governor of Alabama, the post that he wanted the most. "I feel very sure that if I could be sent there," Milroy informed Johnson, "with a proper military force and some discretionary power I could bring Alabama in all right with the machinery of Civil Govt. in good working order."[97]

Johnson did not give Milroy the opportunity for another post, and Milroy's time as major general soon came to an end. General Thomas sent Milroy an order dated July 11, 1865: "In accordance with instructions received from the Lieut. Genl. Comdg. Armies of the United States, Maj.

Genl. *R.H. Milroy* U.S. Vols. will proceed to his residence at Rensselaer, Ind." Milroy's Civil War had come to an end, but the war's impact continued to influence Milroy's life just as it would continue to affect the life of our nation. Fighting with government officials in Washington continued, his hatred of West Pointers grew, and his defeat at the Second Battle of Winchester remained a central focus for the rest of Milroy's life.[98]

8

"The army of eternal peace"

When he received Thomas' order asking for a resignation Milroy must have been crushed as his time as a major general had ended and he had not achieved a glorious reputation commanding men in a great battle. His career as a Civil War general on the battlefield was mediocre at best, but his real importance was in breaking the resolve of Confederate civilians, enforcing emancipation, and in protecting Unionists wherever he went. While he may have not gained the fame and reputation he desired on the battlefield he left a strong imprint on the memories of those whom he helped. Throughout the war Milroy received kind letters of support from countless Unionist citizens, but perhaps a letter written to him in late April 1865 sums up what he meant to them. We "will be ever grateful to you for the upright and noble course you have pursued with so much vigilance in ridding us of that worst scourges of Guerrillas and bushwhackers," explained a group of citizens from Tullahoma. They continued, "We know that you have beautifully shown in your excellent policy here the most eminent qualities of the warrior the statesman and the Christian … you have our most cordial assurance that with us, aside from our late lamented president, you are esteemed as our bravest defender, our best friend and our noble patriot."[1]

Regardless of what southern Unionists thought of Milroy, his time in the service had ended. The day following receipt of Thomas' order, Milroy departed Tennessee and made his way home to Rensselaer. Late on the night of the 14th he arrived at home and found his "dear wife and children well."[2]

When Milroy arrived home from the "Great Rebellion" he spent little time with his family and immediately began trying to put his life back into order. He spent a rainy Saturday, July 15, sorting through papers at his law office and was shocked to see that his partner, Tatman, had "stolen from and swindled" Milroy out of about $3,000.[3] Milroy had suspected that his partner had stolen from him while he was away; however, he had yet to confirm it.[4] Over the next several days Milroy tried to get his civilian life in order, but also had to submit his formal resignation to President Johnson. He sent the letter to Johnson on July 18, and happily wrote that "[I] expect soon to have my collar off my neck and not again subject to orders by any of the West Point Sparrows."⁵ On July 26, Milroy received Johnson's acceptance and now he was "freed from" his "allegiance to West Point."⁶

Although Milroy thought his feuding with West Pointers and politicians in Washington had ended he was gravely mistaken. Following his formal resignation from the army Milroy learned that generals were entitled to three months' paid leave before being mustered out. Milroy did not want back in the service; rather he wanted the money that would have accompanied that leave of absence. "I am driven to ask of you this favor for the reason that I find on my return home after an absence of four years and three months, that my law business has been ruined, and myself involved over $3000.00 by a rascally law partner with whom I intrusted my business," Milroy complained to President Johnson. He further explained to Johnson that his request was not "unreasonable ... as I see many other Generals retained

This photograph taken after the Civil War shows Milroy with his wife, Mary, and their four sons — Samuel, Valerius, Walter and Robert Bruce (Jasper County Public Library, Rensselaer, Indiana).

in high position who have not served half the service and one tenth of the fighting that I have."[7] Desperate for money, Milroy implored Johnson to help in some way; even if he could not give Milroy his three months' leave perhaps he could give him something to do in the government to earn some money. "I am therefore compelled to ask of you this favor to enable me to support my family to avoid the most painful pecuniary embarrassments till I can get into business.... If my request is impractical I would ask some paying appointment."[8] Milroy would receive no such concession from the chief executive.

Fearing his family was spiraling into financial crisis he knew that he had to put all of his efforts behind his mining company in Tennessee. During the first week of August Milroy left Indiana for New York where he hoped to forge some business relationships. En route to New York City, Milroy stopped in Albany, where his situation got worse when a pickpocket stole $150 in cash from Milroy's coat pocket. By August 7, he was in New York City to hopefully create some partnerships with New York businessmen, but Milroy understood that businessmen would not invest in the company until the oil wells were pumping.[9] Although he had forged some friendships, business partnerships were nonexistent and Milroy decided to return home to Indiana.

Before he returned home to Indiana, however, Milroy went to Washington, D.C. Milroy still had some pay owed him by the federal government—$382.87—and every penny counted. He settled with the government and left the nation's capital on August 12. So close to the Shenandoah Valley and some of his Unionist friends, Milroy opted to make a trip to Winchester. When he arrived in Winchester, Milroy noted that a "large number of my loyal Union friends of both sides called on me. All expressed the greatest pleasure to see me." Milroy remained in the lower Valley for two days, and on the evening of August 15, accepted a dinner invitation with the loyal citizens of Martinsburg where he delivered a speech, undoubtedly thanking them for their support of the Union war effort.[10]

By August 21, Milroy settled into his home in Rensselaer and continued in his preparations to get the oil and mining company operational. He entertained various individuals showing him types of machinery. As he spoke with certain people and learned the costs of running the mining and oil business he became discouraged. Furthermore Milroy knew that he could not operate a business from Indiana so he went to Nashville in the end of August. By the end of September, Milroy and his partners had secured enough funding to get the firm of "Milroy, Waters, and Co." operational. Joyous, Milroy confided in his diary: "The firm of Milroy, Waters, and Co. has now commenced moving aright and will ere long be in full sail."[11]

Confident that the company would prosper, Milroy returned home and spent the final weeks of 1865 with his family. On New Year's Eve there was little celebration in the Milroy household as he had been spending the previous days organizing his papers. As he sat at home that day he contemplated his service as a major general and in particular the occurrences of 1865. "A year that will ever be Memorable in the history of the U.S. as [the one] that brought the Great Rebellion to a close and completed the second birth of our glorious Union — the permanent establishment of Liberty and Free Government on Earth," Milroy wrote. A sense of calm presided over Milroy as he closed his diary in 1865 with the simple line: "A year of misery with me is ended."[12]

The year 1866 dawned with more promise for the Milroy family. Milroy's wife, Mary, was carrying a child, Samuel Clay, who would be born on January 28.[13] Throughout the winter Milroy remained at home with his newborn son and family, but when spring came Milroy returned to Tennessee to check on the progress of the oil drilling. The business appeared to be on the right track, but Milroy was still in debt and desperately needed to find a way to eliminate it. He sold some land, but was presented with a great opportunity in May 1866 when the governor of Tennessee, William G. "Parson" Brownlow, offered Milroy the post of Nashville police commissioner. While the $3,000 annual salary could have helped Milroy easily get out of debt he declined the offer as he was not a citizen of Tennessee and did not want to give up his Indiana citizenship.[14]

As the oil wells pumped throughout the spring, Milroy became melancholy having to be away from his family, but necessity called for it. Debts needed to be paid off and the bills mounted. That June he directed his wife to start selling some of the horses, including the pony of his 10-year old son, Valerius.[15] By early July the family's economic condition worsened and Milroy directed his wife to sell everything except for his horse Jasper and the family home.[16]

Throughout 1866 the family struggled financially, but faith in the oil operation and his family kept Milroy afloat. In 1867 the Indiana legislature elected Milroy a trustee of the Wabash and Erie Canal.[17] After this it is unclear what role, if any, Milroy served in the workings of the fledgling oil and mining business in Tennessee.

The following year Milroy appeared to get involved in politics and from all accounts became a strong supporter of Ulysses S. Grant in the presidential race that year. While it is unclear how much campaigning Milroy did for Grant, it is likely that at least on one occasion Milroy returned to the Shenandoah Valley to garner support for the Republican candidate. Among the stops was Winchester. Three years earlier Milroy returned to

Winchester and was warmly received by the town's Unionists and from all accounts the former Confederate civilians who held so much hatred for him were indifferent to his stay in town. His visit in October 1868 would be very different. According to a history of Winchester published in 1925 Milroy came to Winchester in 1868 to do political campaigning for a friend — more than likely Grant.[18] When Milroy stood on the steps of the courthouse to deliver a message to the crowd, he was met with such fierce contempt from the onlookers that they forced him out of town. Although Milroy never wrote of the incident and it was not reported in area newspapers, it is highly likely that a reception such as this was possible. Animosity toward Unionists and Federal soldiers ran deep in Winchester. The previous year the Unionist Rebecca Wright — the young Quaker School teacher who had supplied information to Gen. Philip H. Sheridan in September 1864 — was driven from town in 1867 when the town's civilians learned of her "traitorous" activities.[19] Milroy, among the most hated post commanders of Winchester, could have received such a horrid reception in 1868.

Following Grant's successful bid for the presidency, Milroy saw another opportunity to make sure that his reputation — tarnished at Winchester — was restored, not for him, but for his children. "Mr. President," Milroy implored Grant in the spring of 1871, "I have four boys growing up to manhood, and for their sakes, I desire that the cloud upon my reputation occasioned by the iniquitous arrest, may be removed."[20] In the records of the War Department Milroy's name had largely been cleared, but in the public's eye Milroy firmly believed that he had been portrayed as a coward. Milroy implored Grant to enforce the House of Representatives' resolution to publish all documents associated with the court of inquiry. "A dark cloud was therefore thrown upon my reputation by that arrest," Milroy explained, "which would have been removed by the publication of the evidence before the Court of Inquiry." Even in 1871, eight years after his defeat at Winchester, he still maintained a tremendous grudge against Halleck, writing: "I made application to have said evidence, synopsis, opinion, and findings published, but Halleck refused to allow it, for the reason that the evidence showed conclusively that he had been guilty of the grossest injustice toward me by that arrest." Milroy pleaded: "Do this act of simple Justice for me Mr. President, and I will teach my boys to reverence your name if possible more than they otherwise would." When he closed the letter to Grant he informed the president: "I am poor and have no heritage to leave my children but my good name, and I desire them to have copies of the evidence with the opinion of Genl. Holt and finding of Presdt. Lincoln thereon, all of which show conclusively that that arrest, which has shadowed my life ... was without cause and wholly unjust."[21] Although Milroy could not have been certain as to what Grant's response would be, he must have been hopeful that his friend Schulyer Colfax, who tried desperately as a congressman from Indiana to get Milroy a better command and was now vice president of the United States, might do something to help him.

While all Milroy's problems with the restoration of his name for posterity's sake and financial crisis made Milroy melancholy, nothing could have depressed him more than the passing of his daughter, Ella Gertrude on March 1, 1870. She was 18 years of age, and the third child that Milroy and his wife buried.[22]

Despite the loss of this child to an unknown ailment, Milroy pressed on in his efforts to restore his name as well as find a more stable postwar career for himself. Whether or not there is any direct correlation to the letter from Milroy to Grant or not is unknown, but on May 19, 1871, President Grant nominated Milroy to be marshal of the United States for the Wyoming Territory.[23] The nomination was approved and by 1872 Milroy found himself back in the government's service.

His time as marshal for the Wyoming Territory was short and soon he found himself in another government post, superintendent of Indian Affairs for Washington Territory. In this post Milroy had to contend with the corruption and ineptness inherent in the Bureau of Indian Affairs, but Milroy had the opportunity to do some good in his new position.

On July 6, 1872, an executive order from President Grant changed an agreement that had designated territory for the Columbia, Kettle, Colville, Okanogan, Kalispels, Spokanes and San Poils tribes, in favor of white settlers.[24] The order changed the boundaries confining the various tribes to land that, unlike their first reservation, was unfit for planting. The tribes were obviously enraged over the reneging on a government treaty that had been in effect only since April 9, 1872, and the Federal government needed to avoid a disaster. The man sent to deal with the problem was Milroy.

Milroy, accompanied on the trip by his son Robert Bruce, spent much of August and September 1873 riding through the Washington Territory trying to find out what had gone wrong with the treaty and examine land that would be more suitable. After meeting with tribal leaders and conferring with other members of the Bureau of Indian Affairs, Milroy negotiated a compromise treaty that although still favorable to the white settlers, was more beneficial to the native tribes as their new reservation would be situated north of the Columbia and Spokane Rivers on land more suitable for living.[25]

Milroy served in his post as superintendent until it was abolished in 1875.[26] When his tenure as superintendent ended, President Grant nominated Milroy to be a United States attorney for the Washington Territory.

Grant hoped Milroy would accept and fill the vacancy left by Samuel C. Wingard, who had been elevated to associate justice of the territory's supreme court.[27] Milroy declined the offer.

Following yet another retirement from the United States government in 1875, Milroy and his family settled in Olympia, Washington. He continued to nurture his family and watched it mature. Undoubtedly proud of his children, he must have been especially satisfied with the success of his sons Robert Bruce and Walter Judson, who followed in their father's footsteps and established the first law firm in Yakima, Washington, in 1885. Milroy must have also been proud of his son Val, who ended up becoming the postmaster of Olympia.[28] As he undoubtedly abounded with joy at the success of his sons, Milroy's final years were not without sorrow. On December 9, 1875, his son Samuel died at the age of nine — the fourth child that Milroy and his wife would have to bury.[29]

Much of his time in retirement was occupied in reading and writing, and it is more than likely during this time that Milroy attempted to write his autobiography, wherein he focused on his role in the Civil War. It was never published.

Amid writing of his wartime experiences, Milroy spent a considerable amount of time reading the works of Charles Darwin and others. Darwin's writings on evolution challenged Milroy's religious views and made Milroy skeptical of his Presbyterian faith to the extent that Milroy strayed from the church in the war's aftermath. The years following the Civil War were not the only time that Milroy questioned his faith. During the winter of 1860–1861, two members of the Indiana state legislature — Gideon Moody (who would serve with Milroy during the Civil War) and Horace Hefner — had an argument and Moody challenged to Hefner to a duel. Milroy played a vital role in organizing the "hostile meeting." Since Hefner was challenged he had the right to choose the weapon. Milroy, acting as Moody's second, did not think it fair for Moody, a much smaller man than Hefner, to fight with a knife. Milroy then proposed he fight Hefner. When the elders of the Presbyterian Church in Rensselaer discovered Milroy's role they decided to consider suspending him from the "privileges of the Church." Brought before the church council on March 28, 1861, Milroy professed his involvement in the case and also informed the elders that "for sometime past, his mind had been undergoing a change upon the doctrine of the future punishment of the wicked." Until Milroy recanted what he had done he could not receive the sacraments of the church. Even though he questioned Presbyterian teachings before and after the war he never lost his basic faith in God. He eventually returned to the church in his final years, "a sincere believer and worshipper of his former faith."[30]

During the winter of 1889–1890, Milroy's health began to fail and the failure of his heart at 10:30 A.M. on Saturday, March 29, 1890, ended his storied life. The *Republican Partizan* reported that Milroy "had fallen before the hoof of the white courser."[31] In the final hours of his life Milroy's family and friends gathered around the dying general. Even then as he breathed his last Milroy focused on his defeat at Winchester and dictated to a local judge, identified in the obituary as Justice Austin, events in that fight, "the supreme occasion of his life," and reiterated that he was only doing as ordered.[32] Milroy left behind three sons and his wife, Mary. Mary lived until February 23, 1904.[33]

The funeral service on March 31 was filled with dignity. An Olympia newspaper reported the scene: "The casket was beautiful decorated with lilies, wreaths of ivy and evergreen." On the center rested one of Milroy's swords—the one presented to him by his command at Winchester in honor of his promotion to major general (it was buried with him)—proving that even in death Winchester was central to his life. "On the center rested the sword worn in battle by the fallen soldier," reported the *Republican Partizan*, "and by its peaceful side the starry emblem for which he battled, fit tokens of the deeds and hopes of the departed hero."[34] A procession from the Presbyterian Church to Olympia's Masonic Cemetery included a "vast concourse of sorrowing people."[35]

Perhaps in a last effort to vindicate Milroy for his defeat at Second Winchester, the *Republican Partizan* reported that his efforts at Winchester were heroic and that had he not fought there Lee's army would have been victorious north of the Potomac River. "General Milroy," the *Partizan* wrote, "resisted the superior forces of the confederate commander [Lee] for three days, and only retreated when driven to it by the failure of ammunition and threatenings of starvation and cutting his way out by night, suffered a heavy loss of his forces. The result of this battle so detained Lee's army that Meade was enabled to fight more advantageously at Gettysburg." The paper concluded that had Milroy not put up a stand at Winchester then Gettysburg, "that decisive battle of the war would have been fought farther North."[36]

Following his passing various groups passed resolutions in his honor. The George H. Thomas G.A.R. post No. 5 in Olympia passed a resolution on the date of Milroy's death honoring the fallen general. The resolution in memoriam began: "The evening gun has fired, and the issuing countersign has carried within the lines of the Grand Army, above the valiant spirit, the courageous heart, the noble and patriotic soul of our comrade ... Milroy ... left this field of strife to accept promotion to that rank where no more is heard the cannon's roar, the musket's wavering rattle, and the shrieks and groans of the wounded and dying." The G.A.R. declaration positively recounted, "When the dark cloud of rebellion hung like a dark pall over our beloved land, [Milroy] issued the first call to the patriots of the north to spring to the rescue of their country from disunion; leading to the front the brave men who responded to that call, and sharing with them the trials and hardships of the battlefields; standing as a bulwark of night between the oppressed and the oppressors." The decree recorded that Milroy stalled Lee's advance to the Potomac River "thereby making it possible for Meade to win the battle of Gettysburg, and thus save the Nations Capitol and honor; bringing order out of chaos in the valley of the Shenandoah." The G.A.R. camp also professed that Milroy was "martyred to the ambition, of incompetent political generals; giving the best years of his life that the highest and lowest in the land might live under 'One country and one flag' has answered the roll-call of the Great Commander and joined the army of eternal peace."[37]

Another resolution passed by the Thurston County Bar Association likewise praised Milroy for his Civil War service. "That in him," the resolution stated, "our country had one of its ablest and bravest defenders and one of its most upright and honorable citizens; that to him our country will ever owe a great debt of gratitude, for his pre-eminent service in its hour of peril; that in him as a citizen, neighbor and friend, we recognized and bear testimony to the most sterling qualities of a noble manhood." The bar association also resolved that Congress should provide a pension for Mary Milroy "that will insure to her during her declining years those comforts, which by reason of the patriotic devotion of herself and her noble husband she so richly deserves."[38]

While by the time of his death Milroy had been forgotten by many in this country, his fellow friends and citizens of Rensselaer, Indiana, had not forgotten him. In December 1902 the city purchased the Milroy homestead, which at that point was in an advanced state of dilapidation. The property cost $1,900; $1,000 of the price tag was paid for through the fund-raising efforts of the Ladies Literary Club and the remaining $900 was paid by the city. The city's original intent was to make a park for the citizens and later construct some sort of public building.

After the land was purchased, some of Rensselaer's citizens felt that a monument should be erected on the site to immortalize Milroy. Guided by Mrs. Mary E. Thompson, a fund-raising campaign was begun and about $2,500 had been raised. To create a bronze life-size likeness of the general the citizens of Rensselaer enlisted the aid of Chicago sculptor Mary Washburn, who graciously donated her artistic talents. A local marble dealer— W.H. Mackey—donated his labor for setting the monument pedestal, erecting the statue, and engraving the names of the soldiers who served from Jasper County during the Civil War.[39]

Monument to General Milroy in Rensselaer, Indiana. The memorial was dedicated on July 4, 1910.

Washburn, Mackey, and volunteers worked diligently to prepare the statue for its July 4, 1910, dedication. Independence Day 1910 was a glorious occasion in Rensselaer, as thousands gathered to see the monument dedicated and unveiled. The keynote speaker at the dedication was Col. E.P. Hammond who recalled Milroy's life and achievements. "He was a man of intense patriotism," Hammond proclaimed. "The cause which he was fighting, his country, the integrity of the Republic, the freedom of the slaves, was constantly present in his mind. It was the advantage won or the injury suffered by his cause that made him rejoice over our victory or mourn over our defeat."[40]

While Hammond paid tribute to Milroy in his speech he also discussed Milroy's uphill battle against West Pointers throughout his life. "It is probable," Hammond stated, "that few officers in the army graduated of West Point, had a better military education than General Milroy: but as the West Pointers were impressed with the belief that no thorough Military education could be obtained outside of that institution, they were during the war inclined to treat Milroy with their overbearing superiority."[41]

Milroy desired from an early age to gain fame on the battlefield. The

Mexican War afforded that opportunity, and the Civil War likewise offered occasion to gain a reputation of the likes of Grant and Sherman. Yet partly because of command assignments, sometimes impulsive battlefield decisions, his defeat at Second Winchester, and a constant perception that West Pointers were out to destroy his career, Milroy was never elevated to the pantheon of legendary Union generals. The Civil War, in Milroy's eyes, afforded him the opportunity to create "a proud heritage for my children and a pride to my posterity and one that would live in history."[42] In his eyes he failed to create a proud heritage because he never achieved great success in combat. Milroy could never see beyond the battlefield as a venue for the creation of his legacy. What he obviously did not realize was that his role as an occupier and emancipator created his legacy and would and should bring a degree of "pride and posterity" to his name.

Enforcing Lincoln's Emancipation Proclamation, seeing to the safety and security of southern Unionists, and punishing those in rebellion were Milroy's preeminent concerns as an occupation commander. Numerous individuals who mentioned Milroy in resolutions after his death, speeches, and other writings always called to the attention of their audiences Milroy's love of union and hatred of slavery. Joseph Warren Keifer, who served with Milroy in the Valley and after the war had a successful political life praised Milroy's role as an abolitionist. "The colored people of America, should erect a monument to his memory. He was their friend when to be so drew upon him much adverse criticism."[43]

Despite his important role in ending the institution of slavery and curbing the activities of irregular forces, Milroy is most remembered in a negative light because of his defeat at Winchester—which after June 15, 1863, became the central focus of his life until his death in 1890. The best opportunity Milroy had to gain military prestige came at Winchester, but unfortunately he faced insurmountable odds and met a disastrous defeat. While Winchester stands as the climactic point of Milroy's military career and his defeat there has been used as the litmus test for measuring his success as a general, it should not be the only standard by which he is judged. Milroy, as other figures in history, should be viewed objectively for all of his shortcomings and positive qualities.

Hated by his enemies and adored by his men and southern Unionists, Robert H. Milroy left his mark on history. While he did not gain "military fame and renown as a general" in combat, Milroy aided in the creation of freedom for slaves, who for more than two centuries had known no liberty or justice. His role in preserving union and emancipation—perhaps the Civil War's greatest legacy—is what Milroy should be remembered for most. In that, few were his equal.

Appendix A: "Sketch of the Military Career of R.H. Milroy Up to the Battle of Allegany Summit Dec. 13/62"

Following the Civil War, Milroy attempted to write his autobiography. Two versions of his story detailing his early life struggles to obtain a military education and experiences in the Civil War through the end of 1862 exist; the one presented here is the longer version. Milroy did make an attempt to write a complete autobiography; however, he noted that he loaned the manuscript out to someone and it was never returned. The following piece was written by Milroy (Milroy identifies himself in the following selection in both first and third person) at some point during the postwar years and discusses his childhood, travails in obtaining a military education, involvement in the Texas Republic, marriage, study of law, involvement in the Mexican War, and his involvement in the Civil War from his early recruiting drives in February 1861 through action in western Virginia in December 1862. This autobiographical sketch also illuminates Milroy's penchant for combat and disdain for certain superior officers. It also provides a sketch of the service of Milroy's original command in the Civil War's early months—the 9th Indiana Volunteer Infantry.

The following document is a transcription of General Milroy's "Sketch of the Military Career of R.H. Milroy Up to the Battle of Allegany Summit Dec. 13/62." I have tried to maintain the integrity of Milroy's manuscript and made only minor editorial changes to assure easy reading. The handwritten original manuscript of Milroy's "Sketch" is in the Gen. Robert H. Milroy Collection at the Jasper County Public Library in Rensselaer, Indiana.—J.A.N.

Robert Huston Milroy was born June 11th 1816 near Salem Washington County Indiana. His father Gen. Samuel Milroy was one of the early settlers of Indiana territory and was a member of this first constitutional convention of that state and afterwards held various offices under the state and General Governments. He removed with his family in the Fall of 1826 to the Wabash and settled near where the town of Delphi now stands and engaged in the severe labor of opening a farm in the heavy forest and afterwards of building a mill on Deer Creek. The old Gentleman was so much of a democrat in theory and practice that he had unconquerable prejudices against a college education for any of his sons. This was a source of the [deepest regret] to Robert whose strongest desire as he approached manhood was to have a fine education. He early acquired a taste for reading and he spent his leisure hours with the books of his father's excellent library which increased his desire for an education. He at one time offered his father to relinquish all claim to an inheritance of his estate if he afford him the means to obtain a collegiate education which was refused. Finally despairing of getting an education with his father's consent and assistance he in the Winter of 1840 and 41 took advantage of a visit which his father permitted him to make to his relatives in P[ennsylvani]a (for the dual purpose of seeing them and of collecting a small claim of $200.00) of pushing on to Norwich University at Norwich Vermont a military institution of which Capt. Alden Partridge (former superintendent of West Point) was President. With the assistance of his uncle (Col. W[illia]m Reed of Mifflin Co. Pa.) and afterward his father he was enabled to remain at this University about 31 months and by the most intense application to study he was enabled to graduate at the commencement of August 1843. Taking the degree of Master of Arts, Master of Military Science, and Master of Civil Engineering. He traveled through New England a few months teaching fencing and drilling companies, returned home in the Spring of 1844 and commenced the study of Law after vainly trying to get a commission as [a] Lt. in the regular army. Being of a restless disposition he went to Texas in the Spring of 1845, took the oath of allegiance to the "Lone Star" and traveled some months looking at the country when hearing of the death of his father and oldest brother he at the urgent solicitation of his Mother returned home in the Fall of that year and resumed the study of law. Upon the breaking out of the Mexican War in the Spring of 1846 he raised a company and was mustered into the service for the term of one year as Capt. Of Company C 1st Ind. Vol. Inf. That Regt. was not in any of the general battles during its terms of service, and near its close he raised a company from the old volunteers to serve for the [duration of the] war as mounted Infantry, but Gen. Taylor to whom he tendered the services of this company refused to accept the company as mounted

Infantry. He then offered his company to the Gov. of Texas but was refused. He then offered them to the Sec[retar]y of War and was refused by him. He then returned with his Regt. To N[ew] Orleans where his old Regt. was mustered out and discharged and he returned home and recommenced the study of law. Attended Law lectures at the Ind[iana] University in the Winter of 1848 and 9 and graduated taking the degree of L.B. (Bachelor of Law). He was married in May 1845 to Miss Mary J. Armitage — Admitted to the bar the same spring. In the Fall was elected a member of the Constitutional Convention to amend the constitution of the State. In 1852 was appointed and served as circuit judge. Moved with his family to Rensselaer, Jasper [County] Indiana in May 1854 and continued the practice of law there till the breaking out of the Rebellion. Seeing plainly from the disposition of the South and the signs of the times that war was inevitable, he on the 7th of Feb. 1861 issued a call in the Rensselaer Gazette for the formation of a volunteer Company and immediately after the attack on Fort Sumter and the call of the Gov[ernor] of Ind. For six vol[unteer] regts. for three months. He tendered his Company to the Gov. and was accepted and mustered in on the 24th of April for the term of three months and upon the organization of the Regts. his co. was one of the companies of the 9th Indiana and he was unanimously chosen Col. by the commissioned officers and his was the first Indiana Regt that entered Va. crossing his Regt. at Bellair, Ohio into Va. on the 31st day of May 1861 and proceeded on the 1st day of June to report to Col. (now Gen.) Kelley at Grafton Va. and on the 3rd day of the same month moved with Col. Kelley to the attack of the Reb forces at Phillippi and participated in that affair. On the 6th of July lead the advance from Philippi to Laurel Hill. Drove in Reb pickets and would have driven them in to their fortifications and attacked them had he not been restrained by order of Gen. Morris who was ordered by Gen. McClellan not to attack the Reb fortifications till he, McClellan, would get into Beverly and come down in their rear. Gen. Morris got down in front of the Reb works to wait for McClellan, but waited in vain from Sunday till Thursday, when McClellan traveling at his usual speed (as since ascertained) of 6 miles per day arrive at Rich Mountain and Rosecrans with a few Regts. got into the Reb rear and whipped them before McClellan knew it. That night the Rebs at Laurel Hill heard the news and fled. Milroy's Regt. which had been constantly skirmishing with and watching the Rebs discovered their flight soon aftery they left and gave notice of it to Gen. Morris and without waiting [for] permission started with his Regt. in pursuit followed by the 7th Ind. and [a] battery. So rapid was the pursuit that at three o'clock they were within three miles of the Reb rear when Gen. Morris who had come up ordered a halt till next morning and sent back for the balance of his forces. In the morning the pursuit was recommenced but was suspended by the continued heavy rain and by the trees fallen by the Rebs in their rear, but notwithstanding all these obstacles the enemy was overtaken at Corricks Ford across Cheat River about 6 o'clock when he made a stand and was defeated with some loss including among the killed Gen. Garnett. The pursuit was discontinued and the forces under Gen. Morris returned to their camp at Laurel Hill and their term of service being nearly out they returned home and Col. Milroy's Regt. was mustered out of service at Indianapolis on the 30th of July. The Col. before disbanding his Regt. appointed a rendezvous at Laport Ind. on the 14th of Aug. following and invited all his Regt. to meet him there to enlist for the war. He returned home after seeing his men paid off. He remained at home four days and then left to make preparations for his new camp for recruiting which was located at Laport Ind. Companies of mostly new recruits commenced assembling on the 12th of August and by the 27th he had about 700 men who were on that day mustered in to service by Col. Wood (afterward Genl. Wood) who had mustered in the Regt. at the beginning of the 3 month service — Col. Milroy rec[eive]d authority from Col. Wood to muster in the balance of his Regt. himself and continue actively recruiting and mustering in till the 12th of Sept. when he lacked only about 40 men of having his Regt filled to the maximum required. He then rec[eive]d orders to get the required number to complete his Regt. from the 28th Ind. Col. Miller recruiting at the same place. He got these men from Col. Miller on the night of the 14th and started on the 15th by R.R. for W.Va. in great haste to relieve Gen. Reynolds then hard pressed by the Reb Gen. Lee at Camp Elk Water and Cheat Mountain. He arrived and reported to Gen. Reynolds at Camp Elk Water on the 18th of Sept. 1861. He had been notified some weeks before leaving Laport that he was appointed a Brigadier Genl. to rank as such from the 3rd of Sept. 1861 but was not assigned to the command of a brigade till about the 10th of Oct. following up to which time he remained in command of the 9th. About the 27th of Sept. Gen. Reynolds consented to go upon and attack the Reb forces at Camp Barto on the Green Brier about ten miles from Cheat Mountain Summitt which place was then in command of Col. Kimble of the 14th Indiana and on that day the 15th the 9th Indiana started for Cheat Mountain Summit from Camp Elk Water. The 9th camped for the night at the foot of the Mountain and went up the next day. A terrible rain storm commenced that day and continued for two days and nights without cessation and the men being without tents or shelter of any kind suffered terribly. It was not till the night of the 2nd of Oct that Gen. Reynolds got ready to advance. At 12 o'clock that night the 9th took up the line of march, preceded by the 32nd Ohio which was to halt before crossing the Green Brier to form a reserve. The night was intensely dark. The 32nd moved very slow being occasionally stopped by a fallen tree across the road which had to be removed to let the artillery and ambulances pass. It was daylight when the 32nd Ohio arrived at this point about six miles from Cheat Mountain Summit where they were to halt and let the 9th Ind pass on and take the advance which it did and the advance guard soon afterwards had a splendid skirmish with the Reb pickets at the bridge across the Green Brier driving them away and crossing the bridge. A portion of the 9th unfortunately fired upon some of their own skirmishers and killed one man and wounded two others. The 9th pushed on some two miles further when coming in sight of the Rebel Camp and fortifications they halted till the other Regiments with General Reynolds should come up and arrange the plan of attack. The 9th was sent to the right across the narrow valley to the back of the Green Brier which bordered the valley on that side and washed the base of the heights on the other side upon which the Rebels had encamped and fortified some two miles further up. Gen. Milroy being still in command of the 9th alone moved rapidly up the left bank of the stream and his advance soon commenced skirmishing with the Reb pickets he ordered the Regiment forward in line of battle and moved up on the double quick firing as he advanced and keeping pace with the 14th Indiana under Col. Kimble who was moving up. The skirmishing became quite brisk as they advanced and the strong picket guard of the Rebs fled rapidly after a short skirmish across the Green Brier to their works. The 9th followed up till within less than half a mile of the Reb works where it was halted in order to give the artillery time to come up and get into position. Being exposed to the fire of the Rebel artillery they lay down. Our artillery (three batteries) soon got into position and a furious artillery duel took place which lasted over three hours without intermission and with much more noise than harm to either side. The 9th being exposed to the fire of the Reb batteries which were in full view and waiting so long without any orders. Gen. Milroy concluded he could get a more safe and eligible position for his Regt. a few hundred yards to the left of the valley up in the timber on the side of the mountain from which position he could be ready to move as ordered. Accordingly he ordered his Regiment to the new position and soon received an order from Gen. Reynolds to attend a council of war at which Gen. Milroy strenuously urged an immediate attack upon the Reb works by our whole force by storm in this he was seconded by a majority of the other Regimental commanders. Gen. Reynolds rather opposed it but finally consented and told us to go. The regiments all moved up along the side of the mountain into position opposite the Reb works and awaited the order to advance but no order came and after waiting an hour, looking over into the Reb works and expecting the order to advance any moment and none coming the Regts. commenced moving back. Gen. Milroy hearing no order to return, remained in position awaiting orders till all the other Regts had left when he moved slowly and sullenly after them gathering up the dead and wounded of other Regts as he went his own had been attended to. After going a mile or two he overtook the 25th Ohio who stated that they had been ordered by Gen. Reynolds to halt and bring up the rear. The 9th got back to their camp at Cheat River some time after night very weary, having been under fire four hours and marched over 20 miles since starting. The 9th returned to Camp Elk Water the next day and remained there till about the 10th when they returned to Cheat Mountain Summit and Gen. Milroy took command of the Brigade at that post consisting of the 24th, 25th, and 32nd Ohio Regts the 9th Indiana Regt and Indiana Battery. Gen. Milroy at once commenced an active system of daily scouting in all direction around his post and particularly in the direction of Camp Bartow, which place he supposed Gen. Reynolds would soon attack again with all his forces and frequently urged Gen. Reynolds strongly to do so, but without success. The months of Oct and Nov were allowed to pass with an inferior enemy laying in front of us. Gen. Milroy's scouts had several times been around Camp Bartow and skirmished with the Rebs on different sides of it. The Rebs began to think their position unsafe and about the 20th of Nov. fell back 9 miles to the Summit of Alleghany Mountain to Camp Baldwin where they fortified themselves strongly. Gen. Milroy with a portion of his forces followed them up the day after they fell back and found a large amount of Camp equipage about their camp and fortifications at Bartow together with several pugnacious epistles to himself and troops. He followed on with a portion of his forces up to the immediate vicinity of Alleghany Summit when he captured a Georgia soldier from whom he learned the strength and situation of the forces there. Gen. Reynolds Division commenced leaving about the 1st of Dec. some for K[entuck]y and some for Cumberland, M[arylan]d and by the 10th of Dec. all had left except the 9th Ind. 25th and 32nd Oh. and 2nd Va. and Gen. Reynolds himself left leaving Gen. Milroy in command of Cheat Mountain District embracing the posts of Beverly, Huttonsville, Elk Water and Cheat Mountain with a single Regt. at each post. Being left to himself he immediately commenced making preparations to attack the Reb workers at Allegany Summit. The 13th Indiana although under orders to leave had not yet left Beverly on the 12th of Dec. and Gen. Reynolds who was also still there sent up with about 300 of the 13th Ind. and bout 100 of the 32nd Ohio under Capt. Hamilton. These with the 9th (or about 500 of them) About 400 of the 25th Ohio and about 250 of the 2nd Va. without about 30 cavalry moved up to Cheat Mountain on the 12th and on the 13th moved up to Camp Bartow I had sent forward a company of skirmishers in the forenoon from Cheat Mountain who had been fired on by a party of Rebles in ambush and ___ [intentionally left blank in Milroy's manuscript] of our men were killed and wounded. (I am not sure of numbers or dead Mr. Hamilton was there and will remember). My force arrived at Camp Bartow about dark and a little after and remained there some hours. The night was cool and clear and pleasant for marching. About 11 o'clock Gen. Milroy divided his forces and sent Col. G.C. Moody with the troops of the 9th Ind. and 2nd Va. to march a detour up a valley to the right get to the left flank and rear of the Rebel position with orders to get to their position and attack the Rebs at daylight. While Gen. Milroy himself was to take the balance of the forces and attack the rebels in front or on the right flank at the same time. Gen. Milroy with that portion of his forces with him left Camp Bartow about an hour after Col. Moody did and moving directly up the Pike and rear of the vicinity of the Rebel works about daylight of the morning of the 13th of Dec./62 and drove in the Rebel pickets by which one of the men of his advance guard was killed. By the time he arrived at his intended position he found the whole Reb force some 2000 strong drawn out to oppose him, his forces were led by Col. Jones of the 25th Ohio. After a desperate engagement of about half an hour the rebles were driven within their works our men charged gallantly and for a time held part of theirs. But the rebels rallied to strong for them and they were forced back. The Rebs attempted to advance beyond their works several times but were repulsed each time with loss. The fight was then kept up till our ammunition became exhausted and still hearing nothing of the attack by Col. Moody on the other side, our men became discouraged and Gen. Milroy was reluctantly compelled to draw off his men and retire from the conflict which he did in good order taking with him his wounded and 30 prisoners. There is little doubt but had Col. Moody attacked simultaneously as ordered it would have been a complete success and the Reb. Genl. Johnson with all his forces captured.

Appendix B: Troops Commanded by Milroy in Combat

The following order of battle lists units commanded by General Milroy when he was either a brigade or division commander. While Milroy had many units under his command during various occupations in western Virginia, the Shenandoah Valley, and Tennessee, these regiments are those commanded by Milroy only in battle.

Engagement at Camp Alleghany, [West] Virginia (December 13, 1861): Milroy commanded the District of Cheat Mountain.
9th Indiana Infantry; 13th Indiana Infantry; 25th Ohio Infantry; 32nd Ohio Infantry; 2nd Virginia Infantry; detachment of 30 of Bracken's cavalry.

Battle of McDowell (May 8, 1862): Milroy commanded a brigade in Maj. Gen. John C. Fremont's army.
75th Ohio Infantry; 25th Ohio Infantry; 32nd Ohio Infantry; 3rd Virginia Infantry.

Battle of Cross Keys (June 8, 1862): Milroy commanded a brigade in Maj. Gen. John C. Fremont's army.
2nd Virginia Infantry; 3rd Virginia Infantry; 5th Virginia Infantry; 25th Ohio Infantry; 1st Virginia Cavalry (detachment); Virginia Light Artillery (Ewing); 1st Ohio Light Artillery; Battery I (Hyman); Ohio Light Artillery, 12th Battery (Johnson).

Second Battle of Bull Run (August 29–30, 1862): Milroy commanded an independent brigade in Maj. Gen. Franz Sigel's corps.
82nd Ohio Infantry; 2nd Virginia Infantry; 3rd Virginia Infantry; 5th Virginia Infantry; 1st Virginia Cavalry (companies C, E, and I); Ohio Light Battery, 12th Battery

Second Battle of Winchester (June 12–15, 1863): Milroy commanded a division in the Union army's VIII Corps.

First Brigade, commanded by Brig. Gen. Washington L. Elliott

110th Ohio Infantry; 116th Ohio Infantry; 122nd Ohio Infantry; 123rd Ohio Infantry; 12th Pennsylvania Cavalry; 13th Pennsylvania Cavalry; Battery L, 5th United States Artillery.

Second Brigade, commanded by Col. William G. Ely

18th Connecticut Infantry; 5th Maryland Infantry; 87th Pennsylvania Infantry; 12th West Virginia Infantry; 1st West Virginia Cavalry (Company K); 3rd West Virginia Cavalry (Companies D and E); 1st West Virginia Artillery, Battery D

Third Brigade, commanded by Col. Andrew T. McReynolds

6th Maryland Infantry; 67th Pennsylvania Infantry; 1st New York Cavalry; Baltimore Battery, Maryland Light Artillery; 14th [1st] Massachusetts Heavy Artillery

Action near Murfreesboro, Tennessee (December 7, 1864): Milroy commanded a detachment of 3,000 men under the command of Maj. Gen. Lovell H. Rousseau. For purposes of maneuvering on the field he divided his force into two brigades.

First Brigade, commanded by Col. Minor T. Thomas

8th Minnesota Infantry; 61st Illinois Infantry; 174th Ohio Infantry; 181st Ohio Infantry; 13th New York Light Artillery (one section); 12th Ohio Artillery (one section)

Second Brigade, commanded by Col. Edward Anderson

177th Ohio Infantry; 178th Ohio Infantry; 12th Indiana Cavalry (dismounted)

Cavalry Detachment, commanded by Col. Gilbert M. Johnson

4th Tennessee Cavalry (detachment); 5th Tennessee Cavalry (detachment); 13th Indiana Cavalry

Notes

Introduction

1. Joseph Warren Kiefer, *Slavery and Four Years of War: A Political History of Slavery in the United States together with a Narrative of the Campaigns and Battles of the Civil War in which the Author Took Part, 1861–1865* (New York: Putnam, 1900), 2:21.
2. Speech of Col. E.P. Hammond at Milroy monument dedication, July 4, 1910, in Margaret B. Paulus, *Papers of General Robert Huston Milroy* (n.p., 1965), 4:24.

Chapter 1

1. Paulus, *Papers of General Milroy*, 4:42.
2. "The Gray Eagle: Maj. Gen. Robert H. Milroy" *Rensselaer Republican*, Jan. 18, 1910; Cary C. Collins, "Grey Eagle: Major General Robert Huston Milroy and the Civil War," *Indiana Magazine of History* 90 (1994): 50.
3. Paulus, *Papers of General Milroy*, 4:216.
4. Collins, "Grey Eagle," 50.
5. Robert H. Milroy, "Sketch of the Military Career Up to the Battle of Allegany Summit, Dec. 13/62," Referred to hereafter as "Sketch," Robert H. Milroy collection, Jasper County Public Library, Rensselaer, Indiana. All items from this Collection will hereafter be cited as RHMJCPL. After the Civil War Milroy wrote two versions of his early story. The longer version is included in Appendix A.
6. For a discussion of the Jacobites see Norman Davies, *Europe: A History, A Panorama of Europe, East and West, From the Ice Age to the Cold War, from the Urals to Gibraltar* New York, 1996), 632; Speech of Col. E.P. Hammond at Milroy monument dedication, July 4, 1910, in Paulus, *Papers of General Milroy*, 4:19.
7. Paulus, *Papers of General Milroy*, 4:19.
8. Jonathan A. Noyalas, "'My will is absolute law:' General Robert H. Milroy and Winchester, Virginia." (Master's thesis: Virginia Tech, 2003), 5.

9. "Sketch," RHMJCPL.
10. Ibid.
11. Ibid.
12. Ibid.
13. Ibid.
14. "The Gray Eagle," *Rensselaer Republican*, Jan. 18, 1910.
15. "Sketch," RHMJCPL.
16. *A Catalogue of the Corporation, Officers and Cadets, of the Norwich University, for the Academic Year, 1843–4.* (Woodstock, VT, 1844), 16.
17. Al Nofi, "From the Grapevine," *North & South*, no. 1 (November 1997): 8. Norwich University produced 12 generals, 25 colonels, 90 majors and lieutenant colonels, and 198 company grade officers to the Union war effort during the Civil War.
18. William Arba Ellis, ed., *Norwich University 1819–1911: Her History, Her Graduates, Her Roll of Honor* (Montpelier, VT, 1911), 2:360.
19. The construction of a typical day for a cadet at Norwich University is based on *A Catalogue of the Corporation of Officers and Cadets, of the Norwich University, for the Academic Year, 1843–4*, 21–3, 25–9.
20. Ellis, ed., *Norwich University*, 1:80.
21. *Catalogue ... Norwich University*, 28.
22. Later in life Milroy was an elder in the Presbyterian Church; however, in 1861 he became disenchanted with the church because of a proposed duel between Gideon C. Moody and Horace Heffren. Milroy maintained his religion throughout the Civil War, but did not return to the Presbyterian Church until after the war's conclusion. Paulus, *Papers of General Milroy*, 4:21. Milroy's religious views are discussed further in this book's final chapter.
23. One of the notebooks that then Cadet Milroy used at Norwich University survives and contains lecture notes on artillery and fortifications. Notebook 1842, Robert H. Milroy Collection, Norwich University Archives and Special Collections, Kreitzberg Library,

Northfield, VT Items from this collection will be cited hereafter as NUA.
24. Ellis, *Norwich University*, 2:360. Athletic activities at Norwich University were limited to military drill, fencing, boxing, and rowing. Milroy was known to have excelled at fencing. Music for flute, 1842, NUA.
25. *Ibid.*
26. Ellis, ed., *Norwich University*, 3:638.
27. 1843 Commencement Program, NUA; Paulus, *Papers of General Milroy*, 4:13, 20.
28. Milroy to Maj. Gen. Robert Schenck, Jan. 18, 1863, Robert Schenck Papers, University of Miami, Ohio.
29. Lewis Wallace, *Lew Wallace: An Autobiography* (New York: Harper 1906), 1:117.
30. "Sketch," RHMJCPL.
31. *Ibid.*; Collins, "Grey Eagle," 50.
32. Noyalas, "'My will is absolute law,'" 7.
33. Handwritten copy of Robert H. Milroy autobiography, RHMJCPL; Collins, "Grey Eagle," 52.
34. Oran Perry, (comp.), *Indiana in the Mexican War* (n.p.: Indianapolis, 1908), 46, 347.
35. Dr. E.H.M. Beck to ?, October 1846 in "Mexican War Letters," *Indiana Magazine of History* 25 (1929): 170.
36. Wallace, *Lew Wallace*, 1:117.
37. Milroy to James Milroy, Oct. 19, 1846, in "Mexican War Letters," 169.
38. Milroy to Mrs. A.A. Grimes, May 9, 1847, in *ibid.*, 172.
39. Dr. E.M.H. Beck to Frances M. Milroy, in *ibid.*, 167.
40. Robert H. Milroy to Mrs. A.A. Grimes, in *ibid.*, 172.
41. Wallace, *Lew Wallace*, 1:145.
42. *Ibid.*, 145–47.
43. *Ibid.*, 145.
44. *Ibid.*, 145–47.
45. *Ibid.*
46. "Sketch," RHMJCPL.
47. Paulus, *Papers of General Milroy*, 1:488.
48. The births and deaths are taken from "The Robert Huston Milroy Family Bible Family Record" in Paulus, *Papers of General Milroy*, 4:1–2. Edwin was born on March 3, 1850, and died on May 12, 1851; Ella Gertrude was born on December 25, 1851, and died on March 1, 1870; Edgar Whitfield was born on November 21, 1853, and died March 18, 1856; Valerius was born on August 17, 1855, and died on May 4, 1927; Walter was born on August 24, 1857, and died on June 26, 1935; Robert Bruce was born on September 25, 1859, and died on January 9, 1940, and was the last of Robert Milroy's family. Following the Civil War Milroy and his wife had another son, Samuel Clay, born on January 28, 1866. He died at the age of nine on December 9, 1875.
49. Robert H. Milroy, "Prepare for War,"

Handwritten copy of article to be sent to the *Rensselaer Gazette*, Feb. 6, 1861, RHMJCPL.
50. *Ibid.*
51. *Ibid.*
52. *Ibid.*
53. Paulus, Papers of General Milroy, 4:99.
54. *Rensselaer Weekly Gazette*, April 17, 1861.
55. Milroy speech of gratitude for Jasper, in Paulus, *Papers of General Milroy*, 4:41.
56. "Sketch," RHMJCPL.
57. *Ibid.*; Paulus, *Papers of General Milroy*, 4:42.

Chapter 2

1. Address to the volunteer army as quoted in *The Life, Campaigns, and Public Service of General McClellan: The Hero of Western Virginia! South Mountain! And Antietam!* (Philadelphia: T.B. Peterson and Brothers, 1864), 25.
2. "Sketch," RHMJCPL; W. Hunter Lesser, *Rebels at the Gate: Lee and McClellan on the Front Lines of a Nation Divided* (Naperville, IL: Sourcebooks 2004), 64.
3. Lesser, *Rebels at the Gate*, 61.
4. Clayton R. Newell, *Lee vs. McClellan: The First Campaign* (Washington: Regnery, 1996), 91; Lesser, *Rebels at the Gate*, 64.
5. Newell, *Lee vs. McClellan*, 94–7; "Sketch," RHMJCPL.
6. Lesser, *Rebels at the Gate*, 84–5.
7. *Ibid.*, 94.
8. "Sketch," RHMJCPL.
9. Speech of Col. E.P. Hammond at Milroy monument dedication, July 4, 1910, in Paulus, *Papers of General Milroy*, 4:22.
10. Ambrose Bierce, *Battlefields and Ghosts* (Palo Alto, CA: Harvest Press, 1931), 8–9.
11. *Ibid.*
12. David L. Phillips, ed., *War Stories: Civil War in West Virginia* (Leesburg, VA: Gauley Mount Press, 1991), 7.
13. William J. Miller, "Gray Eagle on a Tether," *America's Civil War*, 15, no. 5 (2000): 46; Joseph Warren Keifer, *Slavery and Four Years of War*, 1:311.
14. Colfax to Milroy, July 13, 1861, RHMJCPL.
15. "Sketch," RHMJCPL.
16. *Ibid.*; Robert H. Milroy commission to brigadier general of United States Volunteers, RHMJCPL. Although Milroy's commission dates from September 3, 1861, he did not receive the actual commission document until he was in Virginia and when he did receive it there was no one available to administer the proper oath. Milroy noted at the bottom of the commission: "This was received in Va. where there was no Justice of the Peace or other persons legally authorized to administer an oath."

17. U.S. War Department (comp.), *War of the Rebellion: A Compilation of the Official Records of the Union and Confederate Armies* Ser. I, II, (Washington: U.S. Government Printing Office, 1880–1901), 711–15, cited hereafter as *O.R.*
18. "Sketch," RHMJCPL.
19. Ambrose Bierce, *Shadows of Blue & Gray: The Civil War Writings of Ambrose Bierce*, (New York: Doherty, 2003), 197.
20. Lesser, *Rebels at the Gate*, 225.
21. *Ibid.*; Gregg S. Clemmer, *Old Alleghany: The Life and Wars of General Ed Johnson* (Staunton, VA: Hearthside, 2004), 326.
22. "Sketch," RHMJCPL.
23. *Ibid.*
24. *Ibid.*
25. *Ibid.*
26. *Ibid.*; Lesser, *Rebels at the Gate*, 226.
27. "Sketch," RHMJCPL.
28. Lesser, *Rebels at the Gate*, 226; Clemmer, *Old Alleghany*, 326–27.
29. "Sketch," RHMJCPL.
30. Lesser, *Rebels at the Gate*, 227. Brig. Gen. Henry Jackson's three artillery batteries were commanded by Capts. William Rice, Pierce Anderson, and Lindsey Shumaker.
31. "Sketch," RHMJCPL; Clemmer, *Old Alleghany*, 327
32. "Sketch," RHMJCPL.
33. Lesser, *Rebels at the Gate*, 229.
34. "Sketch," RHMJCPL.
35. Lesser, *Rebels at the Gate*, 230.
36. *Ibid.*
37. "Sketch," RHMJCPL.
38. *O.R.* Ser. I, V, 223, 229.
39. "Sketch," RHMJCPL.
40. *Ibid.*
41. *Ibid.*
42. Lesser, *Rebels at the Gate*, 242–43, 306; Much of the information about Benjamin Summit is contained in "Benjamin Summit" in Paulus, *Papers of General Milroy*, 4:36–9.
43. For a discussion in changing attitudes toward emancipation see James M. McPherson, *What They Fought For: 1861–1865* (Baton Rouge: Louisiana State University Press, 1994), 57–69; For more discussion on the actions of Butler, Fremont, and Hunter in the war's early stages see Mark Grimsley, *The Hard Hand of War: Union Military Policy toward Southern Civilians, 1861–1865* (New York: Cambridge University Press, 1995), 123–29.
44. Schuyler Colfax to Milroy, December 12, 1861, RHMJCPL.
45. *Ibid.*
46. Jonathan A. Noyalas, *Plagued by War: Winchester, Virginia, During the Civil War* (Leesburg, VA: Gauley Mount Press, 2003), 27–8; Clemmer, *Old Alleghany*, 349–51; *O.R.*, Ser. I, V, 988–89; James I. Robertson Jr., *Stonewall Jackson: The Man, The Soldier, The Legened* (New York: Macmillan, 1997), 294–96.
47. *O.R.* Ser. I, V, 461; Lesser, *Rebels at the Gate*, 251. In his excellent study of the early battles in western Virginia, Lesser points out that Jeff Glenn, Doc Rogers, William Lynn, Eugene Murphy and Andy Murphy were the five deserters.
48. Lesser, *Rebels at the Gate*, 251.
49. "Sketch," RHMJCPL.
50. *Ibid.*
51. *Ibid.*
52. In his official report of the fight at Camp Alleghany Milroy lists the following numbers and units that comprised his command: 700 men from the 9th Indiana, 400 men from the 25th Ohio, 250 men from the 2nd Virginia, 300 men from the 13th Indiana, 130 from the 32nd Ohio, 30 cavalrymen, and 75 artillerymen.
53. Lesser, *Rebels at the Gate*, 247. Regarding the date of the Confederate withdrawal from Camp Bartow.
54. *Ibid.*, 353–54
55. *O.R.* Ser. I, LI, pt. 1, 51.
56. *Ibid.*
57. *Ibid.*
58. *O.R.* Ser I, V, 461
59. *Ibid.*, 466
60. *Ibid.*, LI, pt. 1, 52
61. *Ibid.*
62. *Ibid.*, V, 466.
63. *Ibid.*, LI, pt. 1, 53.
64. Lesser, *Rebels at the Gate*, 257.
65. "Sketch," RHMJCPL.
66. *O.R.* Ser. I, LI, pt. 1, 54.
67. *Ibid.*, V, 456.
68. *Ibid.*; LI, pt. 1.
69. Lesser, *Rebels at the Gate*, 260.
70. *O.R.* Ser I, LI, pt. 1, 54.
71. *Ibid.*, V, 691.

Chapter 3

1. Mary Milroy to Milroy, January 2, 1862, in Paulus, *Papers of General Milroy*, 4:149.
2. Milroy to Mary Milroy, February 11, 1862, in Paulus, *Papers of General Milroy*, 1:12.
3. Paulus, *Papers of General Milroy*, 1:12.
4. *Ibid.*
5. *Ibid.*
6. *Ibid.*, 1: 12–13.
7. *Ibid.*, 1: 17.
8. Milroy to Mary Milroy, March 6, 1862, in Paulus, *Papers of General Milroy*, 1:17–19.
9. Milroy to Mary Milroy, March 18, 1862, in *ibid.*, 20.
10. Milroy to Mary Milroy, April 4, 1862, in *ibid.*, 26.
11. Virgil Carrington Jones, *Gray Ghosts and Rebel Raiders* (New York, Holt, 1956), 89.

12. *Ibid.*, 89, 92. The length of the prison sentence is not mentioned.
13. Lesser, *Rebels at the Gate*, 285; Patricia L. Faust, ed., *Historical Times Illustrated Encyclopedia of the Civil War* (New York: Harper-Perennial, 1986), 291.
14. Schuyler Colfax to Milroy, March 18, 1862, in Paulus, *Papers of General Milroy*, 1: 25
15. Milroy to Mary Milroy, March 25, 1862, in *ibid.*, 1:23.
16. For a complete study of Winchester's Civil War story see Noyalas, *Plagued by War.*
17. Clemmer, *Old Alleghany*, 385.
18. Lesser, *Rebels at the Gate*, 286.
19. Milroy to Mary Milroy, April 7, 1862, RHMJCPL.
20. *Ibid.*
21. *Ibid.*
22. *Ibid.*
23. *Ibid.*
24. Milroy to Mary Milroy, April 13, 1862, RHMJCPL.
25. *Ibid.*
26. *Ibid.*
27. Miller, "Gray Eagle on a Tether," 49.
28. Milroy to Mary Milroy, April 13, 1862, RHMJCPL. In Miller's "Gray Eagle on a Tether," 49, the author gives the impression that Milroy personally arrived in McDowell on April 13. Milroy's lead elements arrived on that day and Milroy followed in the following days. Milroy's letter to his wife written on the night of April 13 from Monterey proves this point.
29. Robert E. Lee to Gen. Edward Johnson, April 18, 1862, quoted in Clifford Dowdey and Louis Manarin, eds., *The Wartime Papers of R.E. Lee* (New York: Bramhall House, 1961), 147–48.
30. Clemmer, *Old Alleghany*, 391–92.
31. *Ibid.*, 394.
32. For more on the importance of the Virginia Central Railroad especially to Stonewall Jackson see Robert C. Black III, *The Railroads of the Confederacy* (Chapel Hill: University of North Carolina Press, 1998), 176–80; Miller, "Gray Eagle on a Tether," 50.
33. Milroy to Mary Milroy, May 13, 1862, RHMJCPL.
34. Robertson, *Stonewall Jackson*, 366.
35. James I. Robertson Jr., *The Stonewall Brigade* (Baton Rouge: Louisiana State University Press, 1991), 84–5.
36. Milroy to Mary Milroy, May 13, 1862, RHMJCPL.
37. *Ibid.* .
38. *Ibid.*
39. Miller, "Gray Eagle on a Tether," 51.
40. Milroy to Mary Milroy, May 13, 1863; O.R., Ser. I, XII, pt. 1, 465.
41. O.R. Ser. I, XII, pt. 1, 465.
42. *Ibid.*, 462; Robertson, *Stonewall Jackson*, 374.
43. O.R. Ser. I, XII, pt. 1, 463.
44. *Ibid.*,
45. *Ibid.*
46. *Ibid.*, 465–6.
47. *Ibid.*, 466.
48. *Ibid.*, 466; Milroy to Mary Milroy, May 13, 1863; Time Life Books, ed., *Voices of the Civil War: Shenandoah 1862* (Alexandria, VA: Time Life Books, 1997), 74; Archie P. McDonald, ed., *Make Me a Map of the Valley: The Civil War Journal of Stonewall Jackson's Topographer* (Dallas: Southern Methodist University Press, 1973), 41.
49. O.R. Ser. I, XII, pt. 1, 466.
50. Milroy to Mary Milroy, May 13, 1863, RHMJCPL.
51. Robertson, *Stonewall Jackson*, 374–5.
52. Miller, "Gray Eagle on a Tether," 52.
53. O.R., Ser. I, XII, pt. 1, 466.
54. Miller, "Gray Eagle on a Tether," 52.
55. Robertson, *Stonewall Jackson*, 375; Clemmer, *Old Alleghany*, 410.
56. O.R. Ser. I, XII, pt. 1, 469.
57. Robert G. Tanner, *Stonewall in the Valley: Thomas J. "Stonewall" Jackson's Shenandoah Valley Campaign, Spring 1862* (New York: Doubleday, 1976), 172.
58. Milroy to Mary Milroy, May 13, 1863, RHMJCPL.
59. *Ibid.*
60. *Ibid.*
61. *Ibid.*
62. O.R. Ser. I, XII, pt. 1, 467.
63. Robertson, *Stonewall Jackson*, 376.
64. O.R. Ser. I, XII, pt. 1, 464.
65. McDonald, ed., *Make Me a Map of the Valley*, 43–4.
66. Milroy to Mary Milroy, May 13, 1862, RHMJCPL.
67. Robertson, *Stonewall Jackson*, 378.
68. Milroy to Mary Milroy, May 13, 1862, RHMJCPL.
69. *Ibid.*
70. William J. Miller, "Such Men as Shields, Banks, and Fremont. Federal Command in Western Virginia, March-June 1862" in Gary W. Gallagher, ed., *The Shenandoah Valley Campaign of 1862* (Chapel Hill: University of North Carolina Press, 2003), 66.
71. For a complete study of Front Royal and the First Battle of Winchester see Brandon H. Beck and Charles S. Grunder, *Jackson's Valley Campaign: The First Battle of Winchester, May 25, 1862* (Lynchburg, VA: H.E. Howard, 1992).
72. O.R., Ser. I, XII, pt. 1, 643.
73. Miller, "Such Men as Shields, Banks, and Fremont," 66.
74. *Ibid.*, 67.
75. Milroy to Mary Milroy, June 15, 1862, RHMJCPL.
76. O.R. Ser. I, XII, pt. 1, 644.

77. Ibid., 647.
78. Noyalas, *Plagued by War*, 58–60.
79. Darrell L. Collins, *Jackson's Valley Campaign: The Battles of Cross Keys and Port Republic, June 8–9, 1862* (Lynchburg, VA: H.E. Howard 1993), 15.
80. Ibid., 16–17.
81. The fight of June 6, 1862, resulted in the death of Jackson's cavalry commander, Brig. Gen. Turner Ashby.
82. Milroy to Mary Milroy, June 15, 1862, RHMJCPL.
83. Ibid.
84. Collins, *Cross Keys and Port Republic*, 49.
85. Robert K. Krick, *Conquering the Valley: Stonewall Jackson at Port Republic* (Baton Rouge: Louisiana State University Press, 1996), 141, 147. Union Church was a small building that stood near the Keezletown Road and suffered artillery damage during the battle. After the fight it served as a field hospital. *O.R.*, Ser. I, XII, pt. 1, 19.
86. Milroy to Mary Milroy, June 15, 1862, RHMJCPL.
87. Ibid.; Krick, *Conquering the Valley*, 146, 149–50.
88. At the Battle of Cross Keys Fremont felt that the weakest part of the Confederate line was the right flank. Brig. Gen. Julius Stahel launched the attack and after suffering severely was reinforced by Brig. Gen. Henry Bohlen's brigade. Confederate Brig. Gen. Isaac Trimble defended this portion of Ewell's line and although outnumbered Trimble's men fought tenaciously as well as launched a counterattack into the Union attackers. Fremont did not order further support for Stahel and Bohlen. See, Collins, *Cross Keys and Port Republic*, 55–66.
89. Milroy to Mary Milroy, June 15, 1862, RHMJCPL.
90. Ibid.
91. Ibid.
92. Krick, *Conquering the Valley*, 219.
93. Milroy to Mary Milroy, June 15, 1862, RHMJCPL.
94. Ibid.
95. Ibid.
96. Ibid.
97. Ibid.
98. Ibid.
99. Ibid.
100. Ibid.
101. Ibid.
102. Ibid.
103. Milroy to Mary Milroy, July 4, 1862, in Paulus, *Papers of General Milroy*, 1:54.
104. *O.R.* Ser. I, XII, pt. 1, 24.
105. Milroy to Mary Milroy, June 15, 1862, RHMJCPL.
106. Ibid.
107. *O.R.* Ser. I, XII, pt. 1, 24–5.
108. Milroy to Mary Milroy, June 17, 1862, RHMJCPL.
109. "Jasper" in Paulus, *Papers of General Milroy*, 4:40.
110. Ibid.
111. *O.R.* Ser. I, XII, pt. 1, 26.
112. Peter Cozzens, *General John Pope: A Life for the Nation* (Urbana: University of Illinois Press, 2000), 75.
113. Noyalas, *Plagued by War*, 65–6.
114. Milroy to Mary Milroy, July 4, 1862, in Paulus, *Papers of General Milroy*, 1:54.
115. Ibid., 1:55.
116. Ibid.
117. Ibid., 54.

Chapter 4

1. Milroy to Mary Milroy, July 4, 1862, in Paulus, *Papers of General Milroy*, 1:54.
2. John J. Hennessy, *Return to Bull Run: The Campaign and Battle of Second Manassas* (Norman: University of Oklahoma Press, 1993), 9.
3. Milroy to Mary Milroy, July 14, 1862, RHMJCPL. In his study of Gen. John Pope, Peter Cozzens states that General Sigel's corps did not depart the Shenandoah Valley until July 14. This is a misleading statement as Milroy's independent brigade was the lead brigade and crossed the Blue Ridge on July 9. See Cozzens, *General John Pope*, 83.
4. Milroy to Mary Milroy, July 14, 1862, RHMJCPL.
5. Milroy to Mary Milroy, August 2, 1862, in Paulus, *Papers of General Milroy*, 1: 59.
6. Ibid.
7. Milroy to Mary Milroy, July 14, 1862, RHMJCPL.
8. Milroy to Mary Milroy, Aug. 2, 1862, in Paulus, *Papers of General Milroy*, 1:60.
9. Ibid.
10. For further discussion on the treatment of fugitive slaves in the war's early stage see James M. McPherson, *The Negro's Civil War: How American Blacks Felt and Acted During the War for the Union* (New York: Vintage Books, 1993), 22–3, 44, 60–3.
11. Milroy to Mary Milroy, August 2, 1862, in Paulus, *Papers of General Milroy*, 1:60–1.
12. Noyalas, *Plagued by War*, 69.
13. Milroy to Mary Milroy, August 2, 1862, in Paulus, *Papers of General Milroy*, 1:63.
14. Ibid.
15. Milroy to Mary Milroy, July 14, 1862, RHMJCPL; Milroy to Mary Milroy, August 2, 1862, in Paulus, *Papers of General Milroy*, 1:64–5.

16. Milroy to Mary Milroy, August 2, 1862, in Paulus, *Papers of General Milroy*, 1:65.
17. *Ibid.*, 1:64–5.
18. *Ibid.*, 65.
19. Cozzens, *General John Pope*, 90.
20. Peter Cozzens and Robert I. Girardi, eds., *The Military Memoirs of General John Pope* (Chapel Hill: University of North Carolina Press, 1998), 134.
21. Robertson, *Stonewall Jackson*, 523.
22. *Ibid.*, 135; Cozzens, *General John Pope*, 91.
23. Robertson, *Stonewall Jackson*, 525.
24. *O.R.* Ser. I, XII, pt. 2, 25–6.; Hennessy, *Return to Bull Run*, 28.
25. Cozzens and Girardi, eds., *Military Memoirs*, 136; Hennessy, *Return to Bull Run*, 28; Robertson, *Stonewall Jackson*, 527.
26. *O.R.*, Ser. I, XII, pt. 2, 142.
27. *Ibid.*, 26.
28. Milroy to Mary Milroy, August 15, 1862, in Paulus, *Papers of General Milroy*, 1:66.
29. *O.R.*, Ser. I, XII, pt. 2, 142.
30. Milroy to Mary Milroy, August 15, 1862, RHMJCPL.
31. *Ibid.*
32. *Ibid.*
33. *Ibid.*; *O.R.* Ser. I, XII, pt. 2, 143.
34. Milroy to Mary Milroy, August 15, 1862, RHMJCPL.
35. Milroy to Mary Milroy, August 15, 1862, RHMJCPL.
36. *Ibid.*
37. Hennessy, *Return to Bull Run*, 29.
38. Cozzens, *General John Pope*, 97; *O.R.* Ser. I, XII, pt. 2, 143.
39. Milroy to Mary Milroy, August 15, 1862, RHMJCPL.
40. *Ibid.*
41. Hennessy, *Return to Bull Run*, 30–1; Robertson, *Stonewall Jackson*, 539.
42. Robertson, *Stonewall Jackson*, 539.
43. Cozzens and Girardi, eds., *Military Memoirs*, 141.
44. *Ibid.*, 141–42. Fredericksburg was not the only gateway for reinforcements for the Army of the Potomac. Alexandria, Virginia, also served as another gateway if the route from Fredericksburg was blocked. Union troops could have used Pope's major line of supply and communication, the Orange & Alexandria Railroad, to reach Pope's Army of Virginia along the Rappahannock.
45. Robert J. Trout, *Galloping Thunder: The Story of the Stuart Horse Artillery* (Mechanicsburg, PA: Stackpole Books, 2002), 79–80. *O.R.*, Ser. I, XII, pt. 2, 316.
46. *O.R.*, Ser. I, XII, pt. 2, 317.
47. *Ibid.*
48. Robertson, *Stonewall Jackson*, 545.
49. Edward G. Longacre, *Lee's Cavalrymen: A History of the Mounted Forces of the Army of Northern Virginia, 1861–1865* (Mechanicsburg, PA: Stackpole Books, 2002), 117–19.
50. Cozzens and Girardi, eds., *Military Memoirs*, 146.
51. *O.R.* Ser. I, XII, pt. 2, 317; Hennessy, *Return to Bull Run*, 87.
52. *O.R.* Ser. I, XII, pt. 2, 318.
53. Milroy to Mary Milroy, September 4, 1862, RHMJCPL; *O.R.*, Ser. I, XII, pt. 2, 318.
54. *O.R.* Ser. I, XII, pt. 2, 318; Milroy to Mary Milroy, September 4, 1862, RHMJCPL.
55. Hennessy, *Return to Bull Run*, 90.
56. *Ibid.*, 130, 135.
57. *Ibid.*, 136.
58. *O.R.* Ser. I, XII, pt. 2, 319–20; Hennessy, *Return to Bull Run*, 206–14.
59. *Ibid.*, 320.
60. *O.R.* Ser. I, XII, pt. 2, 320.
61. Hennessy, *Return to Bull Run*, 265.
62. Milroy to Mary Milroy, September 4, 1862, RHMJCPL.
63. Milroy to Mary Milroy, September 1862, in Paulus, *Papers of Gen. Milroy*, 1:91.
64. *O.R.*, Ser I, XII, pt. 2, 321.
65. *Ibid.*
66. Speech of Col. E.P. Hammond at Milroy monument dedication, July 4, 1910, in Paulus, *Papers of General Milroy*, 4:24.
67. *Ibid.*; Milroy to Mary Milroy, September 1862, in Paulus, *Papers of Gen. Milroy*, 1:96–7.
68. *Ibid.*
69. *Ibid.*, 1:96.
70. *O.R.* Ser. I, XII, pt. 2, 342.
71. *Ibid.*, 343.
72. *Ibid.*, pt. 1, 320.
73. Charles F. Walcott, *History of the Twenty-First Regiment Massachusetts Volunteers* (Boston: Houghton Mifflin, 1882), 148–49.
74. Milroy to Mary Milroy, Sept. 1862, in Paulus, *Papers of General Milroy*, 1:98.
75. *Ibid.*
76. *O.R.* Ser. I, XII, pt. 2, 323.
77. Milroy to Mary Milroy, September 1862, in Paulus, *Papers of General Milroy*, 1:98.
78. *Ibid.*, 1:122.
79. *Ibid.*, 1:98.
80. *Ibid.*, 1:124.
81. *O.R.*, Ser. I, XII, pt. 2, 323.
82. Milroy to Mary Milroy, September 1862, in Paulus, *Papers of General Milroy*, 1:100–01; *O.R.* Ser. I, XII, pt. 2, 315.
83. Milroy to Mary Milroy, September 28, 1862, RHMJCPL.
84. Milroy to Mary Milroy, September 1862, in Paulus, *Papers of General Milroy*, 1:102.
85. *Ibid.*, 123.
86. *Ibid.*, 102.
87. *Ibid.*, 103.
88. *Ibid.*, 124.
89. *Ibid.*, 124.

90. Milroy to Mary Milroy, September 28, 1862, RHMJCPL.
91. Milroy to Mary Milroy, October 19, 1862, in Paulus, *Papers of General Milroy*, 1:130.
92. *Ibid.*, 131–32.
93. Milroy to Mary Milroy, September 28, 1862, RHMJCPL
94. Milroy to Mary Milroy, November 7, 1862, in Paulus, *Papers of General Milroy*, 1:134
95. Milroy to Mary Milroy, November 16, 1862, in *ibid.*, 139.
96. Spencer C. Tucker, *Brigadier General John D. Imboden: Confederate Commander in the Shenandoah* (Lexington, KY: University Press of Kentucky, 2003), 102.
97. Speech of Col. E.P. Hammond at Milroy monument dedication, July 4, 1910, in Paulus, *Papers of General Milroy,* 4:23.
98. *O.R.* Ser. II, V, 810.
99. General Order No. 39 in Joseph W. Keifer Order Book, General Order No. 2, William R. Perkins Library, Duke University.
100. *O.R.* Ser. II, V, 810.
101. Tucker, *Imboden*, 102.
102. *O.R.* Ser. II, V, 811.
103. Speech of Col. E.P. Hammond at Milroy monument dedication, July 4, 1910, in Paulus, *Papers of General Milroy,* 4:23.
104. Information about Imboden's St. George, Virginia, raid can be found in Tucker, *Imboden*, 103–06.
105. *Ibid.*, 107.
106. *Ibid.*
107. Milroy to Mary Milroy, December 20, 1862, in Paulus, *Papers of Gen. Milroy,* 1:143.
108. *Ibid.*
109. Keifer, *Slavery and Four Years of War,* 1:313; For more on Cluseret see Lowell L. Blaisdell, "A French Civil War Adventurer: Fact and Fancy," *Civil War History* 12 (1966): 246–57; Philip M. Katz, *From Appomattox to Montmartre: Americans and the Paris Commune* (Cambridge: Harvard University Press, 1998).
110. Noyalas, *Plagued by War,* 82.
111. *Ibid.*; Laura Lee Diary, December 24, 1862, Manuscripts and Rare Books Department, Swem Library, College of William and Mary.
112. Officers of Cluseret's brigade to Milroy, January 3, 1863, RHMJCPL.
113. *O.R.*, Ser. I, XXVII, pt. 2, 98.
114. *O.R.* Ser. I, XII, pt. 2, 767.
115. Robert J. Driver Jr., *First and Second Maryland Cavalry, C.S.A.* (Charlottesville, VA: Rockbridge, 1999), 27; Noyalas, *Plagued by War,* 78.
116. Milroy to Mary Milroy, December 20, 1862, in Paulus, *Papers of General Milroy,* 1:144; *O.R.* Ser I., XXI, 33–4.
117. Noyalas, *Plagued by War,* 81.
118. *Partial Record of the Session of the Presbyterian Church of Rensselaer, Jasper County Indiana 1854–1867* in Paulus, *Papers of General Milroy,* 4:84–5.
119. Milroy to Mary Milroy, December 20, 1862, in Paulus, *Papers of General Milroy,* 1:145.

Chapter 5

1. Keifer, *Slavery and Four Years of War,* 1:313.
2. Milroy's speech to his men, January 1, 1863, in Keifer, *Slavery and Four Years of War,* 1:316.
3. For a brief discussion of how Federal soldiers in the Army of the Potomac reacted to the preliminary Emancipation Proclamation see Davis, *Lincoln's Men,* 99-103.
4. Milroy to Mary Milroy, January 5, 1863, in Paulus, *Papers of General Milroy,* 1:226–27.
5. Davis, *Lincoln's Men,* 103.
6. Thomas O. Crowl to sister, January 28, 1863, Thomas O. Crowl Letter Collection, Historical Collections and Larbor Archives, Eberly Family Special Collections Library, Pennsylvania State University. Items from this collection are cited hereafter as PSU.
7. *Ibid.*
8. Kate Sperry, *Surrender? Never Surrender,* January 21, 1863, Stewart Bell Jr. Archives, Handley Library, Winchester, Va. All items from this archives will be cited hereafter as HL.
9. Milroy to Mary Milroy, January 5, 1863, in Paulus, *Papers of General Milroy,* 1:227.
10. Thomas E. Pope, *The Weary Boys: Colonel J. Warren Keifer and the 110th Ohio Volunteer Infantry* (Kent, Ohio: Kent State University Press, 2002), 34.
11. "Freedom to Slaves!," RHMJCPL.
12. *Ibid.*
13. Milroy to Mary Milroy, February 10, 1863, in Paulus, *Papers of General Milroy,* 1:236.
14. Keifer, *Slavery and Four Years of War,* 1:319.
15. *Ibid.*, 1:318, 320.
16. Milroy to Mary Milroy, February 10, 1863, in Paulus, *Papers of General Milroy,* 1:234.
17. Julia Chase Diary, January 1, 1863, HL.
18. *Ibid.*, October 19, 1862.
19. "Journal of the Senate of Virginia," January 10, 1863, RHMJCPL.
20. A.R. Boteler to Governor John Letcher, January 19, 1863, John Letcher Papers, Library of Virginia.
21. *Ibid.*
22. Executive Communication to the Virginia Senate and House of Delegates, January 20, 1863, in *ibid.*; *Journal of the House of Delegates of the State of Virginia for the Adjourned Session, 1863* (Richmond: William F. Ritchie, Public Printer, 1863), 43.

23. Executive Communication to the Virginia Senate and House of Delegates, January 20, 1863, John Letcher Papers, Library of Virginia.
24. *Ibid.*
25. *Ibid.*
26. *Ibid.*
27. Journal of the Senate of Virginia, January 10, 1863 Resolution, in Paulus, *Papers of General Milroy*, 4:58.
28. Milroy to wife, February 10, 1863, in Paulus, *Papers of General Milroy*, 1:237.
29. *O.R.* Ser. I, XXV, pt. 1, 42
30. Harold Hand Jr., *One Good Regiment: The 13th Pennsylvania Cavalry in the Civil War, 1861-1865* (Victoria, BC: Trafford, 2002), 22.
31. Milroy boasted during the fall of 1862 that his practice of forcing the people to take the oath of allegiance was somewhat successful. He wrote to his wife: "This order seemed to have operated like enchantment upon the hitherto stiff necked and rebellious natives.... I am curing traitors rapidly and no treasonable talk is heard among the people any more." Milroy to Mary Milroy, December 20, 1862, in Paulus, *Papers of General Milroy*, 1:147.
32. Keifer, *Slavery and Four Years of War*, 1:312.
33. Mary Lee Diary, January 10, 1863, HL.
34. Milroy to Schenck, January 17, 1863, Schenck Papers, University of Miami, Ohio.
35. There seems to be some discrepancy as to when General Cluseret actually left Milroy's command. Mary Lee in her diary noted that Cluseret resigned on January 10, whereas Cornelia McDonald wrote that Cluseret resigned on January 9.; Minrose C. Gwin, ed., *A Woman's Civil War: A Diary with Reminiscences of the War from March 1862* (Madison: University of Wisconsin Press, 1992); Katz, *Appomattox to Montmartre*, 8.
36. David W. Blight and Brooks D. Simpson, eds., *Union & Emancipation: Essays on Politics and Race in the Civil War Era* (Kent, OH: Kent State University Press, 1997), 125; Goss, *The War within the Union High Command*, 170.
37. Officers of Cluseret's brigade to Milroy, January 3, 1863, RHMJCPL.
38. *Ibid.*
39. Treadwell Smith Diary, January 3 and January 10, 1863, HL.
40. Pope, *The Weary Boys*, 36.
41. Keifer, *Slavery and Four Years of War*, 1:323.
42. Gwin, ed., *A Woman's War*, 119.
43. Circular, January 11, 1863, RG 393, Vol. II, #4906, National Archives and Records Administration, cited hereafter as NARA.
44. Robert M. Rhodes, "Our Forts," in Sam Lehman, Rd., *The Story of Frederick County* (Winchester, VA: n.p., 1989), 33.

45. Gwin, ed., *A Woman's War*, 117.
46. The typical week of a soldier in Milroy's division is derived from Pope, *The Weary Boys*, 35.
47. Laura Lee Diary, January 11, 1863, Swem Library, College of William and Mary.
48. Portia Baldwin Baker Diary, January 1, 1863, HL.
49. Mary Lee Diary, January 2, 1863, HL.
50. Milroy to Mary Milroy, February 11, 1863, in Paulus, *Papers of Gen. Milroy*, 1:237.
51. Special Order No. 25, RG 393, Vol. II, #4906, NARA.
52. Gary B. Mills, *Southern Loyalists in the Civil War: The Southern Claims Commission* (Baltimore: Genealogical Publishing, 1994), 284.
53. Since Hollingsworth's claim was "disallowed" and not "dismissed" she must have proven her loyalty to the United States. More information about the operations of the Southern Claims Commission can be found in Frank W. Klingberg, *The Southern Claims Commission* (Millwood, NY: Kraus, 1980).
54. Mills, *Southern Loyalists*, 284.
55. Special Order No. 11, RG 393, Vol. II, #4906, NARA.
56. *O.R.* Ser. I, XXI, 110.
57. John Bigelow Jr. *Chancellorsville* (New York: Smithmark, 1995), 123.
58. Clifford Dowdey and Louis Manarin, eds., *The Wartime Papers of R.E. Lee* (New York: Bramhall House, 1961), 402. Gen. Fitzhugh Lee was Gen. Robert E. Lee's nephew.
59. *Ibid.*
60. *Ibid.*, 403. The Union corps was believed to be that of Maj. Gen. W.F. Smith.
61. *O.R.* Ser. I, XXV, pt. 2, 85
62. *Ibid.*
63. Milroy to Schenck, January 26, 1863, Schenck Papers, University of Miami, Ohio.
64. *Ibid.*, March 19, 1863.
65. *O.R.* Ser. I, XXV, pt. 2, 27.
66. *Ibid.*, 27, 30, 32.
67. Hand, *One Good Regiment*, 34.
68. Bigelow, *Chancellorsville*, 123–25.
69. For a detailed study of the Jones-Imboden raid see Tucker, *Brigadier General John D. Imboden*, 11-38.
70. Milroy to Mary Milroy, January 18, 1863, RHMJCPL.
71. Grimsley, *Hard Hand of War*, 144.
72. *Ibid.*, 148–51.
73. For an excellent example of mail censorship as a practice under Union martial law see Lee C. Drickamer and Karen C. Drickamer, eds., *Fort Lyon to Harper's Ferry: On the Border with "Rambling Jour," The Civil War Letters and Newspaper Dispatches of Charles H. Moulton 34th Mass. Vol. Inf.* (Shippensburg, PA: White Mane, 1987).

74. Mary Lee Diary, January 3, 1863, HL.
75. Margaretta Barton Colt, *Defend the Valley: A Shenandoah Family in the Civil War* (Oxford: Oxford University Press, 1994), 16.
76. Pope, *The Weary Boys*, 35–6.
77. Special Order Number 42, RG 393, Vol. II, NARA.
78. Pope, *The Weary Boys*, 35.
79. For more on Butler's treatment of the female population of New Orleans see Chester G. Hearn, *When the Devil Came Down to Dixie: Ben Butler in New Orleans* (Baton Rouge: Louisiana State University Press, 1997), 103–07.
80. Mary Lee Diary, January 2, 1863, HL.
81. *Ibid.*, January 10, 1863.
82. *Ibid.*; Noyalas, *Plagued by War*, 86.
83. Special Order Number 4, RG. 393, Vol. II, NARA.
84. Emma Cassandra Riely Macon, *Reminiscences of the Civil War* (Cedar Rapids, IA: Torch Press, 1911), 76.
85. Michael G. Mahon, *The Shenandoah Valley 1861-1865: The Destruction of the Granary of the Confederacy* (Mechanicsburg, PA: Stackpole Books, 1999), 78.
86. Gwin, ed., *A Woman's War*, 123.
87. *Ibid.*, 132.
88. *Ibid.*, 125–26.
89. Milroy to Mary Milroy, January 18, 1863, RHMJCPL.
90. *Ibid.*
91. Gwin, ed., *A Woman's War*, 125–26.
92. Gary W. Gallagher, *The Confederate War: How Popular Will, Nationalism, and Military Strategy Could Not Stave Off Defeat* (Cambridge: Harvard University Press, 1997), 79.
93. Milroy to Mary Milroy, February 27, 1863, in Paulus, *Papers of General Milroy*, 1:244.
94. Middle Department Oaths of Allegiance, RG 393, Vol. I, NARA.
95. Mary Lee Diary, February 12, 1863, HL; For more on the rebellious spirit of Mary Lee see Sheila R. Phipps, *Genteel Rebel: The Life of Mary Greenhow Lee* (Baton Rouge: Louisiana State University Press, 2004).
96. Mary Lee Diary, February 20, 1862, HL.
97. Gwin, ed., *A Woman's War*, 123, 129.
98. Thomas O. Crowl to sister, January 28, 1863, PSU.
99. *Ibid.*, February 16, 1863.
100. Milroy to Schenck, February 15, 1863, Schenck Papers, University of Miami, Ohio.
101. Speech of Col. E.P. Hammond at Milroy monument dedication, July 10, 1910, in Paulus, *Papers of General Milroy*, 4:25.
102. Milroy to Schenck, April 18, 1863, Schenck Papers, University of Miami, Ohio.
103. *Ibid.*, February 15, 1863.
104. *Ibid.*
105. Petition to Abraham Lincoln from residents of Frederick County, Virginia, August 10, 1863, Civil War materials, Jonah H. Lupton, Virginia Historical Society.
106. Milroy to Mary Milroy, February 27, 1863, in Paulus, *Papers of General Milroy*, 1:244.
107. Gwin, ed., *A Woman's War*, 121.
108. Colt, *Defend the Valley*, 217-19. On page 218 there is a rendering of the Valentine; this was a copy made after the fact. The one present in this work is the original sent to Milroy.
109. Gwin, ed., *A Woman's War*, 121.
110. Milroy to Mary Milroy, February 27, 1863, RHMJCPL.
111. Mary Lee Diary, February 23, 1863, HL; Special Order No. 27, RG 393, Vol. II, #4906, NARA.
112. For more on Lee's practices of gathering supplies for Confederate soldiers during Union occupations see Phipps, *Genteel Rebel*, 169–71.
113. Macon, *Reminiscences of the Civil War*, 69.
114. Gwin, ed., *A Woman's War*, 120.
115. Mary Lee Diary, March 6, 1863, HL.
116. Milroy to Schenck, April 18, 1863, Schenck Papers, University of Miami, Ohio.
117. Mary Lee Diary, March 16, 1863, HL; Roger U. Delauter Jr. *Winchester in the Civil War* (Lynchburg, VA: H.E. Howard, 1992), 49.
118. Mary Lee Diary, April 1, 1863, HL.
119. George R. Prowell, *History of the Eighty-Seventh Regiment, Pennsylvania Volunteers: Prepared from Official Records, Diaries, and other Authentic Sources of Information* (York, PA: Press of the York Daily, 1903), 64–5.
120. Treadwell Smith Diary, June 13, 1863, HL.
121. Milroy's commission to major general of United States Volunteers, March 31, 1863, RHMJCPL.
122. Milroy to Mary Milroy, February 10, 1863, in Paulus, *Papers of General Milroy*, 1:234.
123. *Ibid.*
124. *Ibid.*, 233.
125. Milroy to Mary Milroy, February 10, 1863, in Paulus, *Papers of General Milroy*, 1:233.
126. Surveyor of Wheeling, West Virginia, to Milroy, March 9, 1863, RHMJCPL.
127. H.L. Sibley to Milroy, March 10, 1863, RHMJCPL.
128. "Milroy's swords" in Paulus, *Papers of General Milroy*, 4:9.
129. Davidson, ed., *James J. Hartley*, 30; Paulus, *Papers of General Milroy*, 4:137. The original extract about the event was taken from the *Cincinnati Commercial*, April 1863.
130. "Milroy's swords" in Paulus, *Papers of General Milroy*, 4:9.
131. W.H. Ball's address, April 4, 1863, in *ibid.*, 4:139–40.
132. Milroy's response to W.H. Ball's address, April 4, 1863, in *ibid.*, 4:141.
133. Paulus, *Papers of General Milroy*, 4:141.

134. "Milroy's swords" in *ibid.*, 4:9.
135. Delauter, *Winchester in the Civil War*, 36.
136. Mary Lee Diary, April 6, 1863, HL.
137. *Ibid.*
138. Kate Sperry, *Surrender? Never Surrender*, April 7, 1863, HL.
139. Mary Lee Diary, April 7, 1863, HL.
140. *Ibid.*, April 9, 1863.
141. Gettie Miller Diary, April 8, 1863, HL. The entry reads: "They say that some of the yankee officers resigned their office and that the one that boarded at Mrs. Logan's tore off his shoulder straps and thru them down at Milroy's feet and he had been courtmarshaled."
142. Gwin, ed., *A Woman's Civil War*, 137.
143. *Ibid.*, 138. Cornelia McDonald noted in her diary that the woman was a teacher at a school run by a Mrs. Eichelbarger.
144. Cornelia McDonald recorded some of Milroy's actions from April-June. According to her diary Mary McGill was exiled on April 14, and a store owner with the last name of Rumley saw his store and contents seized by Milroy on May 15. Dr. W.H. Boyd and his entire family were sent south on May 22; George and Julian Ward were held captive as ransom for the safe return of a Jessie Scout captured by Confederates; and on June 9, Dr. and Mrs. Robert Baldwin were sent south for not paying wages to a negro woman. See *ibid.*, 139, 141, 151, 154.
145. Milroy to Mary Milroy, May 17, 1863, in Paulus, *Papers of General Milroy*, 1:247.
146. For a detailed account of the events surrounding Jackson's wounding and death see Robertson, *Stonewall Jackson*, 727–62.
147. Delauter, *Winchester in the Civil War*, 50.
148. Mary Lee Diary, June 10, 1863, HL.
149. *Ibid.*, May 10, 1863.
150. Thomas J. Jackson to Alexander R. Boteler, January 21, 1863, Alexander Robinson Boteler Papers, William R. Perkins Library, Duke University, Chapel Hill, N.C. .
151. Milroy to Schenck, February 15, 1863, in Paulus, *Papers of General Milroy*, 4:60.
152. Keifer, *Slavery and Four Years of War*, 2:4.
153. *Ibid.*
154. *Ibid.;* Pope, *The Weary Boys*, 37.
155. Halleck to Schenck, April 29, 1863, RHMJCPL.
156. *Ibid.*, May 29, 1863.
157. Mary Lee Diary, June 5, 1863, HL.
158. Davidson, *James J. Hartley*, 38.
159. Keifer, *Slavery and Four Years of War*, 2:4.
160. *Ibid.*
161. O.R. Ser. I, XXVII, pt. 2, 161.
162. *Ibid.*, 125.
163. Halleck to Piatt, June 11, 1863, RHMJCPL.
164. Milroy to Schenck, in Keifer, *Slavery and Four Years of War*, 2:5.
165. Piatt to Milroy, June 11, 1863, RHMJCPL.
166. Schenck to Milroy, June 12, 1863, RHMJCPL.
167. Brandon H. Beck and Charles S. Grunder, *The Second Battle of Winchester* (Lynchburg, VA: H.E. Howard, 1998), 23–4; Delauter, *Winchester in the Civil War*, 51; Douglas Southall Freeman, *R.E. Lee* (New York: Scribner's, 1935), 3:33.
168. Prowell, *History of the Eighty-Seventh Regiment*, 66. Of the 87 Confederate casualties, 50 were killed or wounded and 37 captured.
169. Prowell, *History of the Eighty-Seventh Regiment*, 67–9.
170. *New York Herald*, June 22, 1863. Milroy deployed the following regiments: 87th Pennsylvania, 110th Ohio, 123rd Ohio, 18th Connecticut, 12th West Virginia Infantry regiments, 13th Pennsylvania Cavalry, and Battery L, 5th U.S. Artillery.
171. Beck and Grunder, *Second Battle of Winchester*, 29.
172. *Ibid.*
173. Delauter, *Winchester in the Civil War*, 52.
174. Keifer, *Slavery and Four Years of War*, 2:5.
175. O.R. Ser. I, XXVII, pt. 2, 92.
176. *Ibid.*, 173.
177. Beck and Grunder, *Second Battle of Winchester*, 32; Collins, "Grey Eagle," 66.
178. W.C. Walker, *History of the Eighteenth Regiment Connecticut Volunteers in the War for the Union*. (Norwich, CT: Published by the committee, 1885), 108.
179. O.R. Ser. I, LVII, pt. 1, 1055.
180. Mary Lee Diary, June 13, 1863, HL.
181. Julia Chase Diary, June 13, 1863, HL.
182. O.R. Ser. I, XXVII, Pt. 2, 55.
183. Prowell, *History of the Eighty-Seventh Regiment*, 72.
184. Terry L. Jones, *Lee's Tigers: The Louisiana Infantry in the Army of Northern Virginia* (Baton Rouge: Louisiana State University Press, 1987), 158.
185. Beck and Grunder, *The Second Battle of Winchester*, 35.
186. *Ibid.*, 80.
187. Keifer, *Slavery and Four Years of War*, 2:11.
188. Terry L. Jones, ed., *The Civil War Memoirs of Captain William J. Seymour: Reminiscences of a Louisiana Tiger* (Baton Rouge: Louisiana State University Press, 1991), 61.
189. Sperry, *Surrender? Never Surrender*, June 14, 1863, HL.
190. Keifer, *Slavery and Four Years of War*, 2:13.
191. O.R., Ser. I, XXVII, pt. 2, 101.
192. Prowell, *History of the Eighty-Seventh Regiment*, 73.

193. Pope, *The Weary Boys*, 42.
194. Mary Lee Diary, June 14, 1863, HL.
195. Macon, *Reminiscences*, 81.
196. Prowell, *History of the Eighty-Seventh Regiment*, 76.
197. Beck and Grunder, *Second Winchester*, 49.
198. Keifer, *Slavery and Four Years of War*, 2:16.
199. *Ibid.*
200. *Ibid.*, 15.
201. *New York Herald*, June 22, 1863.
202. Clemmer, *Old Alleghany*, 450
203. O.R. Ser. I, XXVII, pt. 2, 53.
204. *Ibid.*, 328.
205. William A. Garrison to Americha J. Garrison, June 18, 1863, William A. Garrison Papers, William R. Perkins Library, Duke University, Chapel Hill, N.C.
206. Macon, *Reminiscences*, 84.
207. William G. Bean, *Stonewall's Man: Sandie Pendleton* (Chapel Hill: University of North Carolina Press, 1959), 133.
208. William H. Runge, ed., *Four Years in the Confederate Artillery: The Diary of Private Henry Robinson Berkeley* (Richmond: Virginia Historical Society, 1991), 47.
209. Ann Carey Randolph Jones to Lucy P. Parkhill, June 18, 1863, HL.
210. Julia Chase Diary, June 15, 1863.

Chapter 6

1. O.R. Ser. I, XXVII, pt. 2, 171.
2. Gideon Welles, *Diary of Gideon Welles: Secretary of the Navy under Lincoln and Johnson* (Boston: Houghton Mifflin, 1909), 1:328.
3. *New York Herald*, June 22, 1863.
4. *Ibid.*
5. O.R. Ser. II, VI, 69.
6. Special Order No. 162, Schenck to Milroy, June 17, 1863, RG 393, Vol. I, NARA.
7. Milroy to Schenck, June 22, 1863, Schenck Papers, University of Miami, Ohio.
8. Special Order No. 16, June 26, 1863, RHMJCPL.
9. *Ibid.*
10. Keifer, *Slavery and Four Years of War*, 2:19; Collins, "The Grey Eagle," 67.
11. Milroy to John Usher, June 28, 1863 in Roy P. Basler, ed., *The Collected Works of Abraham Lincoln* (New Brunswick, NJ: Rutgers University Press, 1953), 6:309.
12. Milroy to John Usher, June 28, 1863, Abraham Lincoln Papers, Library of Congress.
13. Milroy to John Usher, June 28, 1863, in Basler, ed., *Abraham Lincoln*, 6:309.
14. *Ibid.*
15. *Ibid.*
16. Lincoln to Milroy, June 29, 1863, in *ibid.*, 308.
17. *Ibid.*
18. Milroy to Halleck, July 2, 1863, Abraham Lincoln Papers, Library of Congress.
19. *Ibid.*
20. *Ibid.*
21. Milroy to Lincoln, July 13, 1863, RHMJCPL.
22. Milroy to Lincoln, July 20, 1863, Abraham Lincoln Papers, Library of Congress.
23. Milroy to wife, June 30, 1863, RHMJCPL.
24. Newspaper clipping in letter from the 116th Regiment, August 23, 1863, in Paulus, *Papers of General Milroy*, 4:159.
25. *Ibid.*, 161–2.
26. *Evening Gazette*, October 1863, in Paulus, *Papers of General Milroy*, 4:174.
27. *Ibid.*
28. Paulus, *Papers of General Milroy*, 4:162.
29. *Ibid.*
30. Lloyd H. Adamson, "Siege of Winchester: A Soldier's Tribute to the Life and Services of His Brave Commander, General Robert H. Milroy," in Paulus, *Papers of General Milroy*, 3:188.
31. Officers in Milroy division to Lincoln from "Camp Milroy" Sharpsburg, Maryland, July 23, 1863, Abraham Lincoln Papers, Library of Congress.
32. 122nd Ohio to Milroy from Sharpsburg, Maryland, July 21, 1863, RHMJCPL.
33. Mark Poore to Milroy, July 29, 1863, RHMJCPL; Senator Samuel Young to Milroy, July 28, 1863, RHMJCPL.
34. Senator Samuel Young to Milroy, July 28, 1863, RHMJCPL.
35. Lloyd H. Adamson, "Siege of Winchester," in Paulus, *Papers of General Milroy*, 3:190.
36. Davidson, ed., *James J. Hartley*, 42.
37. *Ibid.*
38. Ronge, ed., *Four Years in the Confederate Artillery*, 48.
39. *Ibid.*
40. Petition to Abraham Lincoln from residents of Frederick County, Virginia, August 10, 1863, Civil War Materials, Jonah H. Lupton, Virginia Historical Society.
41. O.R. Ser. I, XXVII, pt. 2, 169.
42. *Ibid.*, 88–9.
43. *Ibid.*, 88–91.
44. *Ibid.*, 169.
45. *Ibid.*, 90–1.
46. War Department, *Revised United States Army Regulations of 1861 with an Appendix Containing the Changes and Laws Affecting Army Regulations and Articles of War to June 25, 1863* (Washington, D.C.: U.S. Government Printing Office, 1863), 499.
47. O.R. Ser. I, XXVII, pt. 2, 92–3.
48. Milroy to Schenck, May 20, 1863, Schenck Papers, University of Miami, Ohio.
49. O.R. Ser. I, XXVII, pt. 2, 178.

50. *Ibid.*, 178.
51. *Ibid.*, 178.
52. *Ibid.*, 93.
53. *Ibid.*, 94.
54. *Ibid.*, 97.
55. *Ibid.*, 102.
56. *Ibid.*, 114.
57. *Ibid.*
58. *Ibid.*, 117.
59. *Ibid.*, 113–14.
60. *Ibid.*, 112.
61. *Ibid.*, 115.
62. Milroy to Schenck, June 9, 1863, Schenck Papers, University of Miami, Ohio.
63. *O.R.* Ser. I, XXVII, pt. 2, 156.
64. *Ibid.*, 153.
65. *Ibid.*, 157.
66. *Ibid.*, 158.
67. *Ibid.*, 167.
68. *Ibid.*, 156–168.
69. *Ibid.*, 188.
70. *Ibid.*, 187–8.
71. *Ibid.*, 196.
72. *Ibid.*, 188.
73. *Ibid.*
74. *Ibid.*, 191.
75. *Ibid.*, 190–93.
76. *Ibid.*
77. *Ibid.*, 194.
78. *Ibid.*, 197.
79. *O.R.* Ser. I, XXVII, pt. 2, 194–95.
80. Milroy to Lincoln, September 20, 1863, Abraham Lincoln Papers, Library of Congress.
81. *Ibid.*
82. Milroy to Lincoln, September 26, 1863, RHMJCPL.
83. Milroy to Lincoln, September 13, 1863, Abraham Lincoln Papers, Library of Congress.
84. Mary Milroy to Milroy, October 3, 1863, in Paulus, *Papers of General Milroy*, 1:323.
85. President Lincoln's endorsement of Holt's findings in correspondence sent from John Hay to Milroy, October 27, 1863, RHMJCPL.
86. Milroy to Schenck, September 18, 1863, Schenck Papers, University of Miami, Ohio.
87. *Ibid.*
88. "Hail to the Chief!" broadside, RHMJCPL. Some historians who have examined Milroy claim that during the nearly 10-month period between June 1863 and May 1864 he spent his time in Indiana. This is incorrect. Milroy received letters from his family and wrote to them from Washington in late October, and then by November 23, 1863, Milroy was back in Washington writing letters to his family. See Paulus, *Papers of General Milroy*, 1:329–30.
89. Lincoln to Grant, December 19, 1863, in Basler, ed., *The Collected Works of Abraham Lincoln*, 7:80.

90. Collins, "The Grey Eagle," 70.
91. Milroy to Lincoln, January 1, 1864, Abraham Lincoln Papers, Library of Congress.
92. *Ibid.*
93. Citizens of Martinsburg, West Virginia, to Lincoln, December 1863, in *ibid.*
94. Mary Milroy to Milroy, December 31, 1863, in Paulus, *Papers of General Milroy*, 1: 336.
95. Milroy to wife, February 5, 1863, in Paulus, *Papers of General Milroy*, 1:343.
96. Gov. Francis H. Pierpont to Lincoln, January 11, 1864, Abraham Lincoln Papers, Library of Congress.
97. Milroy to wife, February 28, 1864, in Paulus, *Papers of General Milroy*, 1:348.
98. Milroy to wife, February 5, 1863, in *ibid.*, 343.
99. Milroy to wife, February 28, 1863, in *ibid.*, 1:348.
100. Goss, *The War Within the Union High Command*, 177–78.
101. Milroy to wife, February 5, 1864, in Paulus, *Papers of General Milroy*, 1:343. The 2nd West Virginia Infantry ceased to exist after January 26, 1864. On that date General Order No. 39 changed the regiment to the 5th West Virginia Cavalry. For more information on the regiment see Theodore F. Lang, *Loyal West Virginia From 1861–1865: With an Introductory Chapter on the Status of Virginia for Thirty Years Prior to the War* (Baltimore: Deutsch, 1895), 210–13.
102. Song composed by 9th Virginia Infantry and sung to Milroy at Cumberland, Maryland, February 2, 1864, RHMJCPL.
103. Milroy to wife, February 5, 1864, in Paulus, *Papers of General Milroy*, 1:343.
104. *Ibid.*
105. *Ibid.*, 1:345–46.
106. Collins, "The Grey Eagle," 70; John Y. Simon, ed., *The Papers of Ulysses S. Grant* (Carbondale, IL: Southern Illinois University Press, 1979–1991), 10:278–79; Ulysses S. Grant, *Personal Memoirs of U.S. Grant*, (New York: Webster, 1885), 2:114.
107. Meade to Grant, April 8, 1864, in Simon, ed., *The Papers of Ulysses S. Grant*, 10:279.
108. Milroy to Mary Milroy, February 28, 1864, in Paulus, *Papers of General Milroy*, 1:349.
109. *Ibid.*
110. *O.R.* Ser. I, XXXVIII, pt. 4, 54.
111. *Ibid.*, 289.
112. Anonymous to Lincoln, May 12, 1864, RHMJCPL.
113. *Ibid.*

Chapter 7

1. Milroy to wife, June 19, 1864, in Paulus, *Papers of General Milroy*, 1: 358.
2. *O.R.* Ser. I, XXXVIII, pt. 4, 289.

3. Milroy to wife, May 20, 1864, in Paulus, *Papers of General Milroy,* 1:354.
4. *Ibid.*
5. *Ibid.*, 352.
6. Milroy to wife, June 19, 1864, in *ibid.*, 1:358.
7. *Ibid.*
8. *Ibid.*, 358–59; Michael R. Bradley, *With Blood and Fire: Life Behind Union Lines in Middle Tennessee, 1863–65,* (Shippensburg, PA: Burd Street Press, 2003), 80.
9. Milroy to wife, July 6, 1864, in *ibid.*, 1:361.
10. When Milroy arrived in Tennessee the following infantry was placed under his command: 133rd, 134th, 135th, 136th, and 138th Indiana. He also had the 5th, 10th, and 12th Tennessee Cavalry, along with two companies of the 2nd Kentucky Cavalry. Bradley, *With Blood and Fire,* 68–9.
11. Milroy to wife, June 19, 1864, in Paulus, *Papers of General Milroy,* 1: 359–60.
12. *Ibid.*, 1:359
13. Milroy to wife, August 8, 1864, in *ibid.*, 1:372.
14. Milroy to wife, June 19, 1864, in *ibid.*, 359.
15. Milroy to wife, August 8, 1864, in *ibid.*, 372.
16. Milroy to Thomas, July 30, 1864, Abraham Lincoln Papers, Library of Congress.
17. *Ibid.*
18. Milroy to wife, August 8, 1864, in Paulus, *Papers of General Milroy,* 1:372.
19. *Ibid.*
20. Milroy to Sherman, September 15, 1864, RHMJCPL.
21. *Ibid.*
22. *Ibid.*
23. Milroy to Lincoln, September 22, 1864, Abraham Lincoln Papers, Library of Congress.
24. *Ibid.* .
25. Milroy to Lincoln, September 26, 1864, in *ibid.*
26. Thomas to Milroy, August 11, 1864, in *ibid.*
27. Milroy to wife, August 8, 1864, in Paulus, *Papers of General Milroy,* 1:372.
28. Bradley, *With Blood and Fire,* 69.
29. *Ibid.*, 82.
30. *O.R.* Ser. I, XXXIX, pt. 3, 238.
31. *Ibid.*
32. Bradley, *With Blood and Fire,* 85. Unionist attempts to secure the release of Confederate sympathizers or to prevent reprisals against disloyal citizens were common practices during the conflict because Unionists feared for their safety. For further discussion see Daniel E. Sutherland, *Seasons of War: The Ordeal of a Confederate Community, 1861–1865* (New York: The Free Press, 1995), 127–28; Michael G. Mahon, ed., *Winchester Divided: The Civil War Diaries of Julia Chase and Laura Lee* (Mechanicsburg, PA: Stackpole Books, 2002), 129–31; Stephen V. Ash, *When the Yankees Came: Conflict and Chaos in the Occupied South, 1861–1865* (Chapel Hill: University of North Carolina Press, 1995), 109–11.
33. Bradley, *With Blood and Fire,* 85–6.
34. *Ibid.*, 101.
35. *O.R.*, Ser. I, XXXIX, pt. 3, 172.
36. *Ibid.*, 689.
37. For more on events of the Battle of Franklin see Wiley Sword, *The Confederacy's Last Hurrah: Spring Hill, Franklin, and Nashville* (Lawrence: University Press of Kansas, 1992), 147–271.
38. Herbert S. Norris and James R. Long, "The Road to Redemption" *Civil War Times Illustrated,* 36, no. 4 (1997): 33; Jacob D. Cox, *The March to the Sea: Franklin and Nashville* (Edison, NJ: Cox, 2002), 100.
39. Milroy to wife, December 18, 1864, in Paulus, *Papers of General Milroy,* 1:399.
40. Sword, *The Confederacy's Last Hurrah,* 293.
41. *O.R.* Ser. I, XLV, pt. 1, 614. In the skirmish at Overall's Creek Milroy commanded the 8th Minnesota, 174th Ohio, 61st Illinois, and a section of the 13th New York Artillery; Milroy to wife, December 18, 1864, in Paulus, *Papers of General Milroy,* 1:399; Norris and Long, "The Road to Redemption," 33; Sword, *The Confederacy's Last Hurrah,* 293–95.
42. Milroy to wife, December 18, 1864, in Paulus, *Papers of General Milroy,* 1:399–400; Sword, *The Confederacy's Last Hurrah,* 295.
43. Jack Hurst, *Nathan Bedford Forrest: A Biography* (New York: Knopf, 1993), 238.
44. Sword, *The Confederacy's Last Hurrah,* 296.
45. Norris and Long, "The Road to Redemption," 34.
46. Sword, *The Confederacy's Last Hurrah,* 296.
47. *O.R.* Ser. I, XLV, pt. 1, 617.
48. *Ibid.*; Milroy to wife, December 18, 1864, in Paulus, *Papers of General Milroy,* 1:400.
49. Norris and Long, "The Road to Redemption," 37.
50. *O.R.* Ser. I, XLV, pt. 1, 614.
51. Milroy to wife, December 18, 1864, in Paulus, *Papers of General Milroy,* 1:400.
52. *Ibid.*
53. *Delhi Journal,* December 1864, in *ibid.*, 4:197.
54. Milroy to wife, December 18, 1864, in *ibid.*, 1:400.
55. Milroy to wife, January 1, 1865, in *ibid.*, 1:489–90.
56. Milroy diary, January 1, 1865, in *ibid.*, 2:2.
57. Bradley, *With Blood and Fire,* 113–14.
58. Milroy to wife, February 12, 1865, in Paulus, *Papers of General Milroy,* 1:495.

59. *Ibid.*; "Circular" Headquarters Defences of N & C RR, Tullahoma, Tennessee, February 1, 1865, RHMJCPL.
60. Milroy to wife, February 12, 1865, in Paulus, *Papers of General Milroy*, 1:495.
61. *Ibid.*
62. "Circular" Headquarters Defences of N & C RR, Tullahoma, Tennessee, February 1, 1865, RHMJCPL. Milroy's orders applied to the following counties in Tennessee — Coffee, Lincoln, Bedford, Franklin, Marshall, Grundy, Warren and Cannon. The order also applied to Jackson County, Alabama.
63. *Ibid.*
64. *Ibid.*
65. *Ibid.*
66. *Ibid.*
67. Bradley, *With Blood and Fire*, 103–4.
68. *Ibid.*, 103.
69. Milroy to wife, February 12, 1865, in Paulus, *Papers of General Milroy*, 1:495.
70. *Ibid.*
71. *Ibid.*
72. Milroy to Stanton, February 9, 1865, Abraham Lincoln Papers, Library of Congress.
73. Presentation speech of William H. Wisener, February 22, 1865, in Paulus, *Papers of General Milroy*, 4:198–99.
74. *Ibid.*, 200.
75. *Ibid.*, 201.
76. *Ibid.*
77. *Ibid.*, 202.
78. Milroy diary, January 1, 1865, in *ibid.*, 2:2; Milroy to wife, January 1, 1865, in *ibid.*, 1:489.
79. Milroy to Lincoln, March 15, 1865, Abraham Lincoln Papers, Library of Congress.
80. *Ibid.*
81. *Ibid.*
82. Milroy diary, March 21, 1865, in Paulus, *Papers of General Milroy*, 2:15.
83. Milroy to Don Matia Romero, March 31, 1865, RHMJCPL.
84. *Ibid.*
85. Don Matia Romero to Milroy, April 5, 1865, in *ibid*
86. Milroy to Don Matia Romero, May 21, 1865, in *ibid.*
87. Milroy diary, April 10, 1865, in Paulus, *Papers of General Milroy*, 2:18.
88. *Ibid.*
89. *Ibid.*
90. *Ibid*, 19
91. *Ibid.*, 19.
92. *Ibid.*, 20.
93. Milroy diary, May 7, 1865, in *ibid.*, 2:22; Bradley, *With Blood and Fire*, 106–7.
94. Milroy diary, May 1, 1865, in *ibid.*, 21.
95. Twelve Tennessee citizens to Milroy, April 24, 1865, RHMJCPL.
96. Milroy diary, May 14, 1864, in *ibid.*, 22; For a complete study of Jefferson Davis' flight from Richmond and his capture see William C. Davis, *An Honorable Defeat: The Last Days of the Confederate Government* (New York: Harcourt, 2001), 286–312.
97. Milroy to Andrew Johnson, May 22, 1865, in Paulus, *Papers of General Milroy*, 3:163.
98. Special Orders No. 18, Thomas to Milroy, July 11, 1865, in Paulus, *Papers of General Milroy*, 3:164.

Chapter 8

1. Citizens of Tullahoma to Milroy, Apr. 24, 1865, RHMJCPL.
2. Milroy diary, July 12, 13, and 14, 1865, in Paulus, *Papers of General Milroy*, 2:32.
3. Milroy diary, July 14 and 15, 1865, in *ibid*.
4. Milroy to Mary Milroy, March 1, 1865, in *ibid.* 1:497
5. Milroy diary, July 18, 1865, in *ibid.*, 2:33.
6. Milroy diary, July 26, 1865, in *ibid.*, 34.
7. Milroy to President Johnson, undated, in *ibid.*, 3:166. While this letter is undated it was more than likely written on August 21, 1865. In his diary Milroy penned: "Wrote a private letter to Presdt Johnson today asking him to recall my resignation and grant me the three months leave of absence that is being granted to all other Generals to be mustered out. I done this because I need the pay and have a much better right to it from meritorious services than many Genls who are retained." In *ibid.*, 2:38.
8. *Ibid.*
9. Milroy diary, August 8, 9, and 10, 1865, in *ibid.* 2:36.
10. Milroy diary, August 14 and 15, 1865, in *ibid.*, 37.
11. Milroy diary, September 30, 1865, in *ibid.*, 2;40.
12. Milroy diary, December 31, 1865, in *ibid.*, 51.
13. Family record from Milroy Family Bible, in *ibid.*, 4:2.
14. Milroy to wife, May 20, 1866, Robert H. Milroy Letters, Civil War Research Center, Motlow State Community College, Tullahoma, Tenn. Letters pertaining to Milroy's time in Tennessee may be accessed through www.cwrc.org.
15. Milroy to wife, June 20, 1866, in *ibid.*
16. Milroy to wife, July 2, 1866, in *ibid.*
17. Paulus, *Papers of General Milroy*, 4:26.
18. Frederic Morton, *The Story of Winchester in Virginia: The Oldest Town in the Shenandoah Valley* (Strasburg, VA: Shenandoah, 1925), 186–87.
19. Oscar A. Kinchen, *Women Who Spied for the Blue and the Gray* (Philadelphia: Dorrance, 1972), 113–4.

20. Milroy to Grant, May 1871, in Paulus, *Papers of General Milroy*, 3:168.
21. *Ibid.*, 169.
22. Milroy Family Bible Record, in *ibid.*, 4:2.
23. *Journal of the Executive Proceedings of the Senate of the United States of America, 1871–1873,* Friday, May 19, 1871, Library of Congress.
24. Jerome Peltier, "Milroy and the Council at Kettle Falls," *The Pacific Northwesterner*, no. 3 (30), 1986: 37.
25. *Ibid.*, 39.
26. Paulus, *Papers of General Milroy*, 4:26.
27. "Journal of the Executive Proceedings of the Senate of the United States of America, 43rd Congress," January 19, 1875, Library of Congress.
28. Milroy obituary, *Republican Partizan*, April 5, 1890.
29. Milroy Family Bible Record, in Paulus, *Papers of General Milroy*, 4:2.
30. Partial record of the session of the Presbyterian Church of Rensselaer, 1854–1867 in Paulus, *Papers of Gen. Milroy*, 4: 84–5; Speech of Col. E.P. Hammond at Milroy monument dedication, July 4, 1910, in *ibid.*, 4: 21.
31. Milroy obituary, *Republican Partizan*, April 5, 1890.
32. *Ibid.*
33. Milroy Family Bible Record, in Paulus, *Papers of General Milroy*, 4:2.
34. Milroy obituary, *Republican Partizan*, April 15, 1890.
35. *Ibid.*
36. *Ibid.*
37. Resolution of George H. Thomas G.A.R. Post No. 5, March 29, 1890, Olympia, Washington, in Paulus, *Papers of General Milroy*, 4:212–13.
38. Resolutions by the Bar Association, in *ibid.*, 213–14.
39. "Milroy Monument" in Paulus, *Papers of General Milroy*, 4: 11–12.
40. Speech of Col. E.P. Hammond at Milroy monument dedication, July 4, 1910, in *ibid.*, 4:24.
41. *Ibid.*
42. Milroy to wife, January 1, 1865, in *ibid.*, 1:489.
43. Keifer, *Slavery and Four Years of War*, 2:21.

Bibliography

Primary Sources

Historical Collections and Labor Archives, Eberly Family Special Collections Library, The Pennsylvania State University, University Park, Pennsylvania
    Thomas O. Crowl Letter Collection

Jasper County Public Library, Rensselaer, Indiana
    Papers of General Robert Huston Milroy

Library of Congress, Washington, D.C.
    Abraham Lincoln Papers
    Journal of the Executive Proceeding of the Senate of the United States, 1871–1873, Friday, May 19, 1871.

Library of Virginia, Richmond, Virginia
    John Letcher Papers

Miami University Archives, Oxford, Ohio
    Papers of Gen. Robert C. Schenck

Motlow State Community College, Civil War Research Center, Tullahoma, Tennessee
    Robert Milroy Letters. These can be accessed online at www.cwrc.org

National Archives and Records Administration, Washington, D.C.
    RG 393, Vol. I, #2351, General Orders, June 1862–April 1864
    RG 393, Vol. I, #2376, Judge Advocate, Letters Sent Feb. 1863–May 1866
    RG 393, Vol. I, #2378, Provost Marshal, Press Copies of Letters Sent January 1863–January 1866.
    RG 393, Vol. I, #2390, Oaths of Allegiance, 1861–1865
    RG 393, Vol. II, #4906, Special Orders, Apr. 1862–June 1863

Norwich University Archives and Special Collections, Kreitzberg Library, Northfield, Vermont
    1843 Commencement Program
    Robert H. Milroy Collection

Rare Book, Manuscript and Special Collections Library, Duke University, Durham, North Carolina
    Alexander Robinson Boteler Papers
    Joseph Warren Keifer Order Book
    William A. Garrison Papers

Stewart Bell Jr. Archives Room, Handley Regional Library, Winchesto-Frederick County Historical Society, Winchester, Virginia
    Ann Carey Randolph Jones Papers
    Gettie [Margaretta] Miller Diary
    Harriet H. Griffith Diary
    Julia Chase Diary
    Kate Sperry Diary, *Surrender? Never Surrender*
    Mrs. Mary (Hugh) Lee Diary
    Portia Baldwin Baker Diary
    Treadwell Smith Diary
    Rev. Benjamin F. Brooke Journal

Swem Library, College of William and Mary, Manuscripts and Rare Books Department, Williamsburg, Virginia
    Laura Lee Diary

Virginia Historical Society, Richmond, Virginia
    Jonah Lupton Papers

Government Documents

Journal of the Congress of the Confederate States of America, 1861–1865. Washington: U.S. Government Printing Office, 1905.

Journal of the House of Delegates of the State of Virginia for the Adjourned Session, Richmond: William F. Ritchie, Public Printer, 1863.

Messages of the Governor of Virginia. Richmond: William F. Ritchie, Public Printer, 1863.

United States Government. *The Eighth Census of the United States.* Washington, D.C.: 1864.

U.S. War Department (comp.). *War of the Rebellion: A Compilation of the Official Records of the Union and Confederate Armies.* 128 vols. Washington: U.S. Government Printing Office, 1880–1901.

War Department, *Revised United States Army Regulations of 1861 with an Appendix Containing the Changes and Laws Affecting Army Regulations and Articles of War to June 25, 1863.* Washington: U.S. Government Printing Office, 1863.

Published Primary Sources

Baird, Nancy Chappelear, ed. *Journals of Amanda Virginia Edmonds: Lass of the Mosby Confederacy, 1859–1867.* Stephens City, VA: Commercial Press, 1984.

Basler, Roy P., ed. *The Collected Works of Abraham Lincoln.* 8 vols. New Brunswick, NJ: Rutgers University Press, 1953.

Bierce, Ambrose. *Battlefields and Ghosts.* Palo Alto, CA: Harvest Press, 1931.

_____. *Shadows of Blue & Gray: The Civil War Writings of Ambrose Bierce.* New York: Doherty, 2002.

Buck, Lucy Rebecca. *Sad Earth, Sweet Heaven: The Diary of Lucy Rebecca Buck During the War Between the States, Front Royal, Va.* Birmingham, AL: Cornerstone, 1973.

A Catalogue of the Corporation, Officers and Cadets of the Norwich University for the Academic Year, 1843–4. Woodstock, VT: Vermont Mercury, 1844.

Colt, Margaretta Barton. *Defend the Valley: A Shenandoah Family in the Civil War.* Oxford: Oxford University Press, 1994.

Cox, Jacob D. *The March to the Sea: Franklin and Nashville.* Edison, NJ: Castle, 2002.

Cozzens, Peter, and Robert I. Girardi, eds. *The Military Memoirs of General John Pope.* Chapel Hill: University of North Carolina Press, 1998.

Davidson, Garber A., ed. *The Civil War Letters of the Late 1st Lieut. James J. Hartley, 122nd Ohio Infantry Regiment.* Jefferson, NC: McFarland, 1998.
Dowdey, Clifford, and Louis Manarin, eds. *The Wartime Papers of R.E. Lee.* New York: Bramhall House, 1961.
Drickamer, Lee C., and Karen C. Drickamer, eds. *Fort Lyon to Harpers Ferry: On the Border with "Rambling Jour," The Civil War Letters and Newspaper Dispatches of Charles H. Moulton 34th Mass. Vol. Inf.* Shippensburg, PA: White Mane, 1987.
Freeman, Douglas Southall, ed. *Lee's Dispatches.* Baton Rouge: Louisiana State University Press, 1994.
Gilmor, Col. Harry. *Four Years in the Saddle.* New York: Harper and Brothers, 1866.
Grant, Ulysses S. *Personal Memoirs of U.S. Grant.* 2 vols. New York: Webster, 1885.
Gwin, Minrose C., ed. *A Woman's Civil War: A Diary with Reminiscences of the War from March 1862.* Madison: University of Wisconsin Press, 1992.
Hale, Laura Virginia. *Four Valiant Years in the Lower Shenandoah Valley, 1861–1865.* Strasburg, VA: Shenandoah, 1968.
Jones, Terry L., ed., *The Civil War Memoirs of Captain William J. Seymour: Reminiscences of a Louisiana Tiger.* Baton Rouge: Louisiana State University Press, 1991.
Keifer, Joseph Warren. *Slavery and Four Years of War: A Political History of Slavery in The United States together with a Narrative of the Campaigns and Battles of the Civil War in which the Author Took Part, 1861–1865.* New York: Putnam, 1900.
The Life, Campaigns, and Public Service of General McClellan: The Hero of Western Virginia! South Mountain! And Antietam!, Philadelphia: T.B. Peterson & Brothers, 1864.
Lynch, Charles H. *The Civil War Diary of Charles H. Lynch, 18th Connecticut Volunteers.* N.p., 1918.
Macon, Emma Cassandra Riely. *Reminiscences of the Civil War.* Cedar Rapids, IA: Torch Press, 1911.
Mahon, Michael G., ed. *Winchester Divided: The Civil War Diaries of Julia Chase and Laura Lee.* Mechanicsburg, PA: Stackpole Books, 2002.
McDonald, Archie P., ed., *Make Me a Map of the Valley: The Civil War Journal of Stonewall Jackson's Topographer.* Dallas: Southern Methodist University Press, 1973.
"Mexican War Letters," *Indiana Magazine of History.* June 1929.
Paulus, Margaret B., comp. *Papers of General Robert Huston Milroy.* N.P., 1965.
Phillips, David L., ed. *War Stories: Civil War in West Virginia.* Leesburg, VA: Gauley Mount Press, 1991.
Prowell, George R. *History of the Eighty-Seventh Regiment, Pennsylvania Volunteers, Prepared from Official Records, Diaries, and other Authentic Sources of Information.* York, PA: Press of the York Daily, 1903.
Runge, William H., ed., *Four Years in the Confederate Artillery: The Diary of Private Henry Robinson Berkeley.* Richmond: Virginia Historical Society, 1991.
Simon, John Y., ed. *The Papers of Ulysses S. Grant.* 18 vols. Carbondale: Southern Illinois University Press, 1979–1991.
Vandiver, Frank E., ed. *War Memoirs: Autobiographical Sketch and Narrative of the War Between the States, Jubal Anderson Early, Lieutenant General, C.S.A.* Bloomington: Indiana University Press, 1960.
Walcott, Charles F. *History of the Twenty-first Regiment Massachusetts Volunteers.* Boston: Houghton Mifflin, 1882.
Walker, William C. *History of the Eighteenth Regiment Connecticut Volunteers in the War for the Union.* Norwich, CT: Published by the committee, 1885.
Welles, Gideon. *Diary of Gideon Welles: Secretary of the Navy under Lincoln and Johnson.* 3 vols. Boston: Houghton Mifflin, 1909.
Williams, Ben Ames, ed. *A Diary from Dixie by Mary Boykin Chestnut.* Boston: Houghton Mifflin, 1949.

Newspapers
Cincinnati Commercial
Delhi Journal
Evening Gazette
New York Herald
Rensselaer Republican
Rensselaer Weekly Gazette
Republican Partizan

Articles
Blaisdell, Lowell L. "A French Civil War Adventurer: Fact and Fancy." *Civil War History: A Journal of the Middle Period.* 12 (September 1966): 246–257.
Collins, Cary C. "Grey Eagle: Major General Robert Huston Milroy and the Civil War." *Indiana Magazine of History.* 90 (March 1994): 48–72.
Curry, Richard O., and F. Gerald Ham, eds. "The 'Bushwhackers' War: Insurgency and Counter-Insurgency in West Virginia." *Civil War History: A Journal of the Middle Period.* 10 (December 1964): 416–433.
Jones, Terry L. "Going Back into the Union at Last: A Louisiana Tiger's Account of the Gettysburg Campaign." *Civil War Times Illustrated* 29, no. 1 (1991): 55–60.
Longacre, Edward G. "Target: Winchester, Virginia." *Civil War Times Illustrated* 15, no. 3 (1976): 22–31.
"Mexican War Letters," *Indiana Magazine of History* 25 (June 1929): 167–173.
Miller, William J. "Grey Eagle on a Tether." *America's Civil War* 15, no. 5 (2002): 46–52, 88.
Moore, Maj. Samuel J.C., C.S.A. "Milroy at Winchester." *Winchester-Frederick County Historical Society Journal* 11: 67–75.
Nofi, Al. "Knapsack." *North and South*, no. 1 (November 1997): 8.
Norris, Herbert S., and James R. Long. "The Road to Redemption." *Civil War Times Illustrated* 36, no. 4 (1997): 32–38, 55–57.
Noyalas, Jonathan A. "The Most Hated Man in Winchester." *America's Civil War* 17, no. 1 (2004): 30–6.
Peltier, Jerome. "Milroy and the Council at Kettle Falls." *The Pacific Northwesterner* 30, no. 3 (1986): 33–40.
Phipps, Sheila. "132 North Cameron Street: 'Secesh Lives Here.'" *Winchester-Frederick County Historical Society Journal* 7: 51–68.

Secondary Sources
Ackinclose, Timothy. *Sabres and Pistols: The Civil War Career of Colonel Harry Gilmor.* Gettysburg, PA: Stan Clark Military Books, 1997.
Ambrose, Stephen E. *Halleck: Lincoln's Chief of Staff.* Baton Rouge: Louisiana State University Press, 1962.
Ash, Stephen V. *When the Yankees Came: Conflict & Chaos in the Occupied South, 1861–1865.* Chapel Hill: University of North Carolina Press, 1995.
Bean, W.G. *Stonewall's Man: Sandie Pendleton.* Chapel Hill: University of North Carolina Press, 1959.
Beck, Brandon H., and Charles S. Grunder. *The Second Battle of Winchester.* Lynchburg, VA: H.E. Howard, 1989.
_____. *The Three Battles of Winchester: A History and Guided Tour.* Berryville, VA: The Civil War Foundation, 1997.

Bigelow, John, Jr. *Chancellorsville.* New York: Smithmark, 1995.
Black, Robert C., III. *The Railroads of the Confederacy.* Chapel Hill: University of North Carolina Press, 1998.
Blight, David W., and Brooks D. Simpson, eds. *Union and Emancipation: Essays on Politics and Race in the Civil War Era.* Kent, OH: Kent State University Press, 1997.
Boney, F.N. *John Letcher of Virginia: The Story of Virginia's Civil War Governor.* Tuscaloosa: University of Alabama Press, 1966.
Bradley, Michael R. *With Blood and Fire: Life Behind Union Lines in Middle Tennessee, 1863–65.* Shippensburg, PA: Burd Street Press, 2003.
Brown, William Mosely. *Freemasonry in Winchester, Virginia.* Staunton, VA: McClure, 1949.
Bushong, Millard K. *Old Jube.* Shippensburg, PA: White Mane, 1990.
Clemmer, Gregg S. *Old Alleghany: The Life and Wars of General Ed Johnson.* Staunton, VA: Hearthside, 2004.
Collins, Darrell L. *Jackson's Valley Campaign: The Battle of Cross Keys and Port Republic.* Lynchburg, VA: H.E. Howard, 1993.
Cozzens, Peter. *General John Pope: A Life for the Nation.* Urbana: University of Illinois Press, 2000.
Davies, Norman. *Europe: A History, A Panorama of Europe, East and West, From the Ice Age to the Cold War, from the Urals to Gibraltar.* New York: Harper Perennial, 1996.
Davis, William C. *An Honorable Defeat: The Last Days of the Confederate Government.* New York: Harcourt, 2001.
_____. *Lincoln's Men: How President Lincoln Became Father to an Army and a Nation.* New York: The Free Press, 1999.
Delauter, Roger U., Jr. *Winchester in the Civil War.* Lynchburg, VA: H.E. Howard, 1992.
Driver, Robert J., Jr. *First and Second Maryland Cavalry, C.S.A.* Charlottesville, VA: Rockbridge, 1999.
Ellis, William Arba, ed., *Norwich University 1819–1911: Her History, Her Graduates, Her Roll of Honor.* 2 vols. Montpelier, VT: Capital City Press, 1911.
Faust, Drew Gilpin. *Mothers of Invention: Women of the Slaveholding South in the American Civil War.* Chapel Hill: University of North Carolina Press, 1996.
Faust, Patricia L., ed. *Historical Times Illustrated Encyclopedia of the Civil War.* New York: Harper-Perennial, 1986.
Freeman, Douglas Southall. *Lee's Lieutenants.* 3 vols. New York: Scribner's, 1944.
_____. *R.E. Lee.* 4 vols. New York: Scribner's, 1942.
Gallagher, Gary W. *The Confederate War: How Popular Will, Nationalism, and Military Strategy Could Not Stave off Defeat.* Cambridge: Harvard University Press, 1997.
_____, ed. *The Shenandoah Valley Campaign of 1862.* Chapel Hill: University of North Carolina Press, 2003.
Goss, Thomas J. *The War Within the Union High Command: Politics and Generalship During the Civil War.* Lawrence: University Press of Kansas, 2003.
Grimsley, Mark. *The Hard Hand of War: Union Military Policy Toward Southern Civilians, 1861–1865.* New York: Cambridge University Press, 1995.
Hand, Harold, Jr. *One Good Regiment: The 13th Pennsylvania Cavalry in the Civil War, 1861–1865.* Victoria, BC: Trafford, 2000.
Hearn, Chester G. *When the Devil Came Down to Dixie: Ben Butler in New Orleans.* Baton Rouge: Louisiana State University Press, 1997.
Hennesy, *Return to Bull Run: The Campaign and Battle of Second Manassas.* Norman: University of Oklahoma Press, 1993.
Hurst, Jack. *Nathan Bedford Forrest: A Biography.* New York: Knopf, 1993.
Jones, Terry L. *Lee's Tigers: The Louisiana Infantry in the Army of Northern Virginia.* Baton Rouge: Louisiana State University Press, 1987.

Jones, Virgil Carrington. *Gray Ghosts and Rebel Raiders.* New York: Holt, 1956.
Katz, Philip M. *From Appomattox to Montmartre: Americans and the Paris Commune.* Cambridge: Harvard University Press, 1998.
Kinchen, Oscar A. *Women Who Spied for the Blue & Gray.* Philadelphia: Dorrance, 1972.
Klingberg, Frank W. *The Southern Claims Commission.* Millwood, NY: Kraus, 1980.
Krick, Robert K. *Conquering the Valley: Stonewall Jackson at Port Republic.* Baton Rouge: Louisiana State University Press, 1996.
Lambert, Dobbie Edward. *Grumble: The W.E. Jones Brigade, 1863–64.* Wahiawa, HI: Lambert Enterprises, 1992.
Lang, Theodore F. *Loyal West Virginia from 1861 to 1865: With an Introductory Chapter on the Status of Virginia for Thirty Years Prior to the War.* Baltimore: Deutsch, 1895.
Lehman, Sam, ed. *The Story of Frederick County.* N.p., 1989.
Lesser, W. Hunter. *Rebels at the Gate: Lee and McClellan on the Front Line of a Nation Divided.* Naperville, IL: Sourcebooks, 2004.
Longacre, Edward G. *Lee's Cavalrymen: A History of the Mounted Forces of the Army of Northern Virginia.* Mechanicsburg, PA: Stackpole Books, 2002.
Mahon, Michael G. *The Shenandoah Valley, 1861–1865: The Destruction of the Granary of the Confederacy.* Mechanicsburg, PA: Stackpole Books, 1999.
Maier, Larry B. *Gateway to Gettysburg: The Second Battle of Winchester.* Shippensburg, PA: Burd Street Press, 2002.
Massey, Mary Elizabeth. *Refugee Life in the Confederacy.* Baton Rouge: Louisiana State University Press, 1964.
McPherson, James M. *Antietam: The Battle That Changed the Course of the Civil War.* Oxford: Oxford University Press, 2002.
_____. *For Cause and Comrades: Why Men Fought in the Civil War.* New York: Oxford University Press, 1997.
_____. *The Negro's Civil War: How American Blacks Felt and Acted During the War for the Union.* New York: Vintage Books, 1993.
_____. *What They Fought for: 1861–1865.* Baton Rouge: Louisiana State University Press, 1994.
Miller, Edward A., Jr. *Lincoln's Abolitionist General: The Biography of David Hunter.* Columbia: University of South Carolina Press, 1997.
Mills, Gary B. *Southern Loyalists in the Civil War: The Southern Claims Commission.* Baltimore: Genealogical Publishing, 1994.
Morton, Frederic. *The Story of Winchester in Virginia: The Oldest Town in the Shenandoah Valley.* Strasburg, VA: Shenandoah, 1925.
Newell, Clayton R. *Lee vs. McClellan: The First Campaign.* Washington, D.C.: Regnery, 1996.
Northern Virginia Daily. *Standing Ground: The Civil War in the Shenandoah Valley.* Strasburg, VA: Shenandoah, 1996.
Noyalas, Jonathan A. *Plagued by War: Winchester, Virginia, During the Civil War.* Leesburg, VA: Gauley Mount Press, 2003.
Perry, Oran, comp. *Indiana in the Mexican War.* N.p.: Indianapolis, 1908.
Pfanz, Donald. *Richard S. Ewell: A Soldier's Life.* Chapel Hill: University of North Carolina Press, 1998.
Phillips, Edward H. *The Lower Shenandoah Valley in the Civil War: The Impact of War Upon the Civilian Population and Upon Civilian Institutions.* Lynchburg, VA: H.E. Howard, 1993.
Phipps, Sheila R. *Genteel Rebel: The Life of Mary Greenhow Lee.* Baton Rouge: Louisiana State University Press, 2004.
Pope, Thomas E. *The Weary Boys: Colonel J. Warren Keifer and the 110th Ohio Volunteer Infantry.* Kent, OH: Kent State University Press, 2002.

Quarles, Garland R. *Occupied Winchester, 1861–1865.* Winchester, VA: Winchester-Frederick County Historical Society, 1991.
_____. *The Story of One Hundred Old Homes in Winchester, Virginia.* Winchester, VA: Farmers & Merchants National Bank, 1967.
Robertson, James I., Jr. *Stonewall Jackson: The Man, the Soldier, the Legend.* New York: Macmillan, 1997.
_____. *The Stonewall Brigade.* Baton Rouge: Louisiana State University Press, 1991.
Simkins, Francis Butler, and James Welch Patton. *The Women of the Confederacy.* Richmond, VA: Garrett and Massie, 1936.
Sutherland, Daniel E. *Seasons of War: The Ordeal of a Confederate Community, 1861–1864.* New York: The Free Press, 1995.
Sword, Wiley. *The Confederacy's Last Hurrah: Spring Hill, Franklin, and Nashville.* Lawrence: University Press of Kansas, 1992.
Tanner, Robert G. *Stonewall in the Valley: Thomas J. "Stonewall" Jackson's Shenandoah Valley Campaign, Spring 1862.* New York: Doubleday, 1976.
Time Life Books, eds. *Voices of the Civil War: Shenandoah 1862.* Alexandria, VA: Time Life Books, 1997.
Trout, Robert J. *Galloping Thunder: The Story of the Stuart Horse Artillery.* Mechanicsburg, PA: Stackpole Books, 2002.
Tucker, Spencer C. *Brigadier General John D. Imboden: Confederate Commander in the Shenandoah.* Lexington: University Press of Kentucky, 2003.
Woodward, Harold. *Defender of the Valley: Brigadier General John Daniel Imboden, C.S.A.* Berryville, VA: Rockbridge, 1996.
Wyeth, John Allan. *That Devil Forrest: Life of General Nathan Bedford Forrest.* Baton Rouge: Louisiana State University Press, 1959.

Thesis

Noyalas, Jonathan A. "My Will Is Absolute Law: General Robert H. Milroy and Winchester, Virginia." Master's thesis, Virginia Polytechnic Institute and State University, 2003.

Index

Abercrombie, Gen. J.J. 124
Alabama units: Infantry, 15th Regt. 47
Andrews, Col. R.S. Snowden 111
Appomattox 161
Argenbright, Capt. Asher 37
Armentrout House 47
Armitage, Mary Jane *see* Milroy, Mrs. Mary
Army of Northern Virginia 61, 72, 89, 103–105, 107, 115, 120, 132, 161
Army of the Cumberland 140
Army of the Potomac 65, 71–72, 77, 89, 120, 123, 127, 139
Army of Virginia 52–53, 65, 71
Ashby, Turner 46

Baker, Jacob 19
Baker, Portia Baldwin 88
Baldwin, Col. John B. 37
Ball, Col. W.H. 99–100
Banks, Gen. Nathaniel P. 35, 38, 44–45, 51–52, 58–59
Barry, Gen. W.F. 124
Barton, Fanny J. 97
Bate, Gen. William 151–153
Bayard, Gen. George 60
Beck, Dr. E.H.M. 11
Belington, VA 19
Ben Hur 10
Berryville, VA 86, 98, 106, 128
Bierce, Ambrose 21
Blackwell, Robert B. 148–149
Bleeding Kansas 14
Blenker, Gen. Louis 50–51, 57–58
Boteler, Alexander R. 84
Brady, Matthew 70
Brain, John C. 23
Brandy Station, Battle of 105
Brawner's Farm, Battle of 65
Bridgeport, AL 142
Brown, John 14, 78, 82, 84

Brownlow, William G. 168
Buchanan, President James 15
Buchanan, Lt. Col. Robert 68–69
Bull Run, Second Battle of 65–70
Burbridge, Gen. Stephen 26
Bureau of Indian Affairs 170
Burnside, Gen. Ambrose 77
Butler, Gen. Benjamin F. 26, 80, 92
Byrne, Maj. Martin 90

Camp Alleghany 27–29, 31, 35–36
Camp Bartow 23–26, 28
Camp Elk Water 23, 25, 180, 182
Captain Partridge's Military Academy, Norwich, VT *see* Norwich University
Carter's Woods, Battle of 111
Carvajal, Gen. Jesus Maria 12–13
Castle Thunder 117
Cedar Mountain, Battle of 59–60, 62
Chancellorsville, Battle of 103
Chapman, Lt. Col. William 68
Chase, Julia 83, 107, 115
Chase, Salmon P. 52
Cheat Mountain District 23, 28, 31
Cheat Mountain Division 73, 149
Chewning, Frederick W. 34
Cluseret, Gen. Gustave Paul 47, 76–77, 85–86
Colfax, Schuyler 21, 27, 32–34, 170
Conrad's Store, VA 37
Contraband slaves 36, 56–57, 148
Couch, Gen. Darius N. 117–118
Cox, Gen. Jacob 45, 73
Cross Keys, Battle of 46–50
Crowl, Thomas 80, 94–95

Davis, Pres. Jefferson 19, 32, 75, 89, 163
Department of the Susquehanna 117
Department of West Virginia 135
Dinkle, Lal 91
Dumont, Col. Ebenezer 18–19

209

Early, Gen. Jubal A. 63, 105, 107–109
Elliott, Gen. Washington 107, 109, 111, 127
Emancipation Proclamation 2, 5, 7, 77, 79–82, 84, 137, 175
Ewell, Gen. Richard S. 38, 46, 105–108, 111–113

Ferrero, Col. Edward 69
Forrest, Gen. Nathan Bedford 151–154
Fort Ethan Allen 70
Fort Jackson 114
Fort Milroy 87, 108–109, 114
Fort Sumter 15–16
Fortress Rosecrans 150, 152–153
Fraley, Mary 23
Franklin, TN 150
Fredericksburg, VA 45, 55, 58, 62
Free Blacks 149
"Freedom to Slaves!" 82–84, 87
Frémont, Gen. John C. 26, 32, 34–36, 38–40, 43–47, 49–53, 90
Front Royal, VA 45–46, 56, 86–87
Fugitive Slave Law (1850) 78
Funk, Lt. Col. John H.S. 77

Garnett, Gen. Robert S. 21, 180
Geary, Gen. John 77–78
Georgia units: Infantry, 12th Regt. 24, 42
Gettysburg, Battle of 112, 115, 120, 123, 127, 136, 172–173
Gordon, Gen. John B. 108
Grafton, VA 18–19, 179
Grant, Gen. Ulysses S. 86, 126, 136–137, 140–141, 150, 168, 170–171, 175
Great South Western Oil and Mining Co. 160, 163
Grover, Gen. Cuvier 67

Halleck, Gen. Henry 58, 70, 75, 91, 99, 104–105, 107, 116, 119, 120, 124–125, 128, 130–131, 135–136, 144, 154, 169
Hammond, Col. E.P. 5, 174
Hampton, Gen. Wade 89
Hansbrough, Lt. Col. George W. 27, 29
Harper, Adam 74
Harpers Ferry 19, 46, 77, 80, 107, 109, 111, 116–117, 125–126, 128, 130
Hatch, Gen. John P. 101
Hays, Gen. Harry T. 109
Hefner, Horace 171
Hitchcock, Gen. E.A. 124
Hollingsworth, Mary E. 88
Holt, Joseph 131–133, 135–136, 139
Hood, Gen. John Bell 150–151, 154
Hooker, Gen. Joseph 89, 125, 130–131
Hotchkiss, Jedediah 44
Hurlburt, Gen. Stephen 155

Houston, Sam 10
Hunter, Gen. David 26
Huston, Martha 8

Imboden, John D. 73–75, 85, 89–90
Indiana units: (Cavalry) 13th Regt. 151; (Infantry) 7th Regt. 25; 9th Regt. 16, 19, 21–25, 28, 31, 35–36, 142, 177, 179–182; 13th Regt. 29, 183; 14th Regt. 24–25, 180–181; 15th Regt. 55, 180; 28th Regt. 22; 73rd Regt. 26

Jackson, Gen. Henry 25
Jackson, Gen. Thomas J. "Stonewall" 27, 35, 37, 38, 40, 44–47, 58–61, 65, 77, 87, 103, 105
Jasper (Milroy's Horse) 17, 49–51, 168
Jessie Scouts 98, 102–103
Johnson, Pres. Andrew 163, 166–167
Johnson, Edward "Old Alleghany" 24, 27–31, 35–38, 40, 42, 105, 107, 111–112, 183
Jolliffe, John 124
Jones, Ann Carey Randolph 114
Jones, Gen. William "Grumble" 77–78, 85, 89–90
Jones-Imboden Raid 91
Juarez, Benito 160–161

Kelley, Benjamin F. 18–19, 77, 80, 99, 118, 179
Kellogg, Capt. Horace 79
Kernstown, First Battle of 35, 106
Kiefer, Col. Joseph W. 5, 21, 79, 81, 92, 103–105, 109, 111, 132, 175
Kimball, Col. Nathan 24, 180–181
King George II (England) 7
Kitchen, George W. 92

Latham, Capt. George 40
Laurel Hill, VA/WV 19–21, 179
Lawton, Gen. A.R. 65
Lee, Gen. Fitzhugh 89
Lee, Laura 76
Lee, Mary Greenhow 92, 94, 97, 102–104, 107, 111
Lee, Gen. Robert E. 19, 23, 37, 55, 62, 75, 89, 104, 115–116, 120, 127, 131, 139, 139, 161–162, 172
Letcher, Governor John 84
Lieber's Code 91
Lincoln, President Abraham 2, 5, 7, 15, 27, 34, 45, 50, 70, 71, 80–82, 84, 95, 102, 119–120, 122–123, 129–131, 133, 135, 137–138, 141, 146–147, 150, 154, 160, 162–163, 169
Logan Family (Winchester, VA) 101–102
Longstreet, Gen. James 62, 65, 77
Loring, Gen. William 27

INDEX

Louisiana units: (Infantry) 2nd Regt. 111; 10th Regt. 111
Luray Valley 46

Mackey, W.H. 173–174
Manassas, Second Battle of *see* Bull Run, Second Battle of
Maryland Units: Infantry, 1st Regt. (CSA) 106
Mason, Sen. James 78, 87
Massachusetts units: Infantry, 21st Regt. 69
Matamoras, Mexico 11–12
McClellan, Gen. George B. 18–21, 27, 55, 58–59, 62, 71–72, 77, 179
McDonald, Cornelia 93–94, 96–97
McDowell, Gen. Irvin 45, 52, 68
McDowell, Battle of 37–44
McElroy, John (Earl of Annandale) 7
McGuire, Dr. Hunter H. 103
McLean, Col. Nathaniel 43
McReynolds, Col. Andrew T. 98–99, 106, 111, 127–129, 132
Meade, Gen. George G. 68, 139–140, 172–173
Meem's Bottom 46
Meigs, Gen. Montgomery 91
Mexican War 11
Milroy, Edgar 14
Milroy, Edwin Bruce 14
Milroy, Ella Gertrude 14, 58, 76, 170
Milroy, Henry 8
Milroy, Mary (wife of Robert H.) 13, 26, 31, 35, 50, 76, 101–102, 116, 134–135, 138, 168, 172–173
Milroy, Robert H.: appeal for new command in 1863 134–141; colonel of 9th Indiana Infantry 17–22, 180; court of inquiry in 1863 124–133; death of 172; delegate at Indiana State Constitutional Convention 14; early life 7–9; fencing instructor 10, 178; first call to put down Confederacy, February, 1861 14–16; judge in Indiana 14; occupation of Tennessee in 1864 141–163; occupation of Winchester in 1863 79–106; officer in Mexican War 11–13, 178; postwar life 165–170; scapegoat for defeat at Second Battle of Winchester 116–124; service as brigadier general 22–74; student at Indiana State University 10–11, 13–14, 179; student at Norwich 9–10, 178; superintendent of Indian Affairs, Wyoming Territory 170–171; time in Texas 10, 178
Milroy, Samuel 7, 8, 11
Milroy, Samuel Clay 168, 171

Milroy, Valerius 14, 168, 171
Milroy, Walter 14
Milroy, Walter Judson 171
Monroe Doctrine 161
Monterey, Mexico 11–12
Moody, Col. Gideon 28–30, 171, 183
Morris, Gen. Thomas A. 18–21, 179–180
Morton, Gov. Oliver P. 16
Mount Jackson 51
Mountain Department 34
Murfreesboro, TN 150–152, 158–159, 162

Nagle, Col. James 67
Nashville, TN 140, 143, 150–151, 156, 167–168
New Orleans, LA 13, 80, 92, 179
New York Herald 112–113, 117, 120
New York Tribune 120
New York units: Cavalry, 1st Regt. 90
Norwich University 6, 9, 178

Ohio Units: (Artillery) 9th Btty. 39; 12th Btty. 63; (Infantry) 24th Regt. 25; 25th Regt. 25, 28–29, 40, 42, 49, 53, 182; 32nd Regt. 23–25, 28–29, 38–40, 42, 181–183; 75th Regt. 40, 42–43; 82nd Regt. 40, 42, 64–65; 110th Regt. 79, 81, 87, 109, 111; 116th Regt. 99, 106, 109, 121; 122nd Regt. 99, 122–123

Paine, Gen. Eleazer 143–144
Parker, Judge Richard 78
Parson, Job 74–75
Partridge, Capt. Alden 178
Pea Ridge, Battle of 53
Pegram, Joh 21
Pelham, Capt. John 63
Pennsylvania units: (Cavalry) 12th Regt. 118, 139; 13th Regt. 83, 85, 90, 106; (Infantry) 87th Regt. 80, 94–95, 106, 111–112
Phillipi, VA/WV 18–19, 75
Piatt, Lt. Col. Donn 105, 107, 131
Pierce, Col. L.B. 118–119
Pierpont, Governor Francis 138
Pope, Gen. John 52–59, 61–63, 65, 69–71
Port Republic, VA 46, 50
Porter, Gen. Fitz-John 67
Porterfield, George 18–19

Ramsey, Col. James 24
Ransom, Gen. Truman B. 10
Rasin, Capt. W.L. 106
Rensselaer Gazette 16
Reynolds, Gen. John F. 68
Reynolds, Gen. Joseph 23–25, 28, 141, 180–182

Rich Mountain, Battle of 19–21, 179
Richmond Dispatch 117
Riely, Emma Cassandra 93, 114
Rodes, Gen. Robert 105
Romero, Don Matia 160–161
Romney, VA/WV 27
Rosecrans, Gen. William S. 21, 31, 33–34, 179
Ross, Maj. John 28
Rousseau, Gen. Lovell 150–151, 157, 163

Schall, Col. John W. 106
Schenck, Gen. Robert C. 39–40, 43–44, 50, 65, 80, 86, 89–90, 95, 98, 103–105, 107, 116–118, 120, 125–136
Schofield, Gen. John M. 150
Schurz, Gen. Carl 64–65, 67
Scott, Capt. R.N. 124
Sharpsburg, MD 72, 122
Shasteen, Capt. Elijah 162–163
Shenandoah Valley 5, 23, 27, 35, 37–38, 44–45, 51, 76, 89, 120, 134, 137–138
Sheridan, Gen. Philip H. 102–126, 134, 169
Sherman, Gen. William T. 140, 146–147, 150, 175
Shields, Gen. James 35, 45–46, 50
Shumaker, Maj. Lindsay M. 65
Sigel, Gen. Franz 51–53, 55, 58–59, 63–65, 67–70, 138
Southern Claims Commission 88
Speese, Capt. Samuel 90
Sperry, Kate 80, 102
Stahel, Gen. Julius 67
Stanton, Edwin 7–71, 117, 157
Star Fort 87, 108–109
Star of the West 15
Starke, Gen. William 65
Staunton, VA 27, 29, 37–38, 75
Stephenson's Depot 111
Steuart, Gen. George H. 77, 111
Stones River, Battle of 144
Strasburg, VA 45–46, 55, 76, 78, 86
Stuart, Charles Edward (Bonnie Prince Charlie) 7
Stuart, Gen. J.E.B. 62–63, 89, 90
Summit, Ben 26, 31, 56, 75–76
Sumner, Charles 14

Taliaferro, Gen. William 42
Taylor, Gen. Zachary 12, 13, 178
Taylor Hotel 88
Tennessee units: Cavalry, 5th Regt. (US) 149
Texas Republic 10

Thomas, Gen. George 140–142, 146–147, 150, 163, 165
Thompson, Mary E. 173
Thornton, VA 19
Traveller's Repose 23–24
Tullahoma, TN 142–143, 150–151, 154–155, 157, 162

Unionists 33–34, 58, 71, 73–74, 82–83, 88, 91, 95–96, 99–100, 107, 115, 123, 126, 137–138, 144–145, 148, 155–156, 158, 163, 165, 169, 175
United States Colored Troops: Infantry, 23rd Regt. 26
United States Regular Troops: Artillery, 5th Btty. 106, 109
Usher, John P. 119

Van Cleve, Gen. Horatio 144
Virginia units (CSA): (Cavalry) 7th Regt. 90; 11th Regt. 90; 14th Regt. 106; (Infantry) 2nd Regt. 106; 5th Regt. 77, 9th Bttln. 27; 31st Regt. 42; 52nd Regt. 25, 28, 37
Virginia units (US): (Cavalry) 1st Regt. 59; (Infantry) 1st Regt. 18; 2nd Regt. 28, 33, 35, 40, 66, 139, 182; 3rd Regt. 40, 42, 67; 5th Regt. 65

Wabash and Erie Canal 168
Wabash Invincibles (Co. C, 1st Indiana Volunteers, Mexican War) 11–13
Walker, Gen. James 111
Wallace, Lew 10–12, 141
War of 1812 7
Washburn, Col. James 89
Washburn, Mary 173–174
Washington, D.C. 8, 18, 62, 70, 81
Welles, Gideon 116
Welton, F.W. 51
West Fort 108–109
White, Gen. Julius 77
Williams, Gen. Alpheus 142
Winchester, VA 27, 35, 45–46, 76–77, 79–87, 137, 139, 146, 168; Second Battle of 95, 102, 106–113, 120–121, 129, 132, 134, 140, 147, 150, 152, 164, 172, 175
Winchester Academy 88
Wingard, Samuel C. 171
Wisener, William H. 158–159
Wood, Col. James 76
Wright, Rebecca 109, 169

Young, Samuel 122

www.ingramcontent.com/pod-product-compliance
Ingram Content Group UK Ltd.
Pitfield, Milton Keynes, MK11 3LW, UK
UKHW041959140426
5217IPUK00015B/875